The Complete
IDIOT'S
Guide to WORKS
FOR WINDOWS™

by Susan Spector

que®

A Division of Prentice Hall Computer Publishing
201 W. 103rd Street, Indianapolis, Indiana 46290 USA

International Standard Book Number:1-56761-451-5
Library of Congress Catalog Card Number: 93-74017

96   8 7 6 5 4

Interpretation of the printing code: the rightmost number of the first series of numbers is the year of the book's printing; the rightmost number of the second series of numbers is the number of the book's printing. For example, a printing code of 94-1 shows that the first printing of the book occurred in 1994.

Screen reproductions in this book were created by means of the program Collage Plus from Inner Media, Inc., Hollis, NH.

Printed in the United States of America

Publisher
Marie Butler-Knight

Managing Editor
Elizabeth Keaffaber

Development Editor
Faithe Wempen

Production Editor
Michelle Shaw

Copy Editor
Audra Gable

Cover Designer
Scott Cook

Designers
Amy Peppler-Adams, Roger Morgan

Illustrations
Steve Vanderbosch

Indexer
Jeanne Clark

Production Team
*Gary Adair, Katy Bodenmiller, Brad Chinn, Kim Cofer, Meshell Dinn,
Terri Edwards, Mark Enochs, Stephanie Gregory, Jenny Kucera, Beth Rago,
Marc Shecter, Greg Simsic, Carol Stamile*

*Special thanks to C. Herbert Feltner for assuring
the technical accuracy of this book.*

Contents at a Glance

The Complete Idiot's Reference Card

The Anatomy of a Works Window

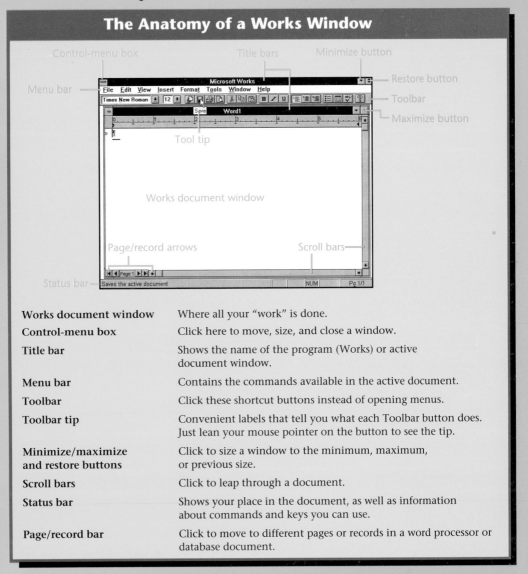

Works document window	Where all your "work" is done.
Control-menu box	Click here to move, size, and close a window.
Title bar	Shows the name of the program (Works) or active document window.
Menu bar	Contains the commands available in the active document.
Toolbar	Click these shortcut buttons instead of opening menus.
Toolbar tip	Convenient labels that tell you what each Toolbar button does. Just lean your mouse pointer on the button to see the tip.
Minimize/maximize and restore buttons	Click to size a window to the minimum, maximum, or previous size.
Scroll bars	Click to leap through a document.
Status bar	Shows your place in the document, as well as information about commands and keys you can use.
Page/record bar	Click to move to different pages or records in a word processor or database document.

The Power of 8

- Use 8 characters in a file name.
- Keep 8 Works document windows open at the same time.
- Choose from 8 basic chart types, or create one of the many variations.
- Save 8 different charts with one spreadsheet file.
- Create and save 8 special reports with each database file.
- Align text and data in any kind of column at least 8 different ways.
- List 8 of your most recently dialed phone numbers in the Easy Connect dialog box.
- Store the last 8 Works files you saved in the Recently used files list box.

cut here

Mouse Moves

Point	Move the mouse so the pointer rests on what you're aiming at.
Click	One swift press and release of the left mouse button. (Ta-Da!)
Double-click	Two swift clicks in a row. (Ta-Da-Ta-Da!)
Drag	Press and hold down the left button and move the mouse.
Drop	When you are dragging and you get where you want to go, release the left button (that's the drop!).

Getting Someplace with the Keyboard

To move . . .	Press . . .
Up or down one line or entry	Up or down arrow keys
To the beginning of a line or entry	Home
To the end of line or entry	End
To the beginning of a document	Ctrl+Home
To the end of a document	Ctrl+End
To the next document window	Ctrl+F6

Taking Your Mouse Out for a Scroll

To move . . .	Do this . . .
To the beginning of a document	Click the first Page arrow on the left.
To the previous page or record	Click the second Page arrow on the left.
To the next page or record	Click the first Page arrow on the right.
To the end of a document	Click the second Page arrow on the right.
Up, down, left, or right slowly	Click up, down, left, or right scroll arrow.
One screen at a time	Click the scroll bar nearest an arrow that points in the direction you want to go.
Pages at a time	Drag the scroll box through the scroll bar.

Selecting Stuff

To select . . .	Use the mouse . . .	Or the keyboard . . .
Any amount of text, or objects	Starting at the top left corner, click and drag the mouse across the selection.	Press Shift+ the appropriate arrow key.
A line	Click in the left margin beside the line.	Press Shift+End.
A word	Double-click the word.	Press F8 twice.
A sentence	Click and hold the mouse button as you drag across the sentence.	Press F8 three times.
A field or cell entry	Click the entry.	Press an arrow key.
An entire record or row	Click the record or row number.	Press Ctrl+F8.
An entire field or column	Click the field or column name.	Press Shift+F8.
An entire database list or spreadsheet	Click the upper left corner of the document window.	Press Ctrl+Shift+ F8.

Contents

Introduction

If you've never used a computer before, or your last attempt left you hoarding paper and pencils and running for shelter, you'll be amazed at how quickly you can become productive with Works for Windows. In fact, thanks to Microsoft, you can be writing letters and memos, generating reports, and creating charts that only yesterday you never dreamed you could.

Why Do You Need This Book?

You need this book because you're no Dummy! Your life and your work mean more to you than merely trying to *look* functional. You've got a job to do, and you're determined to get it done right. Whether you work at home, in an office, factory, or large corporation; or at a school, campus, or big institution, it's time you joined the information age.

For decades now, the world has been waiting for computers to revolutionize our work and our way of life. We sat back and watched in amazement as geeks in white shirts sent computers to the moon and back. We let computers fly our planes, run our cars, invade supermarket checkouts, even change the way we play our music. And what do we have to show for all of our patience, but answering machines and VCRs that we can't understand! Until now.

Payback time is here. In this book, you'll learn Works skills that can change your way of life. You'll see why a computer is nothing more than a tool, as revolutionary as the ball point must have seemed next to the fountain pen. You'll come to understand what they mean by productivity gains, information management, and getting home early.

So why do you need this particular book? Because this book will show you how to use Works to work smarter, not harder!

How Do I Use This Book?

Sit on this book if it'll make you feel taller.

But if you want to learn how to use Works for Windows as quickly as possible, here's what I recommend:

If this marks your first computer experience, read Chapter 2 to make sure Works is really what you need. Once you figure out that it is, and you will, jump into Chapter 3 and stay there for a while. Learn Windows. Play with Windows. Take two hours if you must. Then go on to Chapters 4 and 5 to get a firm grasp of Works. Read it at your computer so you can try everything out. You'll learn a whole lot faster when you spend your time doing it, rather than reading it!

Once you've mastered the essence of Works, find the tool you want to use first and start working in that section of the book. Don't bother reading the whole book at once. Use the chapters you need, when you need them.

The same message is true for experienced users. Give the whole book a quick once-over and then use the chapters you need, when you need 'em. It's called "just-in-time learning," and that's how I got through school. Trust me, it Works!

To get you started, here's a rundown of the conventions used in *The Complete Idiot's Guide to Works for Windows*:

- ☛ Text that you're supposed to type appears in **bold**.
- ☛ Keys that you need to press also appear in **bold**.
- ☛ Mouse clicks appear as "click ons," as in "click on this" or "select this" (which is simply another way of saying click on).

Special boxes run rampant throughout this book. If you're wondering what they're for:

By the Way . . .

These boxes contain some useful information and some things that I just wanted to "put out there" for you to think about.

Easy to understand **definitions** of intimidating computer terms will appear like this.

These boxes are few and far between because I rarely understand Techno Nerds. They're here for those of you who truly enjoy this stuff.

These are tips that cut to the chase. When there's a really easy way to do something, you'll find it here.

A little "heads up" about things that could go wrong, but probably never will. Check here if something already did.

Works for Windows made a lot of changes in the leap from version 2.0 to 3.0. Where there are differences, this icon points out the appropriate 2.0 instructions.

Acknowledgments

Thanks to Scott and everyone else who kept me fed, focused, encouraged, and quiet.

And special thanks to Que Books for giving me Faithe and a little bit of hope.

Trademarks

All terms mentioned in this book that are known to be trademarks or service marks are listed below. In addition, terms suspected of being trademarks or service marks have been appropriately capitalized. Que Books cannot attest to the accuracy of this information. Use of a term in this book should not be regarded as affecting the validity of any trademark or service mark.

Cuisinart and Mini-Mate Chopper/Grinder are registered trademarks of Cuisinart Inc.

Correction Tape is a registered trademark of Dennison Manufacturing Co.

Lotus 1-2-3 is a registered trademark of Lotus Development Corporation.

Microsoft Windows, Microsoft Excel, Word for Windows, and Microsoft Office Suite, are registered trademarks of Microsoft Corporation.

White Out is a registered trademark of Gillette Co.

WordPerfect is a registered trademark of WordPerfect Corporation.

Part I
How the Darned Thing Works

Have you ever bought a gadget and yanked it out of its box the minute you got home—only to find out you have no idea how it works? Well, I do that all the time, and (judging from the shape the world's in) I bet a lot of you do, too!

So, let's say you just bought Microsoft Works, ripped open the box, and scattered all the pieces out onto your desk. Maybe you were lucky enough to crack the hieroglyphics in the book that came with it, and actually got Works installed on your hard drive. Great! Now what? Life's too short to spend deciphering the rest of that book, and you're stuck with a program that you don't even know how to use. What's a non-geek to do?

Just turn the page. I can help.

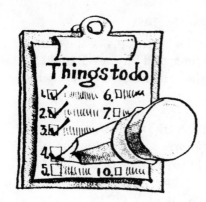

Chapter 1
The Least You Need to Know

Some of you may have no intention of reading this book. You just bought it to be a part of the *Idiot's Club*. Well, you're more than welcome to join, under one condition: Promise to read this chapter so I can honestly say I did my part. (You'll find this to be a "short form" of all you might need to know in order to try Works on your own, or at least to speak intelligently about it to a flock of pigeons.)

1. ". . .for Windows" means that you must "do Windows" in order to use this version of Works.

But rather than thinking of Windows as just one more thing for you to learn, think of it as your *window of opportunity!* Windows not only makes your computer look and feel as gentle and friendly as that other brand, but it also runs today's most popular software packages. So when you know how to "do Windows," whole new worlds open up! Besides, it's easy and fun, and it's covered pretty thoroughly in Chapter 3. (And, if you don't even know what "windows" are, there's no way you're joining the club till you read that chapter—the pigeons won't even believe you!)

2. There are many ways to start working—fast.

Works is a "learn by doing" program. Start out by using any of the thirteen WorksWizards to produce databases, form letters, and business letterhead (stationery). Select **Use a WorksWizard** on the Startup screen, and then sit back and watch the Wizard do your job!

When you're feeling more ambitious, use a Works template to create your own document using one of the many Works formats. You can be guided in every step of the way by selecting **Show Instructions Cue Cards** on the **Use A Template** screen. Take a look at Chapter 4 to start using WorksWizards, AutoStart templates, and Cue Cards.

3. Do yourself a favor—use a mouse!

I can't think of anything you can do from the keyboard (except enter text) that you can't do more quickly and easily with a mouse. You can do all of your editing, formatting, and filing right from the Toolbar or menus, without having to memorize millions of keyboard commands. (Not to mention the contortions you have to put your hands through trying to reach the key combinations!) So if you want to start using Works the minute you get it—and you don't want to keep referring to a chart of key combinations (or the kid next door)—just use the mouse! Everyone else does it. See what I mean in Chapter 3.

4. Works is most accommodating.

No matter which Works tool you're using, you can tell Works what you want it to do (print the document, for example) in any of three ways: by selecting commands from a menu list, by clicking on a Toolbar button, or by pressing key combinations. To check out the accommodations, see Chapter 3.

5. Wherever you are in Works, you can always start a new document.

If you're engrossed in a spreadsheet and remember that a memo has to get out to the troops by noon, you can stop what you're doing and open a new word processing document without closing the spreadsheet. Just select **Create New File** from the File menu, or click the **Startup** button on the Toolbar. Once you've finished the memo, close the memo window and automatically return to your place in the spreadsheet. You can have as many as eight different document windows open like this at the same time.

6. You can easily change the "look" of any Works document.

When all your words and numbers seem to look the same, or you just want to change a dull document's image, select the lifeless text and give it a makeover. If, for example, you can't tell where a heading leaves off and new text begins, use your mouse to highlight the heading and then choose the **Font and Style** command from the Format menu. Change the type, style, size, and/or color of the heading until you find something a little more exciting, or at least convincing.

You'll find formatting hints for each Works tool sprinkled throughout, but formatting is covered in the greatest detail in Chapter 9.

7. Works has its limits, so it's up to you to SAVE!

It's true, there are some very expensive programs out there that will hound you until you save, or that will do it for you when you're not even looking. But not too many of them pack as many tools into one simple program as Works does. So it's not too much to ask in order to avoid one of life's little tragedies (lost time and work) to have you click the **Save** button on the Toolbar once in a while. Or, if you prefer, open the File menu and select Save. In Chapter 6, I go into my little Save song and dance, if you want to hear it.

8. Re-engineer your own Works processes.

If you've used earlier versions of Works, you'll notice that like everything else these days, the menus have been "re-engineered" to maximize productivity and efficiency. But in addition to that, Microsoft looked at the BIGGER picture and decided maybe some of us don't even want to bother opening menus to find the commands we need. So they gave us customizable Toolbars, which means all we have to do is click on one button: one button to Save, one button to Cut, one button to Paste, one button to do just about everything the menus can do.

There's just one catch. Since there's only enough room on the Toolbar for so many buttons, Microsoft chose the ones they thought we'd use the most. But if you're like me, they may not be the right ones for you, so you'll have to re-engineer your own Toolbar. All you have to do is open the Tools menu and choose the **Customize Toolbar** command. There's more on this in Chapter 5.

9. Help clean up the environment.

Don't keep filling up boxes of paper for that long-awaited trip to the recycling center because what you thought was a final draft, wasn't. Use the Print Preview command on the File menu to check page breaks, margins, and obvious errors before you print. What you see is what you get in Chapter 6.

10. Don't forget to share!

There are plenty of reasons to share Works files, or pieces of them, with other Works tools and Windows programs. Aside from the fact that it's silly to reinvent the wheel every time you have information in one place that will work well in another, Works was made for sharing! (Didn't Microsoft share their Word and Excel programs when they made Works?)

Works lets you copy information almost effortlessly from one Works tool to any other Works tool or Windows program. You can also import a spreadsheet from Excel or 1-2-3 for Windows, import text from Word or WordPerfect for Windows, or import files from other database programs to create a form letter mailing list. You can even link an imported file (or part of one) to a Works document so that your Works document will be updated automatically every time the link's source document is changed.

Let's face it—if you can only write one good page, create one great list, or crunch one heck of a number a week, can you really afford to wait around for the next good one? Just use what you've got wherever it fits. At least you'll look productive till the next good one comes along! Read Chapter 23 to see how much there is to share.

**Recycling tip: tear out this page
and photocopy it.**

Chapter 2
The Wonderful World of Works

In This Chapter

☞ Why we all need computers

☞ What you can do with Works tools

☞ How you can use Works as soon as you get it

☞ What exactly are word processors, spreadsheets, and databases?

Do you remember how long it took you to learn to read? How awkward it felt using a pencil? Making words with the pencil? Then numbers? I remember being done with long division long before I figured out what it was. Do you remember calculus? Was that a foreign language, *or what?* I could go on like this forever, but the point is: I still don't know how to do calculus, I make a lot of mistakes with a pen, my long division's rusty, and I wouldn't handwrite a report if you paid me!

That's what computers and Windows and Works are all about. They're changing not only the way we do business, but also the way we learn and think and imagine. They may as well be part of the evolutionary process—because they're definitely here to stay.

By the Way . . .

We used to think that the ability to use language and tools were what ensured our dominance and survival as a species. But, if you've been to the zoo or watched TV lately, you know that dolphins most likely have language, chimpanzees are able to learn, and bears use a stick to get honey. Don't look now but they're gaining on us! In the natural scheme of things, computers may be our only hope for survival!

Ask What Works Can Do for You

There's probably no better way to learn about computers, and what they can do for you, than to use Works for Windows. First off, Works operates in the Windows environment; that means it's menu-driven, fun to use, and idiot-proof (even I can't break it!).

As an integrated package, Works is an exceptionally powerful program that includes elements of just about every kind of software and work tool you'd ever want to use: a *Word Processor* to create documents; a *Spreadsheet* to crunch numbers and hypothesize (what if?); and a *Database* to keep track of all your lists of clients, friends, relatives, addresses, and birthdays. You name it, it tracks it.

What's more, Works integrates a drawing program in the Word Processor so that you can embellish your words with art, and a chart maker in the Spreadsheet to let you turn your numbers into meaningful pictures of comparison. It even includes an easy-to-use Communications tool that lets you swap files with friends and coworkers, or tap into on-line databases for the latest stock quotes, world news, and other information.

And Works makes it easy to do something that computers never used to let you do: share documents between the different tools without using scissors and a glue stick! You can conveniently copy data from a database report to a spreadsheet, turn the spreadsheet into a chart, and then use the chart and the data in a word-processed report. You can even transfer files between entirely separate programs, such as MS Word or Lotus 1-2-3.

Speaking of Productivity

Works not only lets you become productive almost immediately, it dares you not to be! For starters, there are Works Wizards that actually create your customized databases, and form letters and letterheads for you (to name just a few). Autostart Templates give you ready-to-go formats for most of the documents you'll ever need to create. They even have templates for personal things, like home inventories, address books, recipes, and more. And, like your very own tutor, Cue Cards walk you through every step of the Autostart Template. They're even there when you have to create something from scratch (which you may never need to do in Works)! You can use Works Wizards, Autostart Templates, and Cue Cards wherever you work: in a home business, an office, or school.

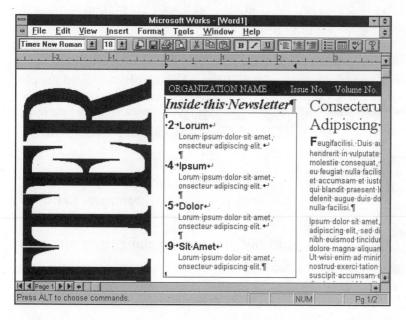

Use a Works template to create your own newsletter.

Recycle Your Works Skills!

When you learn to use one Works tool, the Word Processor for instance, you've already learned most of what you need to use the others.

Since the word processor included in Works is based on Word for Windows, and the database and spreadsheet are based on Excel, you'll find your Works skills transfer to many of Microsoft's powerful stand-alone programs. As a matter of fact, once you learn your way around Works for Windows, you shouldn't have any problem learning and using other Windows or even Macintosh programs.

The Word Processor and Microsoft Draw

I never really learned how to type; writing doesn't come easy; and I don't know the difference between an antonym, synonym, or homily. Why would I need a word processor?

Probably for all of those very reasons. Word processors of all flavors have probably saved people more time (and the world more trees) than anyone could ever imagine. Here's a small sample of what the Works Word Processor can do for your written word:

- Make it look better and easier to read and understand with different formats, fonts, and colors.

- Identify and correct spelling errors with spell checker.

- Find a creative (and correct) word to use instead of old, overworked ones.

- Search for common mistakes that run rampant, and replace them in one step.

- Correct errors before you print.

- Keep track of footnotes so you can add them as you type, without worrying about what page they land on.

SPEAK LIKE A GEEK

Document refers to the file of information created in a word processor, database, or spreadsheet to make it sound like the legal evidence it could someday be.

A **word processor** lets you enter, edit, format, and print text. Word processors are used in lieu of typewriters because they make it easier to correct mistakes and make changes to letters, reports, and other documents.

Spreadsheet comes from the term worksheet, which is what men in little green visors used to use to crunch numbers before there were spreadsheets.

A **database** is a collection of similar records, such as names and addresses or accounts, that you can organize in a way that will actually let you sort out valuable information.

☛ Remember and repeat information so that you type footers and headers just once.

☛ Line up columns and tables with ease.

☛ Let you use one document as the basis for creating another.

☛ Incorporate any graphics and clip art you want to add.

☛ Incorporate documents and data from other Works tools.

☛ Link database reports and spreadsheet charts to a word processed document, so the linked document can be automatically updated whenever the source document is.

Microsoft Draw is the tool you can use to illustrate Works documents or to modify Works' canned ClipArt and WordArt. You can use Draw to create a company logo, illustrate a report for school, or design your own personalized stationery and letterhead. You can even import pictures created in other drawing packages and then add them to word processor documents and database forms.

Since Draw is not a full-fledged stand-alone program, you can only access it from within the word processor. And pictures and illustrations created in Draw or imported to Draw can only be saved to the word-processed document. Despite these minor limitations, you'll be glad you have Draw in your creative toolbox.

The Spreadsheet and Charts

Because spreadsheets can calculate anything from columns of numbers to scientific equations, they're most often used to keep track of financial or statistical information, and to prepare, analyze, and present financial reports. Spreadsheets are made up of intersecting rows and columns called *cells*. Cells can contain text, formulas, or values that are related to each other by the relationships you set up. So when you change a value in one cell, related values will change too.

That's why spreadsheets are perfect for creating business plans and budgets, estimating costs, tracking expenses, and calculating anything you might want to calculate—in a million different ways. You can use them to figure out WHAT would happen IF this variable were different (for example, what if I charged fifty cents more for this widget, or paid twenty dollars a month extra on this loan?) Think of the time and trees a spreadsheet can save if you don't have to do these kinds of jobs yourself!

Business projections based on last year's data, created by Works' Spreadsheet.

	Microsoft Works - [BUSPLAN1.WKS]					
File Edit View Insert Format Tools Window Help						
Arial 10		B I U			Σ $	
B21						
	A	B	C	D	E	F
3		Last Year	Current Year	Next Year?		
4						
5	**Income**					
6	Gross Sales	$248,765	$286,079	$302,450		
7	Less Returns and Allowances	$29,851	$30,645	$32,350		
8	Less Cost of Goods	$94,530	$108,700	$111,400		
9	Gross Profit:	$124,384	$146,734	$158,700		
10						
11	**Operating Expenses**					
12	Selling	$12,321	$13,432	$14,500		
13	Administrative	$23,980	$25,400	$26,800		
14	Other	$14,560	$14,500	$14,800		
15	Total Expenses:		$53,332	$56,100		
16						
17	**Summary**					
18	Net Income Before Taxes	$124,384	$93,402	$102,600		
19	Taxes on Income	$19,234	$23,200	$23,200		
20	Net Income After Taxes:	$105,150	$70,202	$79,400		
21						
22						
Press ALT to choose commands, or F2 to edit.					NUM	

Works can also create meaningful charts from your spreadsheet data that let you highlight relationships between variables or spot emerging trends. You can choose from 12 different chart types and styles, based on your business needs. Charts can really simplify your data and add impact to word-processed reports.

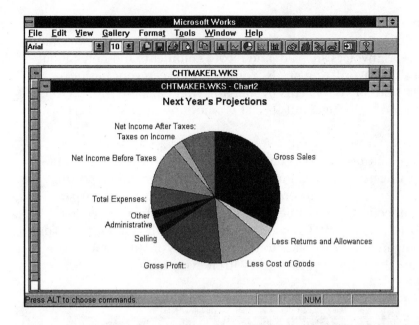

Everybody wants a piece of the pie.

By the Way . . .

The first spreadsheet I ever used was in Works for DOS. I was so taken with the rows and columns, I decided to try to design my own business card with it. Yeah, I know it wasn't intended for that, but I was trying to be creative, and my graphics program didn't have such a great grid. It might have worked, too, if the DOS version had as many font styles and formats as Works for Windows has.

The Database

The Works Database can be used to organize all kinds of information either alphabetically, numerically, or in groups you assign. You can convert your entire address book to a database and print mailing labels at holiday time or prepare a glossary for that science report. For business, you can create a client database and use it to track and mail invoices, calculate amounts due as invoices are paid, and record comments and notes about each client's special ordering needs. You can even keep your business name out in front of your clients by merging your database with a Word Processor document to send out special promotions and newsletters regularly.

Once you've created a Works database, you have a wealth of information at your fingertips. You can use the Database's query and reporting functions to locate specific information (such as how many clients are based in Connecticut). You can even find out how many Connecticut clients did more than $150,000 worth of business with you last year. Then you can compare this year's sales to last year's sales on an ongoing basis, and hit your sales team over the head with it every month.

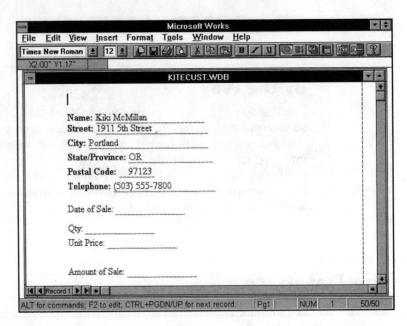

The start of a client database in form view.

Communications

You need a modem (and Works version 3.0) to be able to do anything constructive with Works' communication tool. But if you have a modem and the latest version of Works, you can dial on-line information services or exchange files with friends, neighbors, and coworkers who also have modems. If no one you know is connected, you can always make friends on a network bulletin board.

The Least You Need to Know

☛ Computers are our friends. We need computers.

☛ Works is a powerful tool that can boost your productivity.

☛ When you learn one Works tool you almost learn 'em all!

☛ Word processors help us look good and sound halfway intelligent.

☛ Databases create junk mail, but they also let you sort through tons of information to get the data you need.

☛ Spreadsheets let you ponder "what if." What if I change this number, and this one, and this one . . .without ever erasing? And the answer is usually right.

☛ Spreadsheets can't really do graphics, but they make their own very impressive charts.

☛ You need to have a modem hooked up to your computer in order to benefit from communication tools. Otherwise, you can talk, but there'll be no one to listen.

☛ Works version 2.0 deosn't have the communications tool, so 2.0 users may want to skip Chapter 25.

This page unintentionally left blank.

Chapter 3
Windows: A Room with a View

In This Chapter

- ☛ How to start Windows
- ☛ Window anatomy
- ☛ Using a mouse
- ☛ Menus and dialog boxes
- ☛ Opening, closing, and resizing a window
- ☛ Exiting safely

When I finally finished school I thought I would quickly make my mark in the world. Little did I know that it would take almost four years just to get my own office, and two more to get a window! By that time, I'd almost forgotten what the world looked like, let alone what mark I had intended to make!

To those of you who spend most of your days in small dark cubicles, think of Windows as your very own room with a view. Those days of losing yourself in the dark black hole of DOS and propping your eyes open just to stay awake are over. Windows will liberate your senses, stir your imagination, and let you juggle umpteen different projects—and a compelling game of Solitaire—without ever leaving the *ergonomic* comfort of your chair!

In this chapter, you'll learn just enough about Windows to be able to use it wisely and to get other programs, like Works, started.

SPEAK LIKE A GEEK

A **program** is a software application or tool that accomplishes a particular task. Some examples are a calculator, word processor, database, and spreadsheet. Even Solitaire is a program.

SPEAK LIKE A GEEK

Configured—a big word for "set up." Configuration can mean something as major as what type of hard disk you have, or something as minor as which programs run automatically when you turn on your computer.

Your computer and all the extras attached to it, such as your monitor, your keyboard, and your printer, make up your **system**.

Getting Into It

Just as the way to open a real window depends on the type of window installed, opening Windows depends on how your *system* was *configured*.

Let's assume your computer is all hooked up, turned on, and ready to go. If you're lucky, your computer is set up to load Windows automatically when you start up. You can tell you're in Windows when the Windows logo is splashed across the screen and then, after what seems to be forever, the Program Manager window appears on-screen. If this just happened to you, you're definitely not in Kansas anymore! Go on to the next section.

If Windows didn't start when you turned on your computer, try one of the following tips:

- ☛ If you get an option menu that lists Windows as one of your choices, type the number shown in front of the Windows option and press **Enter**.

- ☛ If you get a menu that doesn't list Windows as an option, choose a command, such as Exit or Quit, to get to a DOS prompt. Then try the next tip.

- ☛ If you get a *DOS prompt* that looks something like this: C:> or C>, be grateful you don't have to stay there; just type **WIN** and press **Enter**.

Welcome to Windows-land

Now that you're in Windows, you may feel a bit like you've landed in Oz. Actually, that's a pretty fair assessment because, like the Wizard, the Program Manager runs just about everything in her domain. The Program Manager operates out of her own window to control all of the programs that you run in windows—and in Windows-land, *everything* runs in windows.

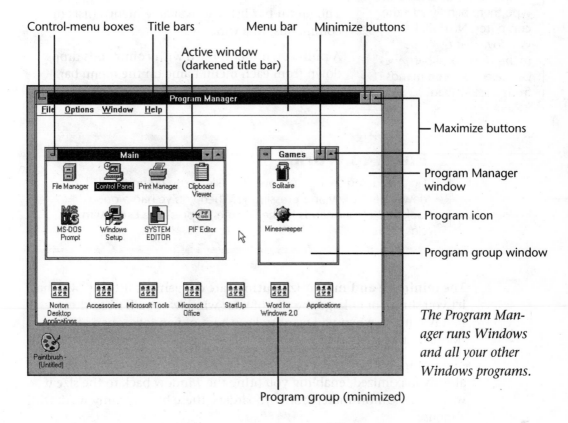

The Program Manager runs Windows and all your other Windows programs.

Except for being larger than other windows, the Program Manager's window is typical of most. Let's see what the Program Manager is made of:

Commands are orders that tell the computer what to do. Before Windows, computer users had to memorize commands and type them blindly into the computer. Now that Windows has given us menu boxes and bars, we can select our commands from a list instead.

The **Program Manager window** is the grand-poobah window. It contains smaller windows and icons (little pictures).

The **title bar** at the top of each window tells you the name of the window. The color of the title bar changes when the window is active. (You'll learn what this means soon.)

The **menu bar** lists the available menus (lists of commands) in a window.

A **pull-down menu** filled with commands drops down from each menu name on the menu bar.

Put It to Work

Go ahead and try it. Pull down the **File** menu by holding down the **Alt** key and pressing **F**. When you've had a good look at the commands in the **File** menu, press the **Esc** key to close it again.

The **minimize and maximize buttons** are convenient little arrows that let you shrink or enlarge the size of your window. You'll need these handy buttons when you want to keep a lot of windows open at once. (More on this later.)

The **restore button** replaces the maximize button when a window is already maximized, enabling you bring the window back to the size it was before. Unfortunately for keyboarders, these buttons only work with a mouse.

You can use the **Control-menu box** if you're a keyboarder who needs to resize a window. It's an equal opportunity box that lets you use either a mouse *or* the keyboard to change window sizes. It can also be used to open and close windows.

A **program group window** holds **program icons** that represent programs you can run. To make more room for the programs you use most often, program group windows can be reduced (minimized) to icons themselves when not in use.

The **active window** is the program group window within Program Manager that Windows is paying attention to at the moment. Even though you might have many windows open at once, only one can be active at a time.

Every Picture Tells a Story, Don't It?

Each of the smaller windows within the Program Manager holds a program or group of programs. That's why these smaller windows are called *program groups*. A program group can be either open or closed. When it's open, it appears as a window with its own title bar. When it's closed, it appears as a little picture of an open window (an *icon*) at the bottom of the Program Manager window.

A **program icon** is a graphic symbol of a program (like Works for Windows) that appears in a program group. You can start the program by double-clicking the icon.

Within an open program group, you'll see *program icons*, which represent tools and applications that you can use. Some of them come free when you buy Windows; these are usually kept in the Main, Accessories, or Games program groups. The others that you install, like Works for Windows, have their own program groups.

> ## By the Way . . .
> You aren't stuck leaving icons in the program groups they start out in—you can move any program icon to any program group you want. Just drag it there with your mouse. You'll learn how to drag shortly.

Playing by the Rules

The Program Manager's sole purpose in life is to start and manage your programs. Once a program (like Works) is started, you have to play by *its* rules instead of the Program Manager's. Fortunately, most programs that work in Windows use the same rules and speak the same language, so you'll find it very easy to catch on. In the remainder of this chapter, you'll learn how to get around in Windows. These skills will make your life much easier when you dive into Microsoft Works!

Mousing Around

In Windows, like in life, you must learn to *ask* for what you want! There are many ways to ask for things in Windows. You can have fun and "mouse around" with your requests. Or, you can bang out your demands on the keyboard.

Having finally learned to navigate WordPerfect commands, I was reluctant to switch to Microsoft Word for Mac at a client's request. But when I saw how easy it was to use a mouse and menus, I realized life was too short to ever struggle with keyboard commands again. Now all I need to do is point and *click*, or *double-click*, or *drag and drop*. Who knows, maybe someday I'll learn how to drop click.

Hold onto Your Mouse

If you've never used a mouse before, a few quick lessons are in order. Hold on tight— here we go. Position your mouse in the middle of the mouse pad, with its tail (cord) facing away from you. Wrap your hand around the mouse like you're palming a basketball. Rest your thumb and ring or little finger along the sides of the mouse, touching the mouse pad slightly. Let your wrist rest on the mouse pad too.

Place your index finger on the left button and your middle finger on the right button. Although the right button can do some pretty weird things, most Windows programs are set up to use only one button, and unless you tell your system otherwise, it's the left one.

Using the Program Manager window as a target, move the mouse around on the mouse pad until you can see the pointer on your screen. Don't press any buttons yet, but keep practicing moving the pointer to different boxes and icons on-screen. You can move the mouse pretty far on the screen without really moving your wrist from its resting place.

If you happen to run out of mouse pad before the pointer gets to the edge of the screen, just pick the mouse up and place it back in the middle of its pad. The pointer will stay where it was until you put the mouse back down.

Mouse Moves

Getting work done takes a little more effort than just walking the mouse. You have to train your mouse to work for you. Most of what you'll ever need to do in Windows can be done with these simple mouse moves:

Point　Move the mouse so the pointer rests on what you're aiming at. But don't expect anything to happen yet. A point always needs a swift click in order to accomplish anything.

Click　This maneuver, when coupled with the point, is used to choose things or make a selection. Click by quickly pressing and releasing the left mouse button.

Double-click　This action, also used in conjunction with the point, is used to start a program or make something run. It's a little tougher than a click because you have to be real fast.

Drag　When you're working in a program, a drag is like a lengthy point that's used to move something or select more than one thing at a time. To do a drag, press and hold down the left button, and then move the mouse pointer along the target area.

Drop　When you drop, you let go of a drag. That means you release the mouse button when the mouse pointer has reached its final destination at the end of a drag.

Would You Like to See a Menu?

Now that you've been around Windows a bit, it might be worthwhile to take a closer look at menu bars and pull-down menus. You'll be amazed at what you can learn about a place just by reading the menu.

In case you've forgotten, the menu bar tells you what kind of menus are served. File, Window, and Help are pretty much standard fare. You'll see them listed on most menu bars. More upscale programs also serve Edit, View, Insert, Format, Tools, and more.

So Many Menus, So Little Time

Are you ready to dig in? There are three ways to open a pull-down menu:

- Click on the menu name with your mouse.

- Hold down the **Alt** key on the keyboard and type the underlined selection letter in the menu's name.

- Press the **Alt** key, and then press the down-arrow key to open the first menu. Press the left arrow key until the menu you want is open.

To select a command once the menu is open, you have three more choices. You can:

- Click on the command with your mouse.

- Press the command's selection letter.

- Use the up or down arrow key to high-light the command, and then press **Enter**.

The underlined letter in the name of a command or menu is called the **selection letter**, or hot key. It's your key to keyboard use; press the key that corresponds to that letter to activate the menu or command.

Once you get comfortable with menus, you may want to look at them more closely. Some menus have special features that give more information about various commands. Here's an example:

If you open a menu or select a command by mistake (these things happen), press **Esc** until things look normal again.

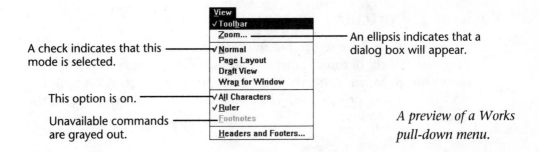

A check indicates that this mode is selected.

This option is on.

Unavailable commands are grayed out.

An ellipsis indicates that a dialog box will appear.

A preview of a Works pull-down menu.

Grayed text   Commands that are not currently available are lighter than the other commands on the menu. They're supposed to be fading into the background so you won't select them, 'cause you can't.

Ellipsis   Three periods that follow a command, like Zoom..., tell you that when you select this command a dialog box will appear, requesting more information before Works can carry out the command.

Check mark   Appears next to options and modes to show you which are turned on or selected.

By the Way . . .

Options work like the rear defroster in a car. When the check mark is displayed, the option is ON, and you need to click it to turn it OFF. When the check mark isn't shown next to an option, it's OFF and a click will turn it ON. You can have more than one option ON at a time.

continues

continued

Modes, on the other hand, are limited to one at a time, like a car's air conditioner and heater. For example, you can't be in the Normal page view while you're also in the Outline or Draft view. To change the active mode, just select another one. The check mark will always go where the action is.

Keyboard Shortcuts

To really get some mileage out of the keyboard, use *shortcut keys*. They're listed to the right of some commands in pull-down menus. When you're lucky enough to remember them, you can press the shortcut key(s) from anywhere in your program—to place your order without even reading the menu.

Pull-down menus offer keyboard "cheat sheets."

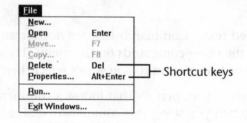

That's All, Folks!

That's basically all there is to selecting menus and commands. Since there are so many ways to make choices in Windows, from now on I'll just tell you *when* to select a command, and you can decide whether to click or type!

Tell It to Your Dialog Box

What? Where? When? Sometimes a simple "please do it" just isn't enough. That's when a dialog box pops up. The dialog box gives you the chance to supply more information about a job or command, so it's done right the first time. Like something out of Mission Control, the File menu's Print dialog box doesn't seem to leave any room for doubt! Here are some creatures you may encounter in a dialog box:

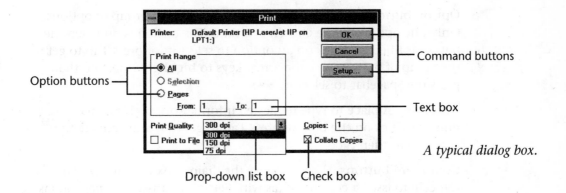

Option buttons ——

Command buttons

Text box

A typical dialog box.

Drop-down list box   Check box

Just Driving Through

You may be familiar with some of the dialog box controls already, but let's just review the rules of the road.

> **List box**   Displays a list of choices. Click on a choice, or use the arrow keys to highlight the choice and press the **Spacebar**.
>
> **Drop-down list box**   Hides a list that's too long to be seen all at once. Click on the down-arrow button to open the list, and then click on the item you want to select. Or, press **Tab** to get to the box, press the down-arrow key to open the list, position the highlighter on the item you want to choose, and then press **Spacebar** to select it.
>
> **Check box**   Indicates whether or not an option is on. When an X appears in a check box, the option is on. Click on it to toggle it on or off, or press **Tab** to get to it and press the Spacebar. More than one check box can be on at the same time.

The best way to select something in a dialog box is to click on it with your mouse. But it is possible to use the keyboard: press **Tab** to move from section to section, or hold down **Alt** and press the selection letter for the section name. Press the arrow keys to move the highlight to a new selection, and press **Spacebar** to select. Press **Enter** to close the box and accept your changes, or press **Esc** to cancel your changes.

Option buttons   Used to select one option from a group of options. Only one option can be chosen at a time. The option is on when the button is filled in. Click on an option to select it, or press **Tab** to get to the group of buttons, use the arrow keys to highlight one, and then press the Spacebar to select it.

Text box   A place to type requested information, such as a name or number. Click on the box, or press **Tab** to get to it and activate the cursor in it; then type.

Command buttons   Used to close the dialog box (as with OK and Cancel), to issue a command (as with Select), to answer a question (as with Yes or No), or to open an additional dialog box (as with Options). If the command opens another dialog box, the button will have an ellipsis following the name. To select a command button, click on it or press **Tab** to get to it, and press Enter.

By the Way . . .

Works for Windows also uses *tabs* in dialog boxes (tabs as in **folder tabs**, not the Tab key). Some dialog boxes are divided into tabbed screens that help organize information logically—just like tabs in a notebook. To move from tab to tab in a dialog box, click the tab or press **Alt** and the selection letter in the tab name. When you're done, click **OK**.

Taking Control of Your Windows

When you're working with several open windows at once, it helps to be able to select and arrange them for comfort and convenience. In this section, you'll learn how.

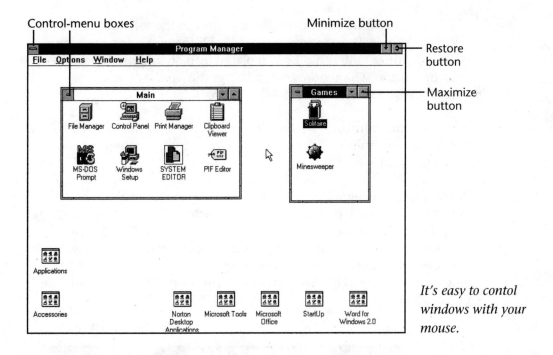

Control-menu boxes — Minimize button — Restore button — Maximize button

It's easy to contol windows with your mouse.

As I mentioned earlier, only one window can be active at a time. The active window has a different-colored title bar from the other windows (usually matching the color of the Program Manager window's title bar). To activate a window, just click on any part of it or press **Ctrl+Tab** until it's activated. To deactivate it, activate a different window.

Window-Sizing, Mouse Style

Ready to try it, mouse users? Start from the Program Manager window and make sure you have two or more program group windows open. If you don't, double-click on some program group icons to open them.

Click on the **maximize** button (the up arrow in the top right corner of the window). Poof! The window expands to fill the entire screen. Notice that the maximize button has been replaced by a double-headed arrow—the restore button. The restore button brings the window back to its previous size (the size it was before it was maximized).

Now click the **minimize** button (the down-arrow) to shrink the window down to an icon. This icon sits quietly on your screen, waiting for you to double-click it back into action.

If you don't like the window's size, resize it by grabbing a side of its border with the mouse pointer (the pointer turns into a double-headed arrow). Then drag to the length or width you want, and drop. Do this repeatedly until you find the size you like. To size a window quickly, size the whole thing at once. Position the mouse pointer on a corner of the window border instead of a side, and drag. Drop when the window is the size you want.

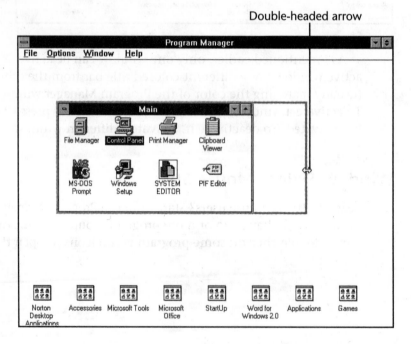

Double-headed arrow

Dragging the border changes the window's size.

To move a window where you want it, point at the title bar and drag the window around. The outline that you see moving around with you is a shadow. The real window is smart enough to stay put until you've made up your mind! Once you have, release the mouse button and drop!

If you think you're seeing double when you grab a window border, it's just the mouse pointer trying to be helpful. Both arrows show you which directions you can drag in.

Window Sizing, Keyboard Style

Resizing windows with the keyboard is not nearly as quick and easy as using the mouse. In fact, it's a real pain. Nevertheless, here's how you do it:

To close an open window quickly, double-click on its control-menu box. If it's the Program Manager window or a program group window, it'll be minimized; if it's an application window, it'll disappear from sight entirely.

☞ Press **Alt+ –** (hyphen) to open the active program group's control menu, or **Alt+Spacebar** to open the Program Manager's Control menu.

☞ To minimize, maximize, or restore the window, choose the corresponding option from the Control menu.

☞ To resize the window, choose **Size**; then use the arrow keys to resize the window. Press **Enter** when you're done.

☞ To move the window, choose **Move**; then use the arrow keys to move the window. (Sounds just like Size, doesn't it?) Again, press **Enter** when you're done.

☞ To close the window, choose **Close**.

Tidying Up the Place

To straighten up all of your windows, select Window from the menu bar. Then pick one of the options there:

☞ If you're the type who goes around straightening pictures on the wall, choose Arrange Icons to line up all of the program icons in the active window.

☞ Choose Tile to spread all of your open windows out across the screen so you can view them at once.

☞ If you prefer to let your work pile up while you do one thing at a time, choose Cascade. Your windows will flow like a waterfall, one upon the other. When you need to work in one of the buried ones, simply click on its title bar to bring it forward.

Although sometimes it can't be helped (like those rare occasions when everything locks up), in general, DON'T turn off the computer until you exit Windows! Wait for that ugly DOS prompt to reappear before you flip the power switch.

Good Night Windows. Good Night Chet.

When everyone else left hours ago and there's nothing more for you to do, close your windows and go home! To exit from Windows safely, take your pick:

☞ Double-click the Program Manager's **Control-menu box.**

☞ Open the Program Manager's **Control** menu and select **Close.**

☞ Press **Alt+F4.**

☞ Choose Exit from the Program Manager's File menu.

At this point, Windows asks if you really want to exit. Select **OK**, and you're outta there.

The Least You Need to Know

We've just packed a lot of Windows stuff into one long chapter. Here's what I hope you'll remember:

- ☞ Windows is a program that runs other programs. Each program within it runs in a window.

- ☞ To start Windows, type **WIN** at the DOS prompt and press **Enter**.

- ☞ Even though the Program Manager's window is bigger than other windows, it looks and feels and works like all the rest.

- ☞ The easiest way to use Windows is to use a mouse. Click the mouse to choose a command, double-click to open a window or start a program, and drag and drop to move an object or make a big selection.

- ☞ You can keep many windows open at once, and arrange, size, and move them to suit your work style.

- ☞ Exit Windows safely before you shut down for the night. Don't turn your computer off until you see the DOS prompt.

**Virtual text page.
(There's virtually no text on it)**

Chapter 4
Out of the Starting Gate

In This Chapter

- Installing Works
- Starting it up
- Running the tutorial
- Using WorksWizards, AutoStart Templates, and Cue Cards
- Getting on-line help

Have you ever lost sleep over the thought of starting something new: the next grade, a new school, a strange neighborhood, a romance, or a job? Why is it we never lose sleep over starting new toothpaste, brand new shoes, a good book, or a fresh pint of ice cream?

What does all this have to do with using Works for Windows? Absolutely nothing. I just don't want anyone losing sleep over starting Works!

Starting on the Right Foot

So you've been practicing the Windows skills and mouse moves you learned in Chapter 3 and you want to get to Works!

First of all, have you installed Works yet? You'll need to do that before you can go any further. If you're not sure whether Works is installed, try to find the Microsoft Works program icon in the Program Manager window. Remember from Chapter 3 that it should be in its own program group window. If it's not, it probably isn't installed yet! Here's how to install it. (Skip to the next section if Works is already installed.)

If you're using Microsoft Works version 2.0, the Microsoft Works program icon will be in the Microsoft Solution Series program group. In version 3.0, the icon resides in the Microsoft Works for Windows program group.

Installing Works

Because installing Works is so simple, I'm just going to get you started and leave you in the hands of those good people at Microsoft. If you have any problems, look in the Microsoft Works for Windows User's Guide, or call their not-so-toll-free help line (the number is listed in the docs).

First, start your computer. Then, since you have to install Works from within Windows to get it to run, make sure you're in Windows. If you happen to still be in DOS, at the DOS prompt (C:\), type **WIN** and press **Enter**. If you worked through Chapter 3, you've probably done all this already.

Once the Windows Program Manager appears, insert the Works Setup and Help Disk into drive A or B, depending on which drive it fits into. (We'll assume you are using drive A.) Select **Run** from the File menu, and type this in the dialog box:

A:**setup**

Now click on **OK** or press **Enter**. The Works Welcome dialog box appears to guide you through the setup process. Keep your eye on the screen and do what the good folks at Microsoft ask. When you're prompted to choose the type of installation you want, choose **Complete Installation** so that all of the Help and Tutorial files we need will be there.

Keep following the instructions on-screen until you're told that the installation is complete. When you restart your computer, a program group for Microsoft Works will have been added to your Program Manager desktop.

Getting to Works

When you can see the Microsoft Works for Windows icons staring back at you from an open program group window, you're ready to go to work.

If the Works for Windows program group is minimized, you won't be able to see the whites of their icons. Double-click on the Microsoft Works for Windows program group icon at the bottom of the Program Manager window to restore the program group. If double-clicking is not your speed, try clicking once and pressing **Enter**. It works just as well.

To get the show on the road, double-click on the program icon labeled **Microsoft Works**. You remember how to double-click, don't you? You just point and put two clicks together. (If you're using the keyboard, press **Ctrl+Tab** until the Works program group is highlighted and then press **Enter**. Press **Enter** again to start Works.)

Works will be there when you arrive. You'll know it's Works by the lighthouse beacon and the welcome mat. Meet me in front of the tutorial.

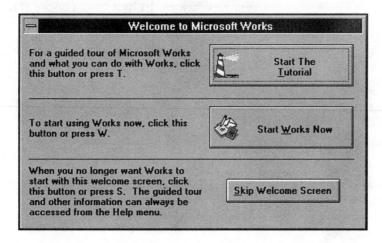

When you get to Works, Microsoft rolls out the welcome mat!

To start the Works program faster, either keep the Microsoft Works for Windows program group window open all the time, or drag the Microsoft Works icon out of this window and place it in another program group (like Applications) that you like to keep open. If you'd rather have Works start automatically as soon as you start Windows, drag the icon to the StartUp program group.

TECHNO NERD TEACHES

When you first enter Works, you land in a Works window, but you read and respond to a Works *dialog box*. How can you tell it's a box and not a window? For one, you can move it, but you can't resize it. And, like other command dialog boxes that you've seen, you can't exit the scene until you've either answered the question or closed the dialog box first.

A Works Tu"tour"ial

Welcome to Works! You might notice that things are kind of different here, a little less hectic and a bit more friendly than Windows. For one, look at the lower-left hand corner of your Works screen. See that "Click on a button or press an underlined letter?" That's a *status bar*. I think of it as a hyperactive road sign that tells me where I am and what I can do. You'll find one on every street and window in Works, so you'll never be at a loss for direction.

There are so many different ways to learn about Works that it's hard to know where to begin:

☞ If you have used other Windows programs before, you may want to go right to the chapter(s) you're most interested in for the Word Processor, Spreadsheet, Database, and Communications. In that case, choose Start Works Now.

☞ If this is all new to you, you might want to stick around. We'll spend the rest of this chapter looking over some of the great tools Microsoft provides in Works that can help you get working quickly.

Now that we're at the Welcome screen, let's look at our options:

Start The Tutorial Click this button (the lighthouse) to take a quick tour of all Works tools and the latest features. I highly recommend it for those of you who have never worked with an integrated software package or have not used other Windows programs. Like the sign says, if you're using the keyboard, press **T** to start the tutorial. Once you're in the tutorial, read the screens to find out what to do next. It's easy and very informative! When you're done, come back to finish this chapter!

Start Works Now Click this button,(the Works icon, of course) or press **W**, if you're already a sophisticated Windower, or you've already viewed the tutorial.

Skip Welcome Screen If you click this button, or press **S**, you'll never see this screen again. The next time you open Works, it will simply start quietly, without asking you if you want to view the tutorial.

Let's click the Start Works Now button to move on. Keyboarders, press **W**, please!

SPEAK LIKE A GEEK

When there are too many ways to carry out a command that you've chosen, or too many important decisions to make, Works will display a **dialog box** to let you decide. That way, you have no one to blame but yourself.

Status bar functions as a "road sign" at the bottom of the Works screen that tells you where you are in a document and what you can do there. It describes what each command or tool you select will do.

By the Way . . .

If you decide to take the on-line tutorial at another time, or you want to refer to the lessons as you need them, open the **Help** menu and choose **Tutorial** (or, press **Shift+F1** from the keyboard). If you are working in a document when you open the tutorial, the document will still be there when you return.

The Startup screen in version 2.0 doesn't look quite the same as this one. But, except for the fact that it lacks the Template and Communications choices, it still takes you where you want to go.

Taxi, Taxi

This is the Startup screen. Think of it as your point of departure for all of your Works.

The Startup screen gives you a lift to any one of four destinations, which you can select by clicking one of the buttons on the left or pressing the underlined hot key. (Use the fifth button—Instructions—to get instructions about the other four buttons.) Here's the itinerary:

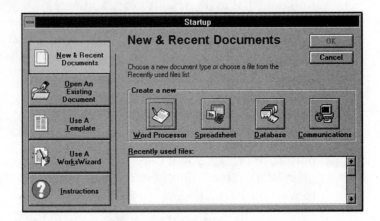

The Startup screen takes you anywhere you want to go in Works.

New & Recent Document   Click on this button, or press **N** to start a word processor, spreadsheet, or database document from scratch, or to access Works Communications. You'll learn how to start documents from scratch in other chapters. For now, we're just looking.

Open An Existing Document   Click on this button or press **O** to open a Word Processor, Spreadsheet, Database, or Communications document that you've worked on before and have already saved to Works files. You'll be able to select the document you want to work on from a list of all your files. We'll be using this button in later chapters. If you press it now, you won't have an existing file to select!

Use A Template   Click on this button or press **T** to use an AutoStart Template or a template that you designed yourself. (Remember from Chapter 2 that templates are pre-formatted document shells that can help you get started and make your work easier to do.) More on this later.

Use A WorksWizard   Click on this button or press **K** to use a WorksWizard when you want Works to create the document for you.

That last one sounds good to me. Let's try it!

To the WorksWizards, Please, and Step on It!

The WorksWizards are really an excellent place to start using Works. WorksWizards can actually perform 12 different jobs for you. Ten of the 12 WorksWizards create specific databases, like customer profiles. If you can't find a database that's quite what you need, use the Quick Database Wizard to design a new one.

The WorksWizard's File Organizer is even easier to use than the Windows File Manager, and it keeps all of the files on your computer organized (not just Works files). If you're like me and you have a footnote phobia, the Footnote Wizard can cure you. It puts them in their proper place.

To find out what each of the WorksWizards does, highlight one of the WorksWizards listed in the selection box and then read a description of it in the Description box below. To highlight a Wizard, click once, or use the arrow keys to make your selection.

When you know which Wizard you want to use, click the **OK** button, or from the keyboard use the arrow keys to highlight it and then press **Enter**. The WorksWizard will be displayed.

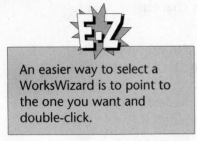

An easier way to select a WorksWizard is to point to the one you want and double-click.

Read each WorksWizard screen carefully. As you can see, everything you need to do will be spelled out on screen.

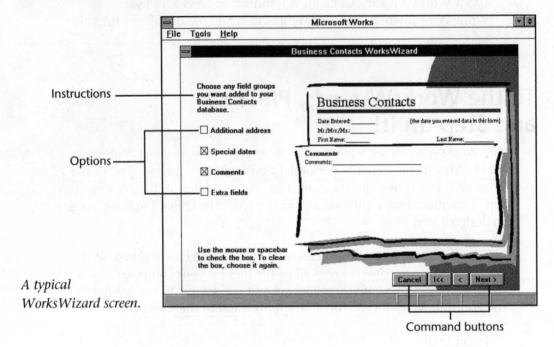

A typical WorksWizard screen.

Here's how to use a WorksWizard screen:

Instructions Usually found in the lower left corner, or boxed off toward the center of the screen, the instructions tell you how to use the screen to respond to WorksWizard's questions. Sometimes, if there's a chance you might need more help, there'll be a Help button right next to the directions.

Options WorksWizards have two kinds of options: option buttons and check boxes. You can select as many check boxes as you want. However, you can select only one option button at a time—when you select one, all the others are deselected. Whichever kind it is, just click on it or press **Tab** to get to it and press the **Spacebar**.

Command buttons   These buttons control the action in the tutorial:

Use this button when you've changed your mind and want to exit the WorksWizard. You can also press **Esc** to cancel.

Click this button to go back to the first screen in the WorksWizard you're working on. You can get back to the beginning from the keyboard by using **Ctrl+←** repeatedly.

Click this button to go back to the previous screen. You can also use the keyboard to go back one screen by pressing **Ctrl+←**.

Click this button when you're ready to move on to the next screen. Or, from the keyboard, press **Enter** instead.

Maybe You AutoStart Here

AutoStart Templates are ready-to-use formats that can help get you started creating many of your home, business, or educational documents and reports. Once you select a template, Cue Cards are available to walk you through each step of the process.

When you want to use an AutoStart Template, click on the Use A Template button on the Startup screen, or press **T**. The template selection box appears. Templates are organized by group and category, so you'll need to select those things first. Select the template group you want to work in by dragging the down arrow in the selection box and scrolling through the selection list. When your choice

> Remember, version 2.0 users, you don't have the Template option, so you can skip to the next section.

is highlighted, drop to select it. If you're using the keyboard, press **Alt+C** and then use the down arrow to make your selection. Next, select the template category you want. Categories differ for each template group, and templates are different for each category. So, as you select a category, the template choices in the template box will change too.

Use the mouse pointer to scroll through the Category selection box, and then click on your choice. Do the same for the template box. From the keyboard, press **Alt+*hot key*** for the selection box that you want, and then use the arrow keys to indicate your choice.

After you've chosen the template, decide if you want to leave the Cue Cards on. It's probably a good idea to leave them on while you're learning Works. If you find they get in the way, you can shut them off at any time. Click or use the Alt+hot key combination to choose which you want.

After you've made your selections, click **OK** or press **Enter**. The template appears. Let the Cue Cards show you how to fill in the template.

Scroll means to move horizontally and vertically through a document or list box, using the arrow keys or a mouse and scroll bars.

A **template** is a preformatted document window that can have pre-set margins, page layout, tabs, and font styles. Templates can save you a lot of time when you create many of the same type documents.

When you've gained more experience with templates, here are some other things you can do:

☞ Rename a template so you can find it more easily.

☞ Customize a template to your specific needs and then rename it so the original template remains intact.

☞ Add your own templates to the selection list.

☞ Set up a template as the default style that you can use whenever you start a new document.

☞ If you find you have too many templates, you can delete some from the selection list by just selecting a template and pressing the **Delete** button on the template Startup screen.

Try with a Little Help from Your Friends

Now that you've had a taste of what WorksWizards and AutoStart templates can do for you, you may be more than a little curious about what kind of help you can get when you need it! No matter where you are in Works, help is never more than a click or a keystroke away.

When You Can't Remember Your Lines

Use Cue Cards whenever you need step-by-step directions for many Works tasks. Cue Cards stay on top of the Works screen so you can use them as you work. They are automatically displayed whenever you open an existing document, create a new document, add data to a WorksWizard, or work with an AutoStart template.

If you want to turn Cue Cards on in your present document and all future documents, open the Help menu and then choose **Cue Cards**. When you want to turn Cue Cards off, choose **Cue Cards** from the Help menu again. Works won't display Cue Cards in any documents until you turn them back on again.

Sorry again, version 2.0 users. There are no Cue Cards for you.

You need a mouse to use Cue Cards. If you are stuck in the middle of a Cue Card without a mouse, press **Shift+F3** to close the Cue Card.

You can turn Cue Cards on or off from the Toolbar by clicking the **Learning Works **?**** button, and then selecting **Cue Cards**.

Help Is Everywhere!

I can think of only one place where you might briefly be without Help: when WorksWizards are preparing your document. But even then, instructions are provided on every screen! If you need help at any other time, click on the **Help** menu or press **Alt+H**, and select the kind of help you need. Here are your options:

Version 2.0 users will find that the **H**elp menu is organized a little differently. But keep reading to find out what is available.

☞ Select Contents to see the Help Table of Contents, which lists all of the available Help categories. The contents are organized as a series of "jumps" (underlined topics that let you move quickly to the Help topics you need). Click on the topic, or jump to the information you want.

☞ Select Search for Help on to look up a particular command or topic by typing the word or phrase you want in the box at the top of the window. Use Search when you know what you're looking for. If you aren't sure of it exactly, type the first few letters of the phrase or command. Then click the Show Topics button, and a list of related topics is displayed. Select the topic you want and choose the Go To button.

☞ Select How to Use Help when you've never used an on-line Help system—or one as extensive as this—before. Then choose the Help topic you need from the Contents selection list.

Jump—a highlighted term or topic in the Works for Windows Help system that, when selected, jumps you right to that section of the Help system.

☞ Select Basic Skills when you need step-by-step instructions on the Works Basic Skills or on each Works Tool. Click on the category you want, and keep clicking on topics to pinpoint the information you need.

Like the Help window shown below, each Help window has a top row of buttons that help you navigate the on-line Help screens.

Click here to see a table of contents.

Click here to go back to the previous screen.

Click here to search for a topic.

Click here to go back to any previous Help screen you've seen.

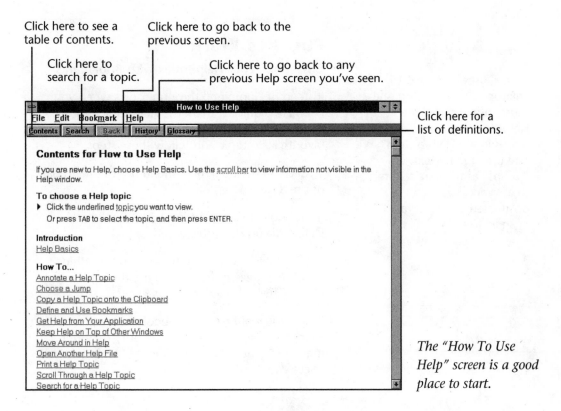

Click here for a list of definitions.

Contents for How to Use Help

If you are new to Help, choose Help Basics. Use the scroll bar to view information not visible in the Help window.

To choose a Help topic
▶ Click the underlined topic you want to view.
  Or press TAB to select the topic, and then press ENTER.

Introduction
Help Basics

How To...
Annotate a Help Topic
Choose a Jump
Copy a Help Topic onto the Clipboard
Define and Use Bookmarks
Get Help from Your Application
Keep Help on Top of Other Windows
Move Around in Help
Open Another Help File
Print a Help Topic
Scroll Through a Help Topic
Search for a Help Topic

The "How To Use Help" screen is a good place to start.

To select any of the options available to you in Help, click on the option, or press **Tab** until you highlight what you want, and then press **Enter**. When you're working in a document and need Help on a specific task, press **F1**. Works displays information about related tools, commands, and dialog box options.

To get a User's Guide reference for a topic that's covered in the on-line Helps, click on the User's Guide jump that's displayed on some Help screens.

TECHNO NERD TEACHES

Works' uses hypertext to link topics of interest in one segment of the on-line Helps to other topics or words in the Help system. The use of hypertext, or "jumps" as they are referred to in Works, was first postulated by Vennavar Bush in 1945.

Put It to Work

Customize Your Help Index with Bookmarks

Instead of "jumping" through topics when you need Help quickly, mark the Help topics you need and use most often. To do so, turn to a favorite Help topic and follow these steps:

1. Click on the Book**m**ark menu on the menu **b**ar or press **Alt+M**.

2. Click on **D**efine or press **D**. The Bookmark Define dialog box is displayed.

3. If you want to change the title to something you'll recognize more easily, type the topic's new name. Then, click **OK** or press **Enter**.

When you want to use the bookmark, open the **H**elp menu and choose the category the book mark is in. Then, open the Book**m**ark menu and select your topic.

The Least You Need to Know

☞ Works must be installed from within Windows. From the Windows Program Manager **F**ile menu, select **R**un. Assuming the Works Setup disk is inserted in your A:\ drive, type:

A:\setup

☞ To start Works from within Windows, double-click on the **Microsoft Works** icon within the Works program group window.

☞ If you are a first-time Works or Windows user, you should Start The **T**utorial for a guided tour of Microsoft Works.

☛ Use A WorksWizard allows you to create 10 different databases, organize all of your files, or add footnotes to documents.

☛ Use A **Template** when you could use a preformatted document to help you get started.

☛ Open the **Help** menu and choose **Cue Cards** to have them appear in your current and future documents. You can always cancel Cue Cards from your document when you no longer need step-by-step instructions.

☛ You need a mouse to use Cue Cards.

☛ When you need on-line Help, you can open the **Help** menu by clicking on it, by clicking on the **Learning Works** tool on the Toolbar, or by pressing **Alt+H**.

☛ To get on-line help for a task you are doing within a document, press **F1**, or open the **Help** menu and click the first item listed, which will relate to the task you are on.

**New lite page—99% less text
than regular pages**

Chapter 5
Works Skills 101

In This Chapter

- ☞ Starting a new document
- ☞ Opening an existing document
- ☞ Parts of a typical Works window
- ☞ Mousing around with the Toolbar
- ☞ Getting around in a document
- ☞ Splitting and switching windows

When I started writing this chapter, I wanted to show you all the neat things you could do with each of the Works tools so you could get started creating your own document—no matter which tool you chose. By the time I finished, though, there was just too much information for one chapter. So, I put "101" at the end of the title to let you know that it's only the first course. There's more in Chapter 6, "Works Skills 102."

Commonality Breeds Content

Works tools let you create many different types of *documents:*

- With the Word Processor you can create text documents that contain words, tables, and pictures.

- In the Database you can either create forms or lists, and then you can sort through lists to create reports.

- Spreadsheets let you create worksheets full of numbers and calculations, and charts from the spreadsheet data.

Although Works documents may differ, many of the windows, commands, and functions used to create them are the same. So, what works in one tool usually works in all. In this chapter, we'll use the Word Processor as a guide to the basic features that are common to all Works tools. I'll also show you how to use these common features and get you started creating Works documents.

Let's Start at the Very Beginning

To work in a document, you must first have one.

- To start a new document, make sure the New & Recent Documents button on the Works Startup screen is highlighted. If it's not, click on it. Then go over to the "Create a new" box to select the Works tool you want to use. If you have a document that you've been working on recently, and you want to work on that one, select it from the recent files list.

☞ To open an existing document, click on the **O**pen An Existing Document button, or press **Tab** to get to it and press **Enter**. When the Open dialog box appears, choose the file you want.

Version 2.0 users: Select the Works tool button you want to use to start a new document.

Type the name of the file . . .

Click here to prevent changes to the document.

. . .or select it from the list.

Select a different directory if needed.

Change the file type if needed.

Select a different drive if needed.

Ready, Aim, Open!

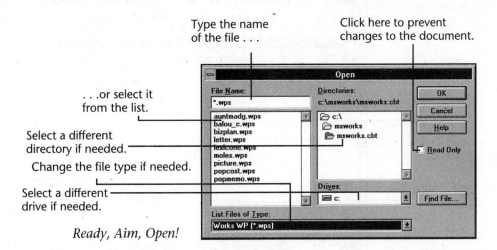

If you can't find your file, change to a different drive or directory. If you still can't find your file, make sure the file type is correct. Works gives you many file types to choose from. Each Works tool has its own file type extensions, so if you're working in the Word Processor you'll most likely be looking to open a Works WP (*.wps) file.

Version 2.0 users: Click on the Open Existing Files button and then use the Open dialog box to select your file.

By the Way . . .

You can always create a new document or open an existing one while you're inside a Works tool by clicking the **Startup** button on the Toolbar, or by choosing the **O**pen option or the **N**ew option from the **F**ile menu.

Haven't I Seen You Somewhere Before?

Once inside a document, you'll recognize some of the old familiar faces from the Windows window: the Control-menu box; title bar; minimize, maximize, and restore buttons; and even some of the commands on the Program Manager menus. But there are still some faces you haven't seen yet! So let's introduce you:

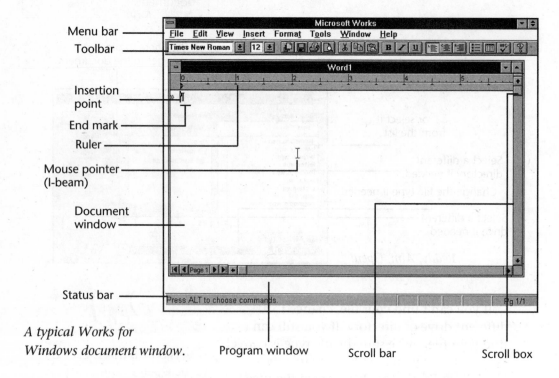

A typical Works for Windows document window.

Menu bar
Toolbar
Insertion point
End mark
Ruler
Mouse pointer (I-beam)
Document window
Status bar
Program window
Scroll bar
Scroll box

Program Window   This is the Works for Windows window, where Works runs the show. It frames all of the tools and menus you need for your current Works document. When you close this window, you exit Works for Windows entirely.

Document Window   This window frames the document file you're working on, as well as related document information. You can have more than one document window open at any time, but as in Windows, only one can be active.

Menu bar   Contains all of the command menus you'll use to create and change documents. Menu commands vary slightly for each Works tool.

Ruler   Provides an easy way to set tab stops, indentation, and margins.

Toolbar   Provides shortcuts for mouse users for the most common commands in the menu bar. The Ruler lets you set tab stops, indents, and margins easily.

Scroll bars   Located on the bottom and right sides of the document window, scroll bars let you display other areas of the document that are out of view. Arrows indicate which direction you want to move in through the document.

Scroll box   Located on the scroll bars, scroll boxes move as you do through the document. Their position on the scroll bar tells you your relative position within the document in relation to the beginning and end.

Status bar   Located on the bottom, underneath the scroll bars, the status bar displays information about your document and commands you are using.

End mark   Shows you where the end of your current document is. As you enter text, the end mark moves down.

Insertion point   The blinking vertical line that tells you where to start typing text is called an insertion point or a cursor.

Mouse pointer   Our fickle friend changes stripes when he's finally doing something constructive. In the text area, he mimics the insertion point, becoming an "I-beam." You can change the real insertion point just by clicking where you want the I-beam.

Mouseketeers, Click Your Toolbar!

In Chapter 3, you learned all about using your mouse or the keyboard to issue commands in Windows. You also learned about menu bars and dialog boxes. All of that applies to making things happen in Works, too.

But now, you can also issue commands directly from the Toolbar. Each Works program (i.e. Word Processor, Spreadsheet, Database, etc.) has it's own special work tools and a toolbar that makes issuing commands with the mouse even quicker.

Your toolbar is still in its infancy. It doesn't have all the buttons and tips, and it can't be customized. But if you need to find out how to use it, chick the Help Index, or keep reading.

An easy way to tell what command an icon on the toolbar represents is to read the Toolbar Tip. To find a Toolbar Tip, just position your mouse pointer over the icon in question.

To use a tool, click your mouse on the tool button and that action will be carried out. If you want your command to cover a lot of territory (to affect multiple paragraphs of a report, for example), highlight the area before you click.

Diehard keyboarders might resent the extra space the Toolbar takes up. Don't worry, we can take care of that! To hide your toolbar, choose Toolbar from the View menu to toggle it off. Do the same thing again later if you change your mind and want to turn it back on. Remember, the check mark next to the View Toolbar command tells you whether it's on or off.

Customizing Your Toolbar

It may be too soon for me to show you how to customize your toolbar before you even test drive it, but it's such a nice feature, I didn't want to forget!

To add a button that you use often to the Toolbar, select Customize Toolbar from the Tools menu. Then choose the type of command you want to add from the Categories list. For example, if the command you want to add is in the File menu, choose **File**. Finally, drag the button from the Toolbar Buttons box to the Toolbar, and drop it where you want it placed. To delete a command from the Toolbar to make room for a different one, select Customize Toolbar from the Tools menu and then drag the command off.

You can always put the Toolbar back the way you found it by selecting Reset in the Customize Toolbar dialog box.

Navigating a Document Window

Believe it or not, you're going to get so good at this that you'll have documents flowing over the edge of your windows in no time. That's why you need to know how to move around in a document window.

If Toolbar Tips drive you nuts, you can shut them off by selecting **Customize Toolbar** from the **Tools** menu. Then click on **Enable Tool Tips** to toggle them off.

They Went That-A-Way

When a document runneth over and you want to see the next page or database record quickly, use the Page arrows on the left-hand side of the bottom scroll bar.

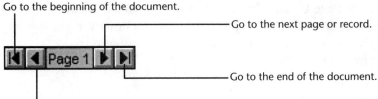

Go to the beginning of the document.

Go to the next page or record.

Go to the end of the document.

Go to the previous page or record.

Use page arrows to move things along.

What a Drag It Is Getting Scrolled!

Scrolling lets you peruse your document as you travel. You can scroll with the keyboard, but like everything else it's much faster to scroll with the mouse in one of these ways:

☞ Drag the scroll box. The scroll box is always positioned on the scroll bar relative to where your window view is in relation to your whole document. Needless to say, if you want to move almost to the end of a document, move the scroll box almost to the end of the scroll bar.

☛ Click a scroll arrow to move one line at a time in the position of the arrow.

☛ Click anywhere between the scroll box and a scroll arrow to move one screen at a time in the same direction as the arrow.

When you scroll with a mouse, the insertion point rides along. To replace the insertion point, click the mouse where you want to start working.

Let Your Fingers Do the Scrolling on the Keyboard

If you want to get nowhere fast, use the up and down arrow keys to scroll one line at time. Use left and right arrows to move one character, cell, or field at a time. Use Page Up to move one full screen back and Page Down to move one screen ahead of where you are in the document. Press **Ctrl+Home** to move to the beginning of the document, and press **Ctrl+End** to move to the end.

Beam Me Up, Scotty

When you know the exact coordinates of your target destination, travel in hyperspace:

Works lets you leave **bookmarks** to mark your place in a document so that you can easily go back to that spot later (like bending the corner of a page).

From the Edit Menu choose Go To, or press **F5** from the keyboard. In the Go To box, type the page number, bookmark name, cell, range, or field reference. Then press **Enter** or click on **OK**. (You'll learn more about cell, range, and field references in Chapters 13 and 14, which discuss spreadsheets in detail.)

Splitting Windows Is Really a Pane

If you have a large document and want to be able to view and work in different parts at the same time, you can split the window to create two window panes. Use the split bar, which is located just under the document window's maximize button, to make a split.

To the computer, a page is only what it can hold in one document window. Consequently, when you Page Up or Page Down, you are really only moving a window's worth, which is approximately half of a printed page, maybe less.

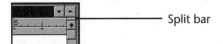

— Split bar

Drag the split bar to split a window.

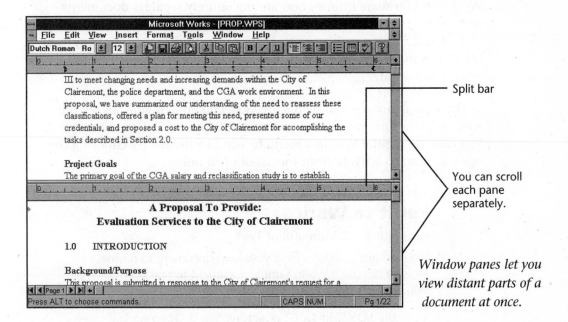

— Split bar

You can scroll each pane separately.

Window panes let you view distant parts of a document at once.

To insert or move a split, scroll to where you want to make the split, and then drag the split bar to where you want to split the document window. Move between panes by clicking on the pane you want to work in, or by pressing **F6**. When you're ready to remove the split, just double-click the split bar. The top pane will stay in the window.

> ## By the Way . . .
> Word Processor documents can be split horizontally into two window panes. Spreadsheets and database lists can be split vertically as well as horizontally to create four window panes.

Switch Hitting

Besides moving around to review information within your document, Works lets you share information among entirely separate documents without having to close one in order to open the other. You can keep up to eight document windows open at the same time. Just open them from the File menu as you need them, and then switch to the one you need when you need it.

There are many ways to switch active documents. If you can see the window you want, just click anywhere in the open window to activate it. You can also use the **W**indow menu to switch windows by choosing the one you want to activate from the list of open ones.

> ## Put It to Work
> ### Navigating a Windowful of Text
> Even though you don't have your own document to navigate yet, you can use a Works sample document to practice your skills. Open a Works file called **letter.wps**.
>
> It's in the MSWORKS.CBT directory. Select **O**pen An Existing File from the Startup screen. When the Open dialog box is displayed, check the Directories: list. Click on the **MSWORKS** directory to display its subdirectories, and then select the **MSWORKS.CBT** subdirectory.

Since we're looking for a Word Processor file (.wps), select **Works WP (*.wps)** in the List Files of Type box. Now, click **OK**. All of the .wps files in that subdirectory will be displayed in the File Name list box.

Select **LETTER.WPS** and then click **OK** again to open the file. Read the warning! It says we can't change this file without renaming it, but since we're just going to look at it, we're all right. Press **OK**. Once the file is displayed, check out the Toolbar and the Toolbar Tips, practice scrolling, and practice using the **E**dit **G**o To command. When you're ready to quit, choose **C**lose from the **F**ile menu.

The Least You Need to Know

You need this chapter to get you going in Works. Here's what I mean:

☛ To start a new document, select the **N**ew & Recent Documents button on the Startup screen, or choose **N**ew from the **F**ile menu.

☛ To open a document you've worked in before and saved, select the **O**pen An Existing Document button on the Startup screen, or choose **O**pen from the **F**ile menu.

☛ Works windows have the same components as the Windows windows—and more.

☛ The Toolbar contains the most often used commands in button form. If a command isn't shown on the Toolbar, you can add it or select it from a menu. You can even delete Toolbar commands you don't use.

☛ The Toolbar can only be used with a mouse.

☛ Use page arrows to scroll quickly ahead to the next page or the end of the document. Or, use them to scroll quickly to the previous page or the beginning of the document.

continues

continued

☞ Drag the scroll box to move through your document in relation to the scroll bar.

☞ Click a scroll arrow to move in the direction of the arrow, or click between the scroll arrow and box to move a full screen.

☞ If you want to scroll using the keyboard, press **Page Up** or **Page Down**, or use the arrow keys.

☞ If you know the page number or have a reference name for your destination, use the **E**dit **G**o To command, or press **F5**.

☞ Split the document window if you need to view two distant sections at once. Scroll to where you want to place the split in your document, and then drag the split bar to that place. Press **F6** to move between window panes.

☞ Keep more than one window open at the same time, and switch between them when you need to work in more than one file or document at a time. Just click on an open window to activate it, or press **Alt+W** to open the **W**indow menu. Select the window you want from the list of open windows.

Chapter 6
Works Skills 102

In This Chapter

- ☛ Selecting the right view
- ☛ Editing a document
- ☛ Previewing before you print
- ☛ Printing it out
- ☛ Save it!
- ☛ Closing a document

What you are about to uncover in this chapter can tap your hidden talents and save you gallons of White-Out and miles of correction tape. Not to mention time, attitude, and lost work!

Changing Your Point of View

You can view an active Works document in one of three modes:

Normal view This is the default viewing mode. In other words, you'll be most comfortable working in normal view, but it won't show you exactly how your page will look when you print. It will also take more time to move around in normal view than in Draft view if your document has many graphics, columns, or fancy fonts.

SPEAK LIKE A GEEK

A **font** is any set of characters that share the same typeface, like Courier, Times New Roman, or Arial. Fonts help set the mood and style of a document.

Format refers to the size, shape, and general layout of something printed.

WYSIWYG is a friendly acronym for "What you see is what you get," which refers to how your document looks on the screen as compared to what it will look like when you print. Before Windows, what you saw on your screen barely resembled what appeared on the printed page.

Page Layout view   This view is as close to WYSIWYG (What You See Is What You Get) as it gets, but it's really slow! Use this view when you want to see your headers, footers, and columns as you write.

Draft view   This view is much faster to work in than the others because even though you might be *using* more styles, it only *displays* one font, font size, and format. You can't view headers, footers, columns, or objects either. But when you change the view or go to print, you'll see that everything is there.

Change your view at any time by selecting the view you want from the View menu.

If you really want to zero in on a portion of your document, use the Zoom command on the **View** menu. Zoom can enlarge the display so you can see every last detail, or shrink it so you can see more information at once. Zooming won't affect how your document prints.

Making Changes

Do you have a boss who just loves to make changes? Like a signature scent, these people feel compelled to leave their mark on all of your work. Fortunately, Works makes it easy to change things. You can move, copy, and delete text in any kind of document by selecting the guilty text and then issuing the command. Here's how it's done.

Every Day Has a Highlight

When you select text, it becomes *highlighted*, which means that it reverses color so you can see how far your mouse has traveled. You can highlight, or select, text in these ways:

☞ To highlight text using a mouse, point at the first character and drag over the text or items you want to edit. When you reach the end of the selection, release the mouse button.

☞ To highlight text with the keyboard, position the cursor where you want the highlight to start. Then press and hold the **Shift** key and press the arrow keys or **Page Up** and **Page Down** to move the highlight through the selected text.

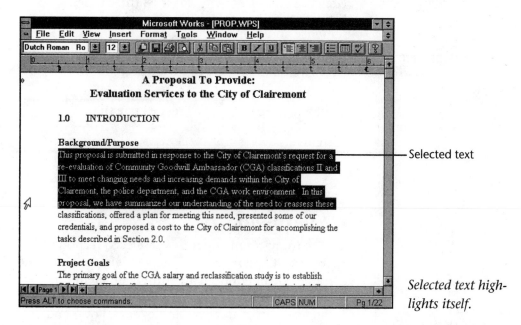

— Selected text

Selected text highlights itself.

The shortcuts in the following table might turn out to be the highlight of your day! Just remember to position the cursor at the beginning of your selection if you're using the keyboard.

To Highlight	Using a Mouse	Using the Keyboard
A word	Double-click the word.	Press **F8** twice.
A line	Click in the left margin of the document window beside the line.	Press **Shift+End**.
Several lines	Click in the left margin and drag the mouse pointer up or down as necessary.	Hold down **Shift** and press ↑ or ↓.
A sentence	Drag the mouse through the sentence and drop.	Press **F8** three times.
A paragraph	Double-click in the left margin beside the paragraph.	Press **F8** four times.
An entire document	Hold down **Ctrl** and click in the left margin.	Press **F8** five times.

You can avoid opening menus entirely by using the Copy and Paste buttons on the Toolbar. Or, use **Ctrl+C** to copy a selection from the keyboard, or **Ctrl+V** to paste it.

Copy Copy

The Copy command lets you select a section of your text and repeat it someplace else, either in the same document or in an entirely different one. (The original selection remains.) You can copy anything over and over and over and over and over and over and over again.

First highlight the text you want to copy, and then select Copy from the Edit menu. Move the mouse pointer to the place where you want to dump the text. Open the Edit menu again and select **Paste**.

Moving Right Along

Moving is almost the same as copying, except this time, the text you select clears out and moves to a new location. Highlight the traveling text first, and then select Cut from the Edit menu. Move the mouse pointer to where you want to place the text, and then select Paste from the Edit menu.

Choosing Select **All** from the **E**dit menu also lets you highlight your entire document at once.

You can use the Cut command without **Paste** to delete text, too. Or, highlight the text you want deleted and press the **Delete** key.

If you select the wrong text, just click anywhere else in the document window and then do it over.

Insert or Overtype?

Works automatically assumes, and rightly so, that you always want to add as much wisdom to your document as you can, so it starts you off in *Insert mode*. You can insert a single character, word, sentence, paragraph, or even an entire document anywhere you want by just positioning the cursor where you want it, and typing.

There may be times, however, when you not only want to add wisdom, but you also want to wipe out the garbage you started with. In that case, use *Overtype* mode. Toggle between Insert mode and Overtype mode by pressing the **Insert** key once. (Or, if you want to do it the hard way, select Options from the Tools menu, and check Overtype.) If watching your old words get massacred doesn't delight you, switch back to Insert mode by pressing the **Insert** key again or by deselecting Tools Options Overtype.

Insert mode is the default typing mode that allows you to insert characters and text to the right of the cursor, without wiping out entire armies of existing text.

Overtype mode is the ruthless typing mode that wipes out anything in its way. When you're in this mode, anything you type at the cursor marches right over existing text in it's path.

You can use the Toolbar buttons to Cut and Paste; or if you're using the keyboard, press **Ctrl+X** to cut your selection and **Ctrl+V** to paste it.

Cut! Print! That's a Wrap

When you finally have a document prepared just the way you think you want it, you'll probably want to touch it, look at it, and hold it in your hands. Printing lets you do all three.

Save a Tree: Print Preview

Even though it takes another minute, it's most ecologically correct to preview your document before printing to make sure everything is just the way you want it. Print Preview, in the File menu, gives you a WYSIWYG view of your document.

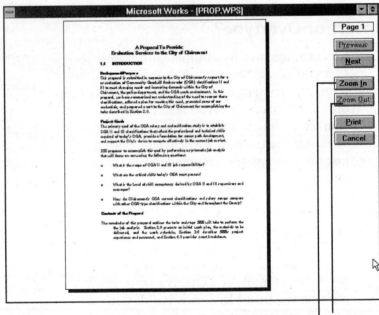

Meet WYSIWYG!

Click here to get a closer look.

Click here to step back.

In standard view, Print Preview lets you look at the whole page at once to check margins and format. Click Zoom In, and you get a half-page view; click Zoom In again, and you get a quarter-page view, but it's actual size. Click Zoom Out twice to get back to standard view. When you're finished looking, press **Cancel** to exit Print Preview, or select **Print** to do just that.

Printing

You can start printing in one of three ways:

- ☞ Click the **Print** button in Print Preview.

- ☞ Select **Print** from the File menu.

- ☞ Click the **Print** button on the Toolbar.

When you tell Works to print with either of the first two methods, the Print dialog box is displayed. (Clicking the Toolbar's Print button tells Works to print immediately using the default settings.) Some of the options in the Print dialog box will vary depending on the type of Works tool you're printing, but some options are pretty standard.

- ☞ You'll always be asked how many copies you want. Type the number in the Number of Copies text box.

- ☞ You can print all or a portion of a document. Choose **All** to print the entire document or **Pages** to print a range of pages. If you choose **Pages**, type the first and last page within the range.

For a quick peek at print preview, click the **Print Preview** button on the Toolbar.

OOPS!

If you clicked on the Print button on the Toolbar, you won't be able to change print options, such as the pages you want to print. Works will automatically use the settings you chose the last time you used the Print dialog box.

☛ Select **D**raft quality printing if you want to print quickly and don't care that font styles, colors and charts, or objects and drawings won't print.

If you delete, cut, or even copy something mistakenly, select **U**ndo from the **E**dit menu and Works may grant you mercy. In other words, if you catch the mistake in time, you can undo it! For copied information, "in time" means right up until you're done pasting. For cut or deleted information, you have to catch your mistake **before** you paste.

Save a Document: Save Yourself!

It's always best to save yourself the possible time and energy you would need to re-create a document if something horrible (like a power outage or the BIG one) were to happen. Always try to save your document file *before* you:

☛ answer the phone

☛ do something complicated, like a major edit

☛ insert text or graphic files

☛ print

☛ leave the Works program

☛ cook dinner

I also like to save my documents *after* I do things like:

☛ perform major edits

☛ insert text or graphic files

☛ rename a file (Just to make sure that I'm actually in the renamed file instead of the one I'm trying to save!)

WHATSHAMACALLIT.WKS Won't Work

When you start a new document, Works gives it it's own original name, like Word 1, Sheet 1, etc. But unless you can remember your documents in their numeric order, you'll want to rename it when you save. Each file has a first and a last name. The last name, called the *extension*, identifies the file type. Works uses a different extension for each of its tools, so you only need to assign a first name.

The trick to naming a document is in choosing a name that you will be able to easily recognize and identify later—in 8 characters or less. (There's always a catch.) You can use letters, numbers, hyphens, and underscores, but don't try to use the Spacebar to leave a blank space, and don't use the * or ? symbols. Here are some valid file names to get you started:

COVLETTR.WPS   94GAMES.WPS

RESUME.WPS   HOME_RUN.WPS

The First Save Is the Hardest

If you've never saved your document before, Works will ask you for some background information, like *what shall we call this thing?* and *where do you suggest we put it?* To save your document for the first time, choose **S**ave from the **F**ile menu. The Save As dialog box is displayed.

Clicking the **Save** icon on the Toolbar is quicker than selecting **S**ave from the **F**ile menu, and it accomplishes the same thing.

Type in the new file name of 8 characters or less. If you want to save your file in a drive or directory different from the one you're working in, change the settings now.

If you want to save your document file so that you can use it in another program, select the type of file you want it to be in the File Type box. Works will convert only the copy. Your original document will remain the same.

If you would like Works to always make a backup copy of your file whenever you save it, check the **M**ake backup copy box. The backup copy will have the same file name, with a different extension. The backup extension will always start with a B and will then use the other 2 letters of the regular extension. For example, a word processing (.wps) backup extension would be .bps. When you are done, press **Enter** or click **OK**.

> ## By the Way . . .
> Rather than reinventing the wheel every time, I often use documents I've created before as the basis for new ones. With minor changes, for example, I can tailor my resumé for each new opportunity that comes along. I start with my basic resumé and use the Save **A**s command from the **F**ile menu to rename it before I change it. Right now I have three resumés going: Truth, Justice, and Amerway (that's DOS for the American Way).

Saving the Second Time Around

If you've already saved and named a file once, saving the latest version is a snap. Either choose Save from the File menu, or click the **Save** button on the Toolbar. If you want to save it to another file, location, or file type so that you can keep changing this version while you keep a permanent record of what you have so far, use the Save As command in the File menu.

Save Everything!

Picture this: you're feverishly juggling six open documents trying to get the figures you need to close out the monthly report. Suddenly the phone rings, and you're called to another urgent meeting upstairs! You know it'll take 5 minutes just to save all those open documents. What do you do?

Answer: Use the Save Workspace command to save the entire workspace at once! It'll save open documents, minimized documents, icons, and everything so that they're available just as you left them the next time you start Works.

To save your workspace, choose Save Workspace from the File menu (this workspace will then appear every time you start Works). Since it's kind of a temporary arrangement, you don't have to name the workspace, either. When you no longer want this workspace displayed every time you start Works, choose Options from the Tools menu and clear the Use saved workspace box.

It's Closing Time Again

When you're finished working with a document, you can either close it and keep Works running, or close it and quit Works. Either way, Works will ask if you want to save the document before closing. It can't hurt to do it again even if you just did, and it might someday save you from losing valuable changes.

To close your document and stay in Works, choose Close from the File menu or press **Ctrl+F4**. To quit Works, choose Exit Works from the File menu or press **Alt+F4**.

The Least You Need to Know

If you're like me, you'll spend a lot of time editing, viewing, and printing your documents before they're done, so here's a quick review to help you:

- ☞ Use Normal View to enter and edit text, Draft View to speed things up, and Page Layout to work with graphics and formats. Access the **V**iew menu to select a view mode.

- ☞ To change the magnification of your document view, choose **Z**oom from the **V**iew menu. It won't affect your document or the way it prints.

- ☞ To select text with a mouse, point to the first character in your selection, and then drag to the last character and drop. To select text with the keyboard, press and hold the **Shift** key while you use the arrow keys to highlight the text.

continues

continued

☞ To copy text quickly, highlight it, and then click the **Copy** button or press **Ctrl+C**. Paste it in another location by clicking the **Paste** button or pressing **Ctrl+V**.

☞ To move text quickly, highlight it, click the **Cut** button or press **Ctrl+X**. Paste it in a new location by clicking the **Paste** button or pressing **Ctrl+V**.

☞ Delete words or sections of text by cutting without pasting, or by selecting the text and pressing the **Delete** key.

☞ If you recognize your mistake before you paste, you can use **U**ndo in the **E**dit menu to undo an incorrect cut, delete, or a copy command.

☞ Use the Insert mode to safely insert text without typing over existing text. Use Overtype to type right over existing text. Press the **Insert** key to toggle between the two.

☞ For WYSIWYG accuracy, preview your document by clicking the **Print Preview** Toolbar button or by selecting Print Preview from the **F**ile menu.

☞ Click the **Print** button on the Toolbar to print a document, or select **P**rint from the **F**ile menu.

☞ To save a document, select **S**ave from the **F**ile menu or click the **Save** button on the Toolbar.

Part II
Processed Any Good Words Lately?

I hate to cook. But I do love to eat. Years ago, in an effort to "domesticate" me, my favorite mother sent me a food processor. A complete do-it-yourself, "now you can really play house" Cuisinart with all the manuals and recipe books that come with it. Not to mention the extra Mini-Mate Chopper/Grinder. Well, the whole package is still sitting in the farthest reaches of my kitchen cabinet. I know that if I'd just take the time to read the books I could be baking my own little Alaska, or at the very least flinging perfect carrot sticks and cucumber slices at whoever happens to be sitting on the couch.

Anyway, although word processing has very little to do with cooking, word processors share some common ground with food processors: both are great timesavers that end up making you look good. Rather than typing and retyping a letter on a typewriter, you can zip it into your PC, make changes, and print it out a dozen different ways—all with the press of a few keys. Isn't technology amazing? Now if I could only learn to eat my words. . . .

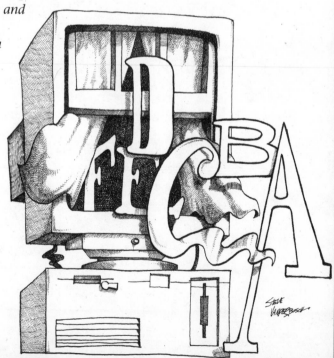

What do you want me to do master?

Chapter 7
More Than Your Basic Typewriter

In This Chapter

- ☛ Starting a document
- ☛ Typing text
- ☛ Typewriting habits you should lose
- ☛ Saving a document to disk

If you read my introduction to Part 2, you already know that I have my very own food processor and a companion Mini-Mate chopper/grinder that's probably more my own speed. In the world of processors, if you consider MS Word for Windows the equivalent of a full-grown Cuisinart, then you might be able to see how the Works for Windows word processor is like my Mini-Mate Chopper/Grinder: A Tiny Wonder, as it says on the box!

Actually, Works' word processor is much more than a tiny wonder. It can do almost all of what Word can do, and it has some very fine tricks of its own. In this chapter you'll learn about word processing, and what you need to know to start processing your own words with Works for Windows.

Word Processing Comes of Age

It wasn't until the early 1980s that word processing really became a mainstream activity. Before that, ordinary people wrote their text on paper by hand (or typed it on a typewriter) and handed it to a Word Processing Specialist, who would type it into a computer via a slow and cumbersome word processing program. Then the author would reread the output and mark the typing errors to be corrected. A lucky soul was he (or she) if he had a Word Processing Specialist who could spell.

Today, almost everyone has his or her own computer and word processing program, complete with a spelling checker. (Works even counts your words, and suggests alternatives to overused ones.) Here's just a sample of some of the things Works' word processing tool can do for you:

- ☛ Insert text into existing words, sentences, or paragraphs, and have everything move down automatically.

- ☛ Delete text just as easily, and have everything automatically self-adjust, leaving no empty hole on the page.

- ☛ Change margins and formats without starting over.

- ☛ Emphasize words, titles, sections, or quotes with bold, italic, or underlined letters, and borders to make them stand out.

- ☛ Create tables for charts and columns for newsletters without taking hours to plan.

- ☛ Automatically merge an address database with a preprinted form letter to send out a mass mailing.

- ☛ Print as many copies of a document as you like without having to run clear across a football field and back to stand in line at the copier.

- ☛ Give you leftover time to actually spend with the kids—anyone's kids.

So You Want to Be a Word Processor?

Before you fully commit to word processing, perhaps you'd like a rundown of what it takes. Here are seven steps required to create every word processing document, more or less.

1. **Open an existing document, or start a new one.** You start each new creation by deciding whether you have a similar document you can "borrow" from or whether this one will be completely from scratch. Either way, you'll learn how to do this later in this chapter.

    If you're opening an existing document, skip step 2 and go right to step 3.

2. **Type in your text.** If you've decided to go with a new document, you'll have to type in some text. Don't worry about rushing out to learn how to type. Works can wait all day for your every word. You'll learn about entering text in this chapter.

3. **Read what you've written and make changes.** This is actually the fun part, where you get the most bang for your buck out of a word processor. In this step you get to edit yourself. You can move text around, add stuff, change the format, delete things that don't make sense, and find alternatives to overused words. You'll learn how to do all of these in Chapters 8 and 9.

4. **Add pictures or graphics.** When a picture can say it better, why struggle with words? Besides, sometimes a picture is just what you need to emphasize an important point or to lighten up a serious one. You'll learn how to use Microsoft Draw and insert drawings and clip art into your documents in Chapter 10.

5. **Save your document.** When you have finished typing, or have made important changes that you wouldn't want to have to make again, save the document! You'll learn how to save later in this chapter.

6. **Spell check your document.** Works uses its own spell checker to make sure that there are no typos. That's word processor talk for spelling errors that occur not from any lack of spelling ability, but rather from a slip of the typing finger. After you've spell checked, guess what—you should save again. You learn about spell checking in Chapter 8.

7. **Choose Print Preview and Print.** Works lets you save a tree by allowing you to see the way your document will look when printed (with all the fancy graphics, fonts, and margin settings). When you've eliminated any potential surprises, like margins being too narrow, or pages breaking in the wrong place, you're ready to print. You'll learn how to make page adjustments in Chapter 11.

Diving into the Word Processor

I used to love to swim, but I never liked getting into the water when the temperature was anything below perfect. So I'd usually dive in just to get it over with, and wait until the water felt warmer than the air. Then you couldn't get me out.

Starting the Works word processor isn't nearly as intimidating as diving half-naked into a pool of ice cubes. Besides, you did it in the last chapter! We'll go over it one more time for those of you who just jumped in.

First, start the program if it's not already running. Open the Works for Windows program group and double-click the **Microsoft Works** icon. The Welcome to Microsoft Works screen is displayed. Select Start **W**orks Now to dive right into the Startup screen. You remember the Startup screen, don't you? It has as many choices as a Baskin Robbins menu board.

By the Way . . .

You can rid yourself of the Welcome to Microsoft Works screen entirely by selecting the **S**kip Welcome Screen button. If you later need to view the tutorial again, you can choose **T**utorial from the **H**elp menu.

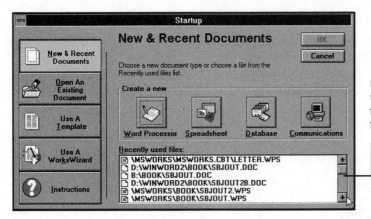

Use the scroll bar
to check
for recently used
files.

*Not as intimidating
as a pool of ice cubes.*

Excuse Me, Is This File New or Used?

As a word processor, your first decision on the Startup screen is *not* which Works tool to work in, as you might expect, but whether or not you have an existing document file you want to work on.

If you want to work on an existing document, first check to see if it's listed in the **R**ecently used files menu list. If it is, Works will automatically load the word processor program as soon as you select the file.

To have the Works for Windows program start up as soon as you start Windows, move the Works program icon into Windows' Startup program group (see Chapter 4).

If you can't find the file in the **R**ecently used files list, it must have already been placed in the existing documents files. Click the **O**pen An Existing Document button and feast your eyes on that dialog box! If you were with us last chapter, you'll remember traversing that box before. Here's a quick run through for those of you who weren't there:

☞ Make sure the Drive and Directories are set for the place you stashed the file.

☞ Check the List of File Types to be sure you're sorting through the Works word processing files (the extension is .wps). You can also have Works open a file created in another word processing program by choosing that file type and letting Works convert it.

☛ Select **OK** to start the sort, and then look for the file to be listed in the File Name menu box. If it's there, select it from the list, and Works will load the file and the tool together.

The terms **file** and **document** are often used interchangeably. While a document in Works is something you create with a word processor, spreadsheet, database, or graphics program, a file refers to the compartment in which it is stored in the computer. A document doesn't become a file until it's saved. And a file won't be a document again until it's opened. If it's all the same to you, it's definitely all the same to me.

If your file's not there, keep trying different directories or file types. If you still can't find it, you might want to start thinking about creating a new file!

Starting from Scratch

If you're sure that you don't want to work on an existing document, especially since you haven't created one yet, select the Word Processor button. Within seconds a fresh clean document page appears.

Betcha Can't Open Just One

When you're finished with a document and want to create another one, or if you just have a sudden burst of energy and feel like working on two or three at once, you don't have to close the word processor and go back out to the Startup screen. Here's how to start another document from inside:

☛ Press the **Startup** dialog box on the Toolbar to go right to the old Startup screen.

☛ Open the File menu and choose Create New File or **Open Existing File.**

☛ If the file you want to work in just happens to be one of the last four documents you opened, it may be listed at the bottom of the File menu. Just select it there.

Windows on the Word

If you're wondering what that blinking vertical line at the top of your Word Processing window is, you obviously didn't read the last two chapters.

When you start the word processor, it automatically places a cursor at the top of an empty document window. As you can see, that's an opportune place to start entering text. That's why they also call it an insertion point. Just stick your text there.

The cursor always stays one step ahead of your text when you type. It's hard to say whether it's trying to lead, or just get out of the way!

Don't Fence Me In

The *end mark* serves as your document's southern text border. And like the cursor, it also moves as you type. Consequently, you can never get any breathing room until you physically move it down the page.

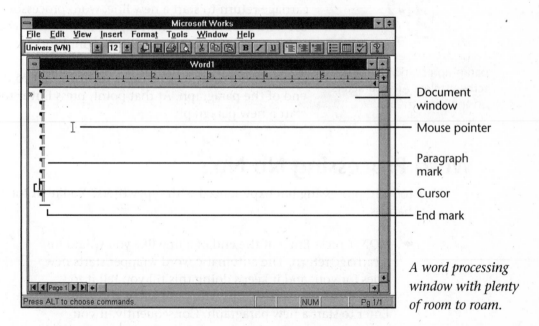

A word processing window with plenty of room to roam.

Sometimes you can't see all of the text you type along the right margin. If you want to stop lines from extending beyond your view, turn on the Wra**p** for Window command in the **V**iew menu. Works will temporarily ignore the margin settings and wrap text at the edge of the window. When you go to print, however, the lines will still wrap at the margins.

To be able to see your paragraph marks on the screen, select A**ll** Characters on the **V**iew menu.

To move the end mark without starting a territorial dispute, just press the **Enter** key repeatedly. This action creates empty paragraphs down your page. You can later fill these paragraphs up with text, pictures, or whatever you'd like, or leave them empty if you prefer.

When you're finished with your document, you might want to remove the empty paragraphs so they don't cause your printer to print an empty page. Just select all of the empty paragraph marks with your mouse and press **Delete**, or place the cursor on the last paragraph mark and press the **Backspace** key repeatedly.

Word 'Rapping

Unlike a typewriter, where you have to press the carriage return to start a new line, word processors use *word wrapping*. Word wrapping means that when you type words past your right margin, Works automatically wraps them to the next line. You don't need to insert a line break until you get to the end of the paragraph. At that point, press **Enter** to start a new paragraph.

Word Processing No No's

New to word processing but experienced with typewriters? You're in for a few changes.

☞ DON'T press Enter at the end of a line like you would for a carriage return. The automatic word wrapper starts new lines for you, and it keeps doing this till you tell it to stop. Word wrap only stops wrapping when you press Enter to start a new paragraph. Consequently, if you press Enter at the end of every line, your document will be filled with one line paragraphs.

☛ DON'T use the Spacebar to move the cursor. The Spacebar will seem to leave empty spaces like you want it to, but if you go back to insert something later, you'll find they weren't empty at all. Use the mouse or arrow keys to move the cursor, or press Enter to insert empty spaces between paragraphs.

☛ DON'T use the Spacebar to indent the first line of a paragraph or to move to columns in a table. When you use Tab, Works makes sure all of your paragraphs and columns are lined up—and it even does most of the work for you.

Call Me Cheap, Call Me Paranoid: I Just Like to SAVE!

As an added precaution, I try to save worthwhile documents often, and I *always* save before I start messing with changes or start printing. Here's how to save:

If you've never saved this document before, choose Save from the File menu. In the File Name box, type the name you want to give to this document—make sure the name is no more than eight characters long. You can use hyphens or underlines, but no spaces in the name. Choose **OK** when you're done. Once the file has been saved, just select Save from the File menu, or click the **Save** button on the Toolbar whenever you want to save it again.

To make a backup copy of your file, choose Save As from the File menu. Keep the same name but choose the **Make** backup copy of old file check box. This tells Works to create a separate file with a different file type extension, such as (.bps), every time you save the document. Then choose **OK**.

For a quick save, nothing beats the **Save** button on the Toolbar. Just click on it.

To save a file to another disk drive, use the Save As command from the File menu and keep the file name the same again. But this time, change the Drives and Directories boxes to match the drive and directory you want to save it to. When you're ready to save, press **OK**.

Closing Time

You can close a document and still keep working in Works, or you can close the document and go home!

No matter which you decide, it's always a good idea to close the active window when you're done with it. Click the **Control-menu** box or press **Ctrl+F4** to close the active document window. If you made changes to the document without saving them, you'll be reminded to do so before closing the active window.

When you're ready to close Works, too, choose Exit Works from the File menu, or press **Alt+F4**. If you try to close Works without closing or saving your active window, you'll be reminded to do so first!

The Least You Need to Know

☞ The cursor marks the point where you start typing. The end mark is the point beyond which you can't type. The end mark moves further down the page as you insert paragraphs (for each time you press Enter).

☞ To stop lines of text from extending beyond your view, turn on the Wra**p** for Window command in the **V**iew menu. It'll trick Works into thinking your right margin is really at the end of the document window.

☞ Word processors use word wrap so you don't have to press Enter to move down a line (as you did with the carriage return on a typewriter). When you type past a margin, word wrap automatically sends words to the next line. It will keep doing this until you press Enter to begin a new paragraph.

☞ Use the mouse or arrow keys, not the Spacebar, to move the cursor.

☞ Use Tab instead of the Spacebar to indent the first line of a paragraph or to move to columns in a table.

☛ 　🖫　Use the **Save** button on the Toolbar or the **S**ave command from the **F**ile menu to save your document.

☛ Use eight characters or less to name your document. Do not use the Spacebar to leave a space in the name. Use a hyphen or underline instead, for example, BUDGET_1.WPS.

☛ Click the **Control-menu** box or press **Ctrl+F4** to close the document window; choose E**x**it Works from the **F**ile menu or press **Alt+F4** to exit Works.

This page unintentionally left blank.

Chapter 8
Editing Magic

In This Chapter

- Adding and deleting text
- Moving text around
- Spell-checking your work
- Finding the right word
- Finding anything and then replacing it!

Wasn't it Franklin Delano Roosevelt who said that we should not fear change, but rather welcome it? He was right, but it never hurts to keep these thoughts in mind when you start changing a document, or "editing" as it's called in the business:

- You will usually run out of enthusiasm before you run out of things to change.
- It's always a good idea to let someone else edit your work, too.
- A document is almost never finished, but it is always due.

Editing is the process of changing existing information. In a word processing document, editing includes changing format and content, and spell checking, until the document is considered complete or a deadline is reached, whichever comes first.

If you don't like what you've added and miss what you deleted, use **U**ndo in the **E**dit menu to pretend your latest action never happened. You can cancel your most recent command whenever **U**ndo is visible in dark type on the **E**dit menu. If the Undo command is grayed, you're out of luck.

In this chapter, you'll learn how to change your text in various ways. Besides the obvious ways, like adding and deleting words, you can cut, copy, and paste text to rearrange it, perform a spelling check, look words up in a thesaurus, and find and replace occurrences of one word with another one. I know, it sounds like a lot of work, but you'll be pleased with the result!

Simple Arithmetic: Adding and Subtracting Words

Add text to your document whenever you want. It's that simple. Just use the arrow keys or the mouse to move the cursor to the place where you want to start inserting, and type. You can insert letters in between letters to correct misspellings, and insert words between words to finish sentences. You can also add paragraphs between paragraphs to expound on a topic.

When you just need to delete a character, or a word, or even a sentence, that's simple subtraction. There are three ways to do simple subtraction:

☛ Place the cursor to the right of the offending text, and press the **Back-space** key until it's gone.

☛ Place the cursor to the left of the offending text, and press the **Delete** key until it's gone.

☛ Place the cursor to the left of the offending text, press the **Insert** key to switch to the Overtype mode, and type right over the text and anything else in your way!

Selecting, Revisited

Most of the more powerful editing moves you can make in Works require that you select the text you want to change first. When you select text, it becomes highlighted in reverse video so that you know where your selection begins and ends. Of course, you probably remember all this from Chapter 6.

When you want to do something to your entire document, like change the font or page margins, choose Select **A**ll from the **E**dit menu, and then make your change.

There are many ways to select text using both the mouse and the keyboard. To select text from the keyboard, position the cursor in front of the first character in the text you want to select. Then press and hold the **Shift** key while you use the arrow keys or Page Up and Page Down to highlight the text you want. To select text using the mouse, point to the first character in the text to be highlighted, and drag over the text you want to change. When you reach the last character in the text you want, release the mouse button.

Chapter 6 contains a list of highlighting shortcuts for both the mouse and the keyboard. You might want to refer to that from time to time.

If you select the wrong text, just click anywhere else in the document window to undo the selection, or press the arrow key again.

Once you have highlighted a block of text, you can work wonders with it. For instance, you can delete it, all of it at once, by pressing the **Delete** key once. Or, you can cut, copy, or paste the block, as you'll see in this next section.

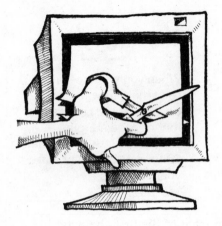

Major Edits Without Scissors and Tape

When you have big changes to make, such as moving or copying big chunks of text, you can use the old Backspace and Delete keys if you have nothing better to do with your time. Or you can learn how to cut, copy, and paste your text quickly, with the click of a button.

    Cut button

    Copy button

    Paste button

You may remember some of this from Chapter 6; if so, you can safely skip it here.

Since the Clipboard belongs to Windows itself and not to Works, you can even cut or copy something from Works, open a different Windows application, and paste it in there instead. For instance, you could cut some text from Works and paste it into Windows' Paintbrush or Cardfile programs.

The Mysterious Clipboard

To understand how Works cuts and pastes, you have to know something about the Clipboard. The Clipboard, strictly speaking, isn't part of Works; it's part of Windows itself. It's a holding tank, off in la-la land. Most Windows programs include a "door" that leads to it, so you can use it while you're in the program. (That's what Works does.)

When you use Works' Cut or Copy commands (or buttons), the text zips off to the Clipboard. (When you copy, the original remains in Works; when you cut, it doesn't.) When you use Works' Paste command (or button), the contents of the Clipboard zips back into Works, and lands wherever the cursor is sitting. Do you see where this is headed? To move an item from one place to another, you would cut it with the Cut command, move the cursor to the new location, and then choose the Paste command.

When you paste, a copy of the item remains on the Clipboard. It doesn't disappear until you cut or copy something else (or until you exit from Windows). That means you can copy something once, and then paste it as many times as you want.

Copying Text: Power Addition

When you copy text, you leave the original where it is, and place a copy of it on the Clipboard. Then you paste the Clipboard copy someplace else. "Someplace else" can range anywhere from another location in the same document, to a spot in an entirely different document, or even in another Windows program! In other words, you can copy text from a document to the Clipboard, open another document, type some text into it, and at the appropriate spot paste the copy into the new document.

To copy, first select the text you want copied. Then open the Edit menu and choose Copy, or click the **Copy** button on the Toolbar. The text zooms off to the Clipboard. When you're ready to paste your copy, position your cursor where you want the copy to appear, and then open the Edit menu again and choose Paste. If you want to put identical copies in many different spots, just keep clicking where you want them and selecting Paste.

Here's a shortcut: to copy text, select it and press **Ctrl+C**. To paste it, press **Ctrl+V**.

Moving Text: Power Subtraction

Moving text is almost the same as copying text, with one big exception. When you move text, you actually delete it from it's present location and place it somewhere else. So instead of using the Copy command, we use the Cut command before pasting.

To move text using the keyboard, select it and press **Crtl+X**. To paste it, press **Ctrl+V**.

First, select the text you want to move. Then open the Edit menu and select Cut. While the text waits for you in the Clipboard, move the pointer to the new location and click. Then open the Edit menu and select Paste.

The text moves from the Clipboard into the document. And like a copy, you can actually paste the cut text in other places as long as you don't copy anything else to the Clipboard in the meantime.

> ### By the Way . . .
>
> One of Works for Windows' new version 3.0 features is drag and drop editing. You can use drag and drop whenever you want to move text to a place that you can still see on your screen without scrolling. To execute a drag and drop move, first select the text. Then click and hold the left mouse button. When the mouse pointer changes to an arrow and box, drag the mouse pointer to the place where you want to insert the text and release the button. You can copy text this way too, by pressing **Ctrl** as you drag.

Spelling for the Linguistically Challenged

Does this ever happen to you? You have this word that you want to use, but you don't know how to spell it, so you look it up—but you can't find it 'cause you can't spell it. I spent an hour once trying to get my spell checker to accept anything for the word "perogative." It wasn't until I called a friend who has a doctorate in Words that I learned about the extra "r"—it's "prerogative." Who would've guessed?

Spell checkers, like dictionaries, are not entirely idiot proof. But for those of you who, like myself, may have lost some of your spell-ability during the sixties, they do come in handy.

The Works spell checker can scan your whole document, or just the part you select, checking for words that are spelled, capitalized, or hyphenated incorrectly. If the spell checker finds a word that it doesn't recognize, it asks if you want to add the word to its memory banks. If you have a typing impediment, like like this, the spell checker asks if the repeat was on purpose.

Spell Bound

When Works checks your document for
spelling errors, it begins its search at the
cursor. If you start in the middle, it will go to
the end and then ask if you want to check the
beginning too! Smart thing, that spell checker!

Instead of selecting
Spelling from the
Tools menu, you can simply
click the **Spelling Checker**
button on the Toolbar.

To start the spell checker, place your cursor
where you want to begin the search. If you
want to search only a word, paragraph, or
section, just highlight the text. If you want to start at the beginning, move
to the top of your document by pressing **Ctrl+Home**. Then open the Tools
menu and select Spelling.

Gotcha!

When Works finds a misspelled or repeated word (and believe me, it's just
a matter of time), it doesn't let you off so easy. Here's the dialog box. See
what I mean?

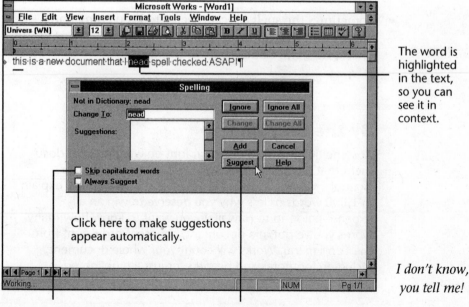

The word is
highlighted
in the text,
so you can
see it in
context.

Click here to make suggestions
appear automatically.

*I don't know,
you tell me!*

Click here to skip acronyms, proper
names, and other capitalization.

Click here for all
the suggestions.

When Spell Checker finds a word it doesn't recognize, it gives you several options:

☞ If you agree with the suggestion in the Change To box, just click on the Change button. If you have your own correction, type it in the Change To box. Or, select one of Works' alternatives from the Suggestions list box. If you want to correct this word throughout the document without going through this every time, click on Change All instead!

☞ If Works finds a word you've used twice in a row, it will ask if it's a mistaken repeat. If it is, click on the Change button, and one of the repeats will be deleted.

☞ If you know your spelling is correct or you just don't want to deal with it anymore, click the Ignore button to skip this occurrence. Click Ignore All to skip it whenever it comes up.

☞ If Works finds a misspelled word that you know is spelled right because you use it a lot at work, at school, or in your jail cell, add it to the dictionary. Once that word is added to the dictionary, you won't be bothered with it again.

☞ Sometimes the spell checker seems to keep going and going and going. When you've checked all you want to check, click the Cancel button to stop.

By the Way . . .

At some time or another, you might be working on a document that needs to be a certain length. You might, for example, want to enter a contest that requires you to explain in 1,000 words or less why you deserve to win an all-expense-paid trip to Hawaii. If you want to know how many words you've got in a document, choose Word Count from the Tools menu. Works will count your whole document, including footnotes and headers, or just a highlighted selection if you prefer.

Thesaurus Rex—For Dino-Mite Synonyms

Are your words feeling tired, run-down, overworked? Works uses a 200,000 word Thesaurus to provide you with synonyms, words with the same or similar meanings.

Remember the hours of fun you had with Mad Libs? This is almost the same thing. You write the sentence and ask Works to fill in the blank word with something similar to what you had. The results are often portentous!

To find a synonym, highlight the word in question and choose Thesaurus from the Tools menu. If more than one word is displayed in the Meanings box, choose the meaning that you want a synonym for. Then do what seems right:

- ☛ To change the synonyms listed, choose one of the variations of the selected word in the Meanings box, and then click **Suggest**.

- ☛ To substitute a synonym for the word in your document, select the synonym you want from the Synonym list box, and click the Change button.

- ☛ To stay with your original word, click **Cancel**.

Mission: Search and Replace

If you've made the same mistake everywhere, Works can search for the mistake and then replace every occurrence with a correction. For example, if you've been referring to Harrisburg, PA as the site of your next sales meeting, but it's really Harrisburg, VA, Works can sort through all of your text, find every error, and change PA to VA for you.

If you've already returned to your document after a text search but decide to check one more time, you can press **F7** to resume the search.

Works can also find and replace special characters, or special characters and text combined. For example, if you've been regrettably using the Spacebar instead of the Tab key to indent paragraphs and now want to straighten everything out, you can have Works find every place where you left five spaces and replace them with one tab. You can do the same with extra paragraph marks.

This table shows you how to tell Works which special characters you're looking for:

Table 8.1   Finding Special Characters in Your Document

To Find	Type
Tab mark	^t
Question mark	^?
Paragraph mark	^p
Page break	^d
Any character	?

The Search Is On!

To find a word, a phrase, or special characters, place the cursor where you want to begin the search. Then choose Find from the Edit menu. Type the text or characters you want in the Find What box. If, for example, you want to find every instance of the word "When" beginning a paragraph, type **^pWhen**.

Before you start the search, choose the options you want.

☞ If you want Works to locate only the word you typed (like finding "side") but not compound words (like "sidewalk"), check Match **W**hole Word only.

☞ If you want to match upper- or lowercase (for example "Word" but not "word"), check the Match Case check box.

When you're ready, click the Find Next button. Works begins the search from the current location. After Works finds the text, click on Find Next to search for the next occurrence. If you want to return to your document, select **Cancel** or press **Esc**.

Add Meaning to a Search: Replace!

To search for a word, a phrase, or special character and replace it with other text, start by opening the Edit menu and selecting Replace. Type the text or characters you're searching for in the Find What box, just like you did when you searched. Then type the text or characters you want to replace that text with, in the Replace With box.

Before you start this mission, don't forget to set the Match **W**hole Word only and Match **C**ase options, like you did in the search mission.

When you're ready to start, click the Find Next button. Press the Replace button to replace found text. When you are confident of the changes being made, choose Replace All so that Works will change all occurrences without your approval. When you've finished this mission, choose the **Cancel** button or press **Esc**.

The Least You Need to Know

Editing a document can be as simple (or as difficult) as you make it. It'll take practice before you feel comfortable, but as you're working, keep these things in mind:

☞ A simple way to add text to a word or sentence is to position the cursor and start typing.

☞ A simple way to delete text from a word or sentence is to position the cursor to the left of the text and press **Delete**, or position the cursor to the right and press **Backspace**.

☞ Drag the mouse cursor across text to highlight it, or press the **Shift** key and use the arrow keys.

continues

continued

☛   Use the Toolbar to copy text and paste it in another location.

☛   Use the Toolbar to move text by cutting it from one location and pasting it someplace else.

☛ 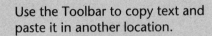   Use the Toolbar or select the **S**pelling command from the **To**ols menu to spell check your work.

☛ To find an alternative to overworked words, highlight the word in question and select the **T**hesaurus command in the **To**ols menu.

☛ Use the **F**ind and Rep**l**ace commands from the **E**dit menu to search for words or characters you want to track down, and to replace them with improved words or characters, if you want.

Chapter 9
Text Makeovers

In This Chapter

- ☞ What is format?
- ☞ Picking a font
- ☞ Changing the type size
- ☞ Using bold, italic, and underline
- ☞ Changing the default font

Whoever said "you can't judge a book by its cover" didn't know much about publishing or life in the twentieth century! Every day, people all over the world do just that. They pick up a book because the cover catches their eye, and then they flip through the pages. What they look at goes way beyond the subject matter. As a matter of fact, it's the format that eventually sells the book. It's also the format that can sell your report to the boss, your research paper to the professor, the memo to your staff, and that poor excuse you're trying to pass off to the judge about the gas pedal being stuck!

So what *is* all this fuss about format? Read on.

Format Defined

Format is easy listening vs. hard rock, fast food vs. nouveau cuisine, *USA Today* vs. *The New York Times*. As Webster's defines it, it's the size, shape, and general makeup of something printed.

To a word processor, format is the style and size of the type and the layout and organization of the page. By changing just the way the type looks on a page, you can emphasize key words, make titles and headings stand out, and control the mood of your document—and that of the reader, too.

There's enough to learn about format at the character level to keep us busy for a while. We'll save page formatting for the advanced class, in the next chapter.

Different Fonts for Different Folks

The type you enter on the page is *text*. The typeface you use is a *font*. There are many different fonts to choose from, depending on your printer and your intent.

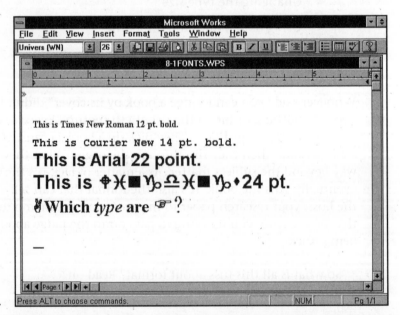

Every font tells a story, some more clearly than others.

The font you choose helps to set the style and tone of your document. *Serif* fonts, such as Times New Roman and Courier, have finely detailed edges that look almost like brush strokes. These fonts are supposed to be easier to read and more soothing, perhaps because they bring us back to a kinder, gentler time in history.

Sans serif fonts, like Arial, Helvetica, and Universe, are no-frills fonts. I use them a lot for business because they're lean and mean and get right to the point!

One thing to remember when you're "type casting" is not to get carried away with font possibilities! Try to limit your document to no more than two or three different fonts: two for titles and headings and a third for the text. Better yet, stick with one font for titles and headings and simply change the *point size* to distinguish levels of importance.

Type Casting

You can use the Toolbar to change the font, style, and point size of your text either before you type it, or after you've lived with it for awhile. If you're going to set the font before you type, move the cursor to where you want to begin typing, and then set the font characteristics you want, as shown in the following figure. If you're out to change existing text, highlight the text you want changed first, as you learned in Chapter 8.

The easiest way to change the type is to use the Toolbar buttons. The font and font size are chosen from drop-down lists, while the font styles (bold, italic, and underline) are controlled with on/off push buttons. Click a button once to turn the attribute on; click again to turn it off.

Type casting with the Toolbar.

Select the font.   Choose a point size.

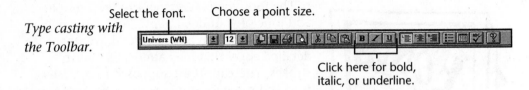

Click here for bold, italic, or underline.

You can also select fonts, styles, and colors in one fell swoop from the keyboard. First select Font and Style from the Format menu, and then choose the font, style, size, and color you want. Preview your selection in the Sample box, and when you think you've created a winner, press **Enter**, or click on **OK**.

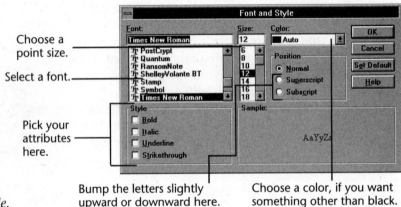

Choose a point size.

Select a font.

Pick your attributes here.

Type casting, dialog box style.

Bump the letters slightly upward or downward here.

Choose a color, if you want something other than black.

Subscript characters are positioned below the rest of the text and are often used in scientific formulas and equations.

Superscript characters are positioned above the rest of the text and are used to denote exponential powers, scientific notation, and temperature

In addition to colorizing your text, using the Font and Style dialog box gives you two other options not available through the Toolbar. The font style Strikethrough is added to your cast of characters. Strikethrough lets 'em think you've made a mistake. You also have the chance to change the Position of selected type to create superscript and subscript, as shown here.

Superscript is like this: Footnote[1]

Subscript is like this: H_2O

If you're a keyboarder, here are some keyboard shortcuts you can use to format your type:

Table 9.1   Formatting Text from the Keyboard

To Make Text	Press
Bold	**Ctrl+B**
Italic	**Ctrl+I**
Underlined	**Ctrl+U**
Subscript	**Ctrl+=** (equal sign)
Superscript	**Ctrl++** (plus sign)
Return to plain text	**Ctrl+Spacebar**

By the Way . . .

The number of fonts you can choose depends on the capabilities of the printer you're using. Different printers support different font styles, sizes, and colors. Works uses the printer you've selected as the active printer to determine the fonts you can use. Whenever you change printers, change your active printer too, through the Printer Setup command from the File menu. Otherwise, the fonts you use in your documents might not match the new printer's capabilities.

Whose (De)fault Is It?

You may not have noticed this, but whenever you open a new document and start to type, there's already a font selected. You may not know this either, but this is the 90s, and you don't have to accept that font anymore!

To change the default font, choose Font and Style from the Format menu. Select the font, size, style, color, and even position that you would like to see on a regular basis, and then click the Set Default button. From this moment on, every time you start a new document, you will be exercising your inalienable right to choose!

You can access the Toolbar with the keyboard to change font settings. Press **Ctrl+F** to open the font box on the Toolbar, or press **Ctrl+K** to open the point size box. Use the arrow keys to highlight your selection, and then press **Enter**.

The Least You Need to Know

Let's do a quick review of the essential formatting basics:

☞ You can change text formatting before you type or by selecting the text after you type.

☞ When formatting text, don't use more than two or three different fonts in the same document. Emphasize titles and headers by using different point sizes and styles.

☞ For quick changes, use the Toolbar buttons. They enable you to change the font and font size and to choose bold, italic, and underline.

☞ For bigger text changes, use the **F**ont and Style command found on the Forma**t** menu. It gives you the extra options of changing the text color, using superscript, subscript, and strikethrough.

☞ Change the default font in all future documents by selecting the **F**ont and Style command from the Forma**t** menu, choosing the new font, and then clicking the S**e**t Default button.

Chapter 10
Adventures in Paragraphs

In This Chapter

- The many ways to indent
- Aligning to suit your fancy
- Making bulleted lists
- Would you like that double-spaced?
- Slapping a border around it

In Chapter 9, I left you hanging with elegantly formatted text floating in a sea of confusion. What you need now is some paragraph formatting to put it all in line.

By the Way . . .

Even though margins affect paragraphs, Works doesn't let you assign margin settings to individual paragraphs. Instead, you assign margins to the entire page, and then use paragraph indents to adjust particular paragraphs in relation to the margins. You'll learn how to set the page margins in Chapter 11.

Let's review some of the things we already know about paragraphs. In Works, as in other word processors, a *paragraph* is any collection of text, graphics, or empty lines that ends with a hard return (created when you press the Enter key). This includes normal paragraphs and single-line paragraphs, such as chapter titles and section headings. When you press Enter in Works, you are marking the end of a paragraph.

When you change the style of your paragraphs, the look of your page changes too. You can adjust the following paragraph styles in Works:

Indents   The amount of distance from the page margins to the edges of a paragraph.

Alignment   The placement of text between the left and right margins in a paragraph. This is left justified (the left margin is straight, and the right margin is left as crooked as it happens to be).

Line and paragraph spacing   The amount of empty space between lines of text and paragraphs.

Border   A line placed on any or all of the four sides of a block of text, a graphic, a chart, or a table.

The rules for formatting text and making edit changes also apply to paragraph formatting:

- ☞ You can format paragraphs you have already typed by selecting them first.

- ☞ If you change the paragraph format to center aligned (to type a heading for example), all your text will be centered until you change the alignment back.

- ☞ You can use either the mouse or the keyboard to change paragraph formatting, thank goodness. Need I say more?

Indentured Paragraphs

An *indent* is the amount of space between the page margin and the edge of your paragraph. Normally a paragraph flows between the margins, but an indent allows you to move an edge of the paragraph closer to or farther from the margin, to mark the beginning of the paragraph. Indents help you visually organize a document by giving you the means of:

- ☞ creating lists using bullets or numbered hanging indents.
- ☞ showing levels of importance in outlines.
- ☞ setting paragraphs apart.
- ☞ identifying quotations.

Indenting with the Ruler

The easiest way to change paragraph indents is to use the Ruler. The Ruler lets you set these kinds of indents:

First Line   Indents the first line of a paragraph the indicated distance from the left margin.

Left   Indents all the lines of a paragraph, except the first, the indicated distance from the left margin.

Right   Indents all the lines of a paragraph the indicated distance from the right margin.

SPEAK LIKE A GEEK

An **indent** is the amount of space between the page margin and the edge of your paragraph. Normally a paragraph flows between the margins, but an indent allows you to move an edge of the paragraph closer to or farther from the margin, to mark the beginning of the paragraph.

When a paragraph has a **hanging indent**, the first line of the paragraph hangs closer to the left margin than the rest of the lines in the paragraph. A hanging indent is often used to create bulleted lists.

Quotation indents are used to offset a paragraph from the rest of the text by indenting both sides of the paragraph. Use quotation indents when you are quoting someone else's work.

This Ruler shows a hanging indent: the first line indent hangs to the left of the regular left indent.

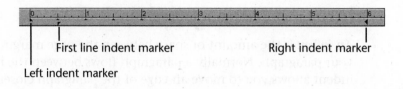

First line indent marker   Right indent marker

Left indent marker

To change paragraph indents, select the paragraph or paragraphs to which you want to apply the indents, or move the cursor to where you want to begin a new indent. Then use the mouse to drag the first line, left, and right markers on the Ruler.

If you want to create a hanging indent, hold the **Shift** key as you drag the first line marker to the left; this allows it to move separately from the left indent marker.

Indents, Keyboard Style

You can easily set these indents using the keyboard:

Hanging indent   Press **Ctrl+H** once for each level of indent you want. To undo the indent, press **Ctrl+G**.

Quotation indent   Press **Ctrl+N** for each level of indent. To undo the indent, press **Ctrl+M**.

If you prefer to work in a unit of measure other than inches, simply type the standard measure abbreviation in the Indents box on the Indents and Alignment tab.

Indents and the Dialog Box

You can also set all types of indents by using Quick Formats in the Paragraph dialog box. From the Format menu, choose Paragraph, and choose the Quick Formats tab. Under Style, choose the type of indent you want. Under Apply relative to, decide whether you want your indent measured from the left margin or the selected paragraph's current indent. Click the **OK** button, and the indents will be applied.

To set precise, custom indents, use the Indents and Alignment tab in the Paragraph dialog box. Just enter your settings in the Indents box.

Bulleted Lists

Let's look quickly at one more kind of indent, the bulleted—or numbered—list. It's really nothing more than a specialized hanging indent, but sometimes it's hard to create one manually with exactly the right amount of "hang." Anyway, since Works 3.0 now comes with the feature for automatically creating a bulleted list, I thought you'd be thrilled to learn more about it.

There are two important things you need to know:

1. I have used bulleted and numbered lists all over this book, including this one.

2. You can create a bulleted list from the Toolbar. Yes!!!

You can also create a bulleted list from selected paragraphs by using the Paragraph dialog box, which is accessed with the Format Paragraph command. Choose the Quick Formats tab and choose the Bulleted check box. Then click OK. If you want bullets, but would rather use your own indents instead of the standard .5" indent, choose the Indents and Alignment tab. Set your indents and check the Bulleted box. Then click OK.

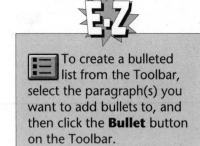

To create a bulleted list from the Toolbar, select the paragraph(s) you want to add bullets to, and then click the **Bullet** button on the Toolbar.

Alignment: Balancing Your Text

Paragraph alignment, not unlike wheel alignment, has to do with which side of the page your text is "wearing" on. There are four ways to align your text and paragraphs on a page:

Align left to have all the text in a paragraph lined up evenly on the left-hand side, like this book. Text on the right remains "ragged," or out of alignment. Works automatically left-aligns your paragraphs until you tell it otherwise.

Align right to have all the text in a paragraph lined up evenly on the right-hand side, causing the left side to look ragged and disheveled. This one doesn't get too much use.

Center to have all the text in a paragraph centered an even distance from both margins. This works remarkably well for headings and titles.

Justify to have all of the text be within reason at the same time. No, not really! Justified is when all of the text is evenly spaced. (Most of my text is evenly spaced, as am I.) One more time. A paragraph is justified when all of the text is evenly spaced and *both* the left and right margins create a straight edge!

It's very simple to align text, and it really gives your document that well-worn look.

To put all of this knowledge to good use, highlight each paragraph you want to align, or position the cursor where you want to begin your new text alignment. Choose one of the Toolbar buttons or shortcut keys shown in Table 10.1.

Table 10.1   Lining Up Text in a Paragraph

To	Click	Or Press
Align left		**Ctrl+L**
Center		**Ctrl+E**
Align right		**Ctrl+R**
Justify		**Ctrl+J**

By the Way . . .

Nope, there's no button on the Toolbar for Justified alignment. If you really must use the mouse to justify a paragraph, but don't want to go to the trouble of customizing your Toolbar, select Paragraph from the Format menu and use the Indent and Alignment tab to justify your preselected paragraphs.

Lost in Spacing

You may want to adjust your document's line and paragraph spacing in order to make your text easier to read and edit, to emphasize special paragraphs, or just to be creative with the layout.

To adjust line and paragraph spacing, and to control when a new page is started in the middle of a paragraph, do one of the following:

☛ Highlight the paragraphs you want to adjust.

☛ Choose Select All from the Edit menu if you want your adjustments to affect the whole document.

Or

☛ Position the cursor where you want to begin typing, and the space adjustments will begin at that point.

The easiest way to change all of these settings at once is to choose the Paragraph command from the Format menu. Click on the Breaks and Spacing tab for the dialog box you need:

Adjust the spacing between lines and paragraphs.

Talking to the head space cadet.

Click here to keep all text in the selected paragraph together.

Click here to keep this paragraph on the same page as the next one.

Here's what the Breaks and Spacing tab wants to know:

Between Lines   Use this box to type the amount of spacing you want between lines of text. You can either use whole numbers (1, 2, 3, and so on) or be creative with fractions (1.25, 1.5, 1.75 and so on). If you want Works to keep adjusting the space for you, type **Auto**, which self adjusts each line to accommodate the tallest character.

Before Paragraphs   Use this box to add extra space before a paragraph. This feature is extremely helpful when you want to control the space between a paragraph border and the first line of paragraph text. (You'll learn about borders soon.)

After Paragraphs   Use this box to add extra space after a paragraph. Use it to highlight special paragraphs, or just to give your layout some breathing room.

If you print a new page and find it starts on a different line than the other pages, it may be because you added space *before* the paragraph. To clear that space, change the setting back to 0li (zero lines).

Don't break paragraph   Check this box if you want to keep all lines in a paragraph together on a page. I use it to keep headings with text.

Keep paragraph with next   Check this box if you want to keep a series of paragraphs, such as a list, together on the same page.

Make Like a Taco and Run for the Border!

Borders are a bold and practical way to offset important paragraphs, create boxes of information, or frame your whole page. You can place a border on any or all of the four sides of a paragraph, table, or graphic.

If you want to add a border to a title or a short line of text without going all the way out to the margin, make the paragraph's left and right indents bigger. This works in reverse too. To extend a border out to the margin, when it dips in for the indent, bring the indent back to the margin.

To create a border, highlight the paragraph or paragraphs on a page that you want framed. Then choose **Border** from the Format menu. Under Border, decide which sides of the text you want framed. Select the Line Style you want, and then press **Enter**. If you have a color printer, change the color of the border line in the Color box; if not, select **Gray** and **Light Gray** to spice up the old black and whites.

If you tire of borders, just highlight the bordered text, access the Border dialog box, and clear your selection.

The Least You Need to Know

☞ An indent is the amount of space between the page margin and the edge of your paragraph.

☞ The easiest way to set indents is to use the Ruler. Use the **I**ndents and Alignment tab in the Paragraph dialog box to set indents more precisely.

☞ Whenever you want to work in a unit of measure other than the one currently being used in a dialog box, type the standard abbreviation for the unit of measure you'd like to switch to.

☞ Paragraphs can be aligned to the left or right, centered, or justified using the Toolbar or the Paragraph dialog box.

☞ Use the Breaks and **S**pacing tab in the Paragraphs dialog box to change line and paragraph spacing and to control page breaks in the middle of paragraphs.

☞ Easily create borders around a paragraph, or a page full of paragraphs, with the **B**order command on the Forma**t** menu.

This page suitable for doodling.

Chapter 11
Page Layouts with Pizzazz

In This Chapter

- Margin mania
- Creative columns
- Building a table
- Headers and footers
- Page breaks

I think by now we can safely assume you've got words on a page, in a carefully selected typeface, with just the right paragraph formats.

Give it the once over and tell me honestly, how does your document look? Is it ready to meet the boss—or is it still wearing sneakers and jeans? Look for these signs that it still needs work:

- Is the text suicidal (marching right up to the edge of the page)?
- Do pages break inappropriately (like right in the middle of the punch line)?
- Could you make your point more clearly by presenting some of that text in a table?

☞ Would readers be interested in knowing what page they're on?

☞ Is this the same document you showed me last Friday, or a new version?

If your document can still use some pizzazz, follow me. We're about to turn you into a real page professional!

Margins determine the distance between the text and the top, bottom, left, and right edges of the paper. The margin number refers to the amount of distance left between the edge of the text and the edge of the paper.

Margins: The Outer Limits

Margin settings may seem unimportant right now. But if you're ever squeezed for space, you'll want to know how to set them to push the limits of your text area. Or, conversely, if you have to write a ten-page report but can only come up with nine pages, it's nice to know you can reset your margins to stretch that point too.

The conventional wisdom on margins is that they should be one inch at the top and bottom, and an inch to an inch and a quarter on the left and right sides. (Works uses an inch and a quarter as the left and right margin default settings.)

Keep the following points in mind when you're adjusting margins:

☞ You need to compensate with a bigger left margin if you plan to bind the document along the left edge—like a book. (A quarter to half inch of extra space is usually plenty.)

☞ The top and bottom margins need to be adjusted if you change the left and right margins dramatically, otherwise the page will look out of proportion.

When you need to use every possible inch of text area you can, you can probably get away with three quarters of an inch on the top, bottom, and left, and as little as a half inch on the right. When you're trying to stretch a document's length, give yourself the extra room for the left binder (no more than two inches), and keep the top, bottom, and right margins within an inch and a half.

You can change the margin settings for the entire document from anywhere inside the document. But once the margins are changed, they affect all of the document. If you want to offset just a section of your text with a different margin, use a quotation indent, as you learned in Chapter 10.

I Want a New Margin Setting

To change your document's margin settings, select Page Setup from the File menu. In the Page Setup dialog box, choose the Margins tab. Type new measurements for any settings you want to change. If your text includes headers and footers (which we'll cover later), you'll want to make sure their margins are smaller than your top and bottom margins. When you're done, click **OK** to accept the changes.

If you get tired of your new margins and want to go back to the old standard, click the R**e**set button on the **M**argins tab in the Page Setup dialog box.

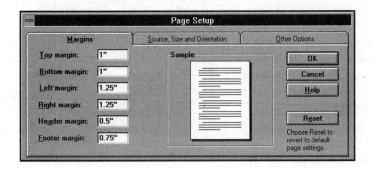

Here's where you change the margins.

Size and Orientation: A Quick Side Trip

While you're in the Page Setup dialog box, why don't you click on the Source, Size and Orientation tab to make sure everything is set up right? This dialog box tells Works what size paper you're using and which way it's oriented. *Orientation* refers to the way you want your document to be read. Overhead transparencies, for example are usually created and read in *landscape*, while letters and other documents are usually in *portrait*.

Document Columnization

Use the Columns command in the Format menu to create your own newsletter or to march your text through the pages like little marines. Set the number of columns you want on a page, and the amount of space you want between them. Works does the rest!

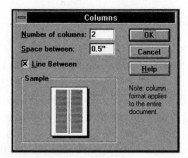

Column-ize your document.

But be warned! Once you set columns, *everything* in your document (except headers and footers) is formatted in columns. That means you'll have to run your newsletter's banner sideways along one of the columns, as they did in the Autostart template you saw in Chapter 2. Or, keep the title short and fit it in at the top of a column. When you type your column text in Normal or Draft view, it unfolds like one long roll of the squeezably soft stuff. To see how it will look in columns, switch to Page Layout view. (Chapter 6 explains how to switch back and forth between document views.)

Setting a Table the Easy Way

While creating tables with tabs may be a noble pursuit, there's no need to with Works 3.0. Use the Insert Spreadsheet/Tables command when you need to arrange text or numbers in side-by-side columns that you can read down and across.

Since a side-by-side table is nothing more than a simple spreadsheet, Works 3.0 uses a spreadsheet as a guide whenever you ask it to make you a table. Like a spreadsheet, the table contains rows of information arranged in columns. You enter all of your information in cells, which are the places where the rows and columns intersect. (Don't worry, you'll learn more about how spreadsheets work when you need to use one to calculate numbers. This is all you really need to know to create a table.)

Table-Making Basics

Here's all you have to do to let Works create a table for you. Position the cursor where you want to insert the table, and click the **Insert Table** button on the Toolbar or choose Spreadsheet/Table from the Insert menu. Choose the New table option and click **OK**. Works will insert an empty spreadsheet into your document.

Even if you think you don't know how to use a spreadsheet, type the text or data you want displayed in each column. If you need more columns or rows, drag the spreadsheet to the size you want. Just click on the spreadsheet to reveal the sizing handles, and then grab one of them with the resize mouse pointer and drag to the size you want.

To format the table, first highlight it, and then select the spreadsheet AutoFormat command from the Format menu. You'll learn how to use AutoFormats in Chapter 17.

To remember what **landscape orientation** is, think of a landscape painting. Landscapes are usually wider than they are long so that you can take in a wider range of scenery.

The celebrated Mona Lisa (the painting, not the pizza place!) is a typical portrait; it's longer than it is wide so our eyes don't have to wander—like her's do. Most word processing documents and reports are done with a **portrait orientation**.

Version 2.0 users, keep a stiff upper lip. Your program doesn't have this handy **I**nsert **S**preadsheet/Table command. You'll have to use the Tab key to create your table the old fashioned way. Or, jump over to the Works Spreadsheet tool, create a simple spreadsheet for your table, and then move or copy it into your word processing document. Take a look at Chapters 13–17 if you need help.

By the Way . . .

You can wrap text around a table or drawing using the Picture/Object command on the Format menu. Just select the object you want to surround with text, and then choose Picture/Object from the Format menu. Select the **T**ext Wrap tab, and then under Wrap choose **A**bsolute. To position the object on the page, use the **H**orizontal and **V**ertical Position boxes to adjust the left/right and up/down coordinates. If you want to center the object, select **Center** in both boxes. To change the page on which the object appears, type a different page number in the **P**age # box. You'll need to switch to Page Layout in the **V**iew menu whenever you want to see, or work with, the wrapped object.

A **spreadsheet** is a computerized program that organizes information in columns and rows, and can make numerous calculations.

The easiest way to create a table is to use the **Insert Table** button on the Toolbar.

Keeping It Straight with Headers and Footers

When you've created more documents than you care to count, headers and footers can help you tell them apart. A *header* floats at the top of every page and usually contains information like chapter titles or the company name. A footer sinks to the bottom of every page, and it usually includes the date and page number.

To create a standard, one-line header or footer, choose Headers and Footers from the View menu. Make sure the Use header and footer paragraphs box in the Headers and Footers dialog box is cleared. Type your text in the Header or Footer box. Works will automatically center align any text that you type.

To insert a page number, type **&p** in either the header or footer box. To insert the date so that it is automatically updated every time you print, type **&d** or **&n** for the long form. Check the Microsoft Works for Windows 3.0 User's Guide for additional codes.

> ## By the Way . . .
> It's not customary to count title pages or cover sheets in a finished document, so Works lets you leave page numbers off the first page by checking the **No** header and **No** footer on 1st page boxes in the dialog box.

Don't Go Breakin' My Page

One of the last things you'll want to do with your almost finished final document, is check it again! This time, check it for page breaks. Page breaks show you where one page ends and another begins. Sometimes, even if you've already told Works when to keep specific paragraphs together on a page, the page breaks can come in the darndest places.

There are two kinds of page breaks to look out for. Works inserts its own automatic page breaks whenever a page gets full. They're indicated by two chevron characters (») in the left margin. Manual page breaks, on the other hand, are man (or woman) made. You can insert them to adjust the flow of text. Manual page breaks are identified by a dashed line (---) that spans the left and right margins.

To enter a manual page break, move the cursor to the beginning of the line where you want to begin a new page. Then choose Page **Break** from the Insert menu, or press **Ctrl+Enter**.

When you insert a manual page break, you throw off all of the remaining page breaks in the document. Works can automatically compensate and adjust for this if, *and only if*, you select my favorite command: Paginate Now! on the Tools menu.

Keep moving forward through the document to check page breaks after each manual break and each new pagination. When you reach the end of the document, you're finished!

Put It to Work

When you've got a document's page setup, paragraph alignment, spacing, and fonts formatted in a way that you'd like to use again, use the Save **A**s command to rename the document. Once it's renamed, delete most of the text, except standard headings and sections that you might need in later documents. Then whenever you need to create a similar document, open that file and rename it before you begin entering text.

Or, press the Tem**p**late button in the Save **A**s dialog box while you're renaming, and save it as a real template that you can always find in the Template files, under Custom templates!

The Least You Need to Know

- ☞ To change your document's margin settings, choose the Pa**g**e Setup command from the **F**ile menu, and select the **M**argins tab.

- ☞ Columns are document-wide. You can't just have a page or two of columns and then go back to regular layout. Use the **C**olumns command in the Forma**t** menu to set them.

- ☞ When you type columns, you can only see them on the screen in Page Layout view.

- ☞ Works uses the Works Spreadsheet to create your document tables. Click the **Insert Table** button on the Toolbar to insert a table.

☛ Standard headers and footers contain one line of center-aligned text. Use the **H**eaders and Footers command from the **V**iew menu to create them. Use special codes to change the alignment and to enter the date and page numbers.

☛ Always make sure your header and footer margins are smaller than the top and bottom text margins.

☛ Press **Ctrl+Enter** to insert a manual page break, and then choose Paginate **N**ow from the T**o**ols menu.

This page unintentionally left blank.

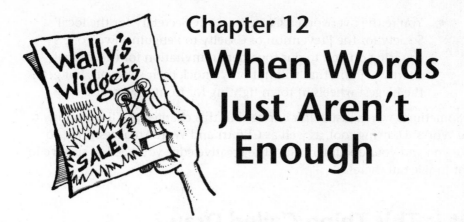

Chapter 12
When Words Just Aren't Enough

In This Chapter

- Drawing with Microsoft Draw
- Making an organizational chart
- Changing a picture
- Adding ClipArt to a document
- Bending text with WordArt

Does one of these scenarios describe your life?

- You're single-handedly working on the biggest proposal your company has ever submitted, for work that will keep you and six engineers busy for the next three years. Your client thinks you've still got a full-time staff, production and graphics capabilities, and everything his firm could possibly need. Little does he know your capital equipment consists of a phone, two file cabinets, a printer, computer, and Works!

- It's coming down to the wire and you just flunked your third quiz this semester. You've still got a chance to ace the final exam, but you'd have better odds in Las Vegas. This research paper just may be your only chance to graduate this year.

☞ You're the overworked Corresponding Secretary for the local Society for the Prevention of Cruelty to Penguins. Everyone's counting on you to put together an invitation for the annual charity auction that will not only knock their socks off, but get the biggest wheels in town fighting for front rows seats.

Sometimes words just aren't enough! In this chapter you'll learn how to use Works' Drawing tool, as well as ClipArt and WordArt accessories, to give you and your documents just the creative edge you need to survive in that jungle out there!

What Is This Thing Called Draw?

Microsoft Draw is a full-fledged Works tool that you can use to add pictures and graphics to word processor documents and database forms. As Microsoft suggests, you can use Draw to create a company logo, illustrate reports, and draw attention to important facts. You can also use Draw to edit your own drawing or to modify ClipArt and drawings that were developed on other compatible drawing programs.

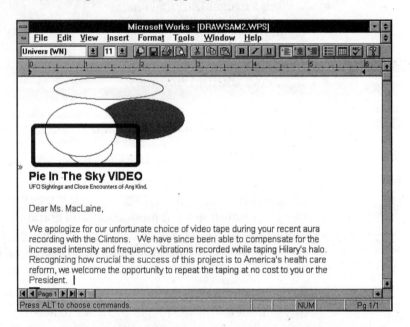

Use Draw to develop your own corporate identity.

Since it's not quite a stand-alone program in Works, you can only use Draw from inside the Word Processor or Database tools. That's true for ClipArt and WordArt, too. But there's no limit to what you can do with any one of these visual enhancements! And when you save your graphically enhanced document, the drawings are saved with them.

Hey, Quick Draw! 'Dis Crazy Tool Has No Switch!

Let me say this one more time: You can't start Microsoft Draw on its own! You have to be using either the Word Processor or Database tool to access Draw. Once you are inside one of these tools, position the cursor where you'd like to place a drawing, and then choose Drawing from the Insert menu.

When the Microsoft Draw window appears, use the toolbox buttons to create lines and shapes. If you need help with any of the tools, press **F1** to access the Microsoft Draw Help index. Or, keep reading.

Tools for the Artistically Challenged

Don't worry if you can't draw the horse on the matchbook cover, let alone a straight line. You don't need talent to be creative in Draw. Draw does all the work, while you get all the credit.

Use the toolbox to create lines, shapes, forms, and even graphic text. Here's a rundown of what you can do with the toolbox:

The **database form** represents one of two ways in which you can enter and view data compiled in a database. In form view, you can only see and work with one record at a time. For example, if you had a recipe database (like a cookbook) and each recipe was a record, the database form would be the index card on which the recipe was written.

Yes, I'm consciously abandoning the keyboard users in this section. Trying to draw without a mouse is like trying to ski without snow. It can be done, but why bother?

Table 12.1   Drawing Tools and Their Descriptions

Tool	Name	Description
	Arrow	Selects one or more objects in the drawing so you can edit or move them.
	Zoom In/Zoom Out	Enlarges the Draw image. Hold the **Shift** key while you click to reduce the image.
	Line	Draws a straight line.
	Ellipse/Circle	Draws a circle and an ellipse. Press **Shift** while you drag to draw a perfect circle.
	Rounded Rectangle/Square	Draws a rectangle or square with rounded corners. Press **Shift** while you drag to draw a perfect square with rounded corners.
	Rectangle/Square	Draws a rectangle. Press **Shift** while you drag to draw a perfect square.
	Arc	Draws an arc. To draw a pie wedge, click on the Filled command and drag the arc to the size and shape you want.
	Free form	Allows you to draw anything you like.
	Text	Allows you to type a single line of text. You can type up to 255 characters. That's enough for one title!

What's the Object of This Game?

In Draw, you create drawings by combining *objects*, like lines, squares, circles, and text. The easiest way to create an object is to click on the one you want in the toolbox, and then drag it in the drawing area to define its size and placement. When you have the size and location you want, just drop it (release the mouse button).

An **object** is any information (such as text, graphics, charts, etc.) that is linked or embedded from one program into another Works document.

Objects (with the exception of lines and text) are made up of two parts: a frame and a fill. The frame is the line around the object, and the fill is the color or pattern that fills it. You can turn off either the frame or the fill at any time by selecting the object, and then selecting or deselecting Framed or Filled from the Draw menu. Or, click on a **Line** or **Fill** button at the bottom of the Draw window.

By the Way . . .

If you have a color printer, you might want to change the frame or fill colors by using the color palettes in the lower-left corner. If you don't have a color printer, there's not much point in changing the colors; they'll print as varying shades of muddy gray.

If you want to make something look transparent, so you can see the object behind it, turn off the object's fill. If you have multiple objects that rest on each other, Bring to Front or Send to Back by using those commands in the Edit menu.

Okay, What Can I Do with Draw?

I've had my own business for the past few years, probably because no one else wants it. But, as a small business owner, I sometimes find myself answering questions about my "organizational capabilities." So I created an organizational chart. This little exercise has really helped me get all my "accountabilities" (great word!), linkages, and relationships down on paper. Now if I could only figure out what "we" do.

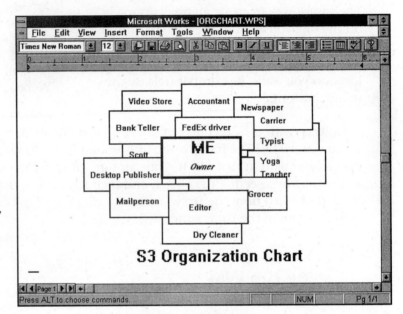

Here's my "org" chart, which I made in Microsoft Draw. As you can see, I'm on top of things—as usual!

If you make a mistake in resizing, select **U**ndo from the **E**dit menu. The object will go back to its previous size without your having to adjust it yourself.

Building a Business

Here's how to build your own org chart. First, decide which shape you want to pigeonhole all your people in: rounded rectangle, rectangle, or square? Then click on the shape of your choice in the toolbox. Next, click on the drawing area and drag the mouse pointer till the outline fills the size you want. When you drop, the shape will fill the dragged area.

Resize your shape by clicking to select it, and grabbing one of the four resizing handles. Remember, the shape needs to be big enough to fit your organizational titles and/or names.

An easy way to make sure all of your organizational boxes match is to duplicate one box. Make an exact duplicate of an object by clicking it, and then choosing Copy from the Draw window's Edit menu. Click on the spot where you want the copy to land and select **P**aste from the Edit menu. If your copy doesn't land where you wanted it, just drag it into place. You can move an object by dragging it by any part except the handles.

Here's the best part. If your organization is really large, save yourself some time by grouping the two objects and copying them again, to make two more boxes. To group objects, press **Shift** and click to select each object in the group. Then choose Group from the Draw menu. Now copy the group and paste . . .and paste . . .and paste.

Once you have all of the boxes in place, add titles and names. To add text, click on the text tool, and then move the insertion point to where you want the text within a box. Click again and start typing. Use the Text menu options to change the style, alignment, or size of your text.

An easy way to line up the boxes when you're moving them is to turn on the Snap to G**r**id and the Sho**w** Guides commands in the **D**raw menu.

TECHNO NERD TEACHES

You can use **G**roup and **U**ngroup any time you want to keep certain objects together for a group move, rotation, or copy. (Unfortunately, it doesn't work for "group" photos.)

If your organization is larger and more "structural" than mine (or you just happen to be "into control"), you can add lines of authority and chains of command. To draw a line connecting boxes, select the Line tool from the toolbox, and then move the mouse pointer to the midpoint of one of the sides. When the cross hairs seem to disappear on the side you're pointing at, the origin of the line is lined up perfectly with the side of the box. Click to start the line, and then drag it to the midpoint of the box or line that you want to connect it to. When the cross hairs line up on that line or side, release the mouse button to drop the line.

By the Way . . .

You can also add drawings that you created with other drawing programs to a word processor document. Just use Microsoft Draw to import them into your Works document. To import another drawing, place the document cursor where you want the drawing to be. Then choose Drawing from the document window's **I**nsert menu. When Microsoft Draw loads, choose **I**mport Picture from Draw's **F**ile menu. Type the name of the file you want or choose it from the list. If you need to locate the file in another directory, you can do that from this File box. When you're finished, choose **OK** and the drawing will be displayed. Use Draw tools to make changes if you like.

Clean-Up Time

When you're finished with your drawing, choose Exit and Return to from Draw's File menu to save the drawing and return to the original document. Microsoft Draw asks if you want to update the document with your drawing. By all means, say yes! Then when you save the document, the drawing will be saved too.

If you want to remove a picture or drawing from a document, just click on the drawing to select it, and then press the **Del** key.

If you want to resize the drawing in your document, just click once on the drawing window and drag the resize handles out to the size you want. You can check the size of your drawing on the page by using Print Preview in the document's File menu. To get back into the drawing to make changes, just double-click on the drawing in the original document, and the Draw window will open.

If, while you're still working or changing a drawing, you want to make sure the latest changes get back into the document file, choose Update from Draw's File menu, which is the equivalent of saving a document every now and then while you work.

ClipArt Creations

If you just don't have the time or confidence to create your own drawing, use any of the ClipArt pieces that Microsoft so thoughtfully included with Works. Not only can you insert ClipArt anywhere in your word processing document or database forms, you can also use Microsoft Draw to "customize" the ClipArt!

To insert a ClipArt picture in a document, move the document cursor to where you want the picture placed. From the Insert menu, choose ClipArt. Narrow your ClipArt Gallery selection down to the category you want, and then choose one of the pictures displayed. Press **OK** when you're ready. The picture will be added to your document.

If you want to modify the ClipArt picture, make a copy of it in your document using the Edit Copy command. Then open a Draw window by choosing Drawing from the document's Insert menu. Paste the copy into Draw from Draw's Edit menu. Once inside, you can use all of Draw's tools to modify the ClipArt. When you're finished, choose Exit and Return to from Draw's File menu. Update the document, and Draw will automatically insert the modified drawing back where it was.

By the Way . . .

You can add your own ClipArt selections to the Works ClipArt Gallery by choosing **O**ptions in the ClipArt dialog box. Choose **R**efresh, and Works will search all your files for other clip art pictures and add them to its files.

Word Twisting

Remember the newsletter template you saw way back in Chapter 2, with the title running sideways up the left column? (If not, flip back there real quick and check it out.) I've always wanted to learn how to do that!

As it turns out, you don't need to use a template to rotate your titles. With the WordArt accessory you can create special effects and twist all your words around!

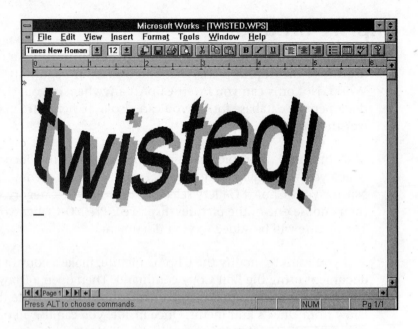

Brought to you by WordArt!

WordArt has its own toolbox, and it's even simpler to use than Draw. Table 12.2 gives you a closer look at the WordArt toolbox. If you need more Help, press **F1** while using WordArt, or use the **Help** menu.

Table 12.2   WordArt Tools and Their Functions

Tool	Function
▶ Curve Down ⬆	Selects the shape the text will conform to.
Arial ⬆	Selects the text font.
50 ⬆	Selects the point size.
B	Makes the text **bold**.
I	*Italicizes* the text.

Tool	Function
	Makes all the letters, capital and lowercase, the same height.
	Turns all the characters 90 degrees to read text sideways.
	Stretches the text to fill the WordArt frame.
	Aligns the text within the frame.
	Adjusts the space between characters.
	Rotates or inclines the text.
	Adds a shading pattern and colors for foreground and background.
	Adds shadows to text.
	Changes the thickness of the text's border.

WordArt Turned On

Add WordArt to a document in the same way you add ClipArt or drawings. Move the cursor to where you want to add WordArt, and then choose **WordArt** from the Insert menu. Type your text in the Enter Your Text Here box of the WordArt window. You can type more than one line by pressing **Enter** to begin each new line.

With the mouse, click on the Toolbar buttons to change your text however you want to. With the keyboard, you can use the menu commands to create the same effects. Experiment, and be creative. To add the WordArt to your document and return to Works, click anywhere outside the Enter Your Text Here box, or press **Esc** twice.

If you want to change the WordArt later, double-click on the WordArt in the document to display the WordArt window. Make your changes, and then choose the Update Display button to update the document too.

Put It to Work

Use Microsoft Draw, ClipArt, and WordArt to design your own letterhead or personal stationery. Now that you've got the skills, you don't need to use the AutoStart template. Unless, of course, you don't have the time.

To get started, just open a new word processing document. If you already have a name picked out, save the document file before you start drawing. Then press **Enter** to move down the page to the point where you'd like to start being creative. Choose the tool you want to use from the **I**nsert menu and have fun, unless, of course, this is business!

The Least You Need to Know

- ☞ Although Microsoft Draw is a complete Drawing program, you can use it only from inside a word processing document or database form.

- ☞ Use Microsoft Draw to create a company logo, illustrate reports, add impact to brochures, or modify ClipArt.

- ☞ Add your own clip art collection to Microsoft Works' Gallery by choosing **O**ptions and **R**efresh once you're inside the ClipArt dialog box.

- ☞ Use WordArt to create interesting titles, logos, and headings. WordArt will rotate, twist, turn, invert, shadow, squish, and stretch text.

- ☞ To get Help with the Draw, ClipArt, or WordArt tools, press **F1** when you're in that window, or use the **H**elp menu.

Part III
Creative Counting with Spreadsheets and Charts

This whole business of spreadsheets actually started when man ran out of fingers and started counting on his toes. He learned how easy it was to double, triple, even quadruple what he could charge based on the number of appendages he could count. The real problem arose when he had to depend on his family's body parts to conduct the really big deals. It got to be that a man's wealth was only limited by the size of his family. Anyway, that's why the first thing new fathers always do is count their newborn's fingers and toes.

You'll learn other more interesting tidbits about figuring numbers once we get inside and start looking at spreadsheets and charts.

Chapter 13
What *Is* a Spreadsheet Anyway?

In This Chapter

- ☛ What spreadsheets do, and how they do it
- ☛ A tour of a typical spreadsheet
- ☛ Getting around in Works' Spreadsheet window
- ☛ Selecting cells and ranges of cells

It's estimated that nearly one out of ten couples searching for a new home break up in the process. While champagne wishes and caviar dreams may account for some separations, statistically, more love has been lost because the passenger seat partner can't read a map!

That's why, in the interests of preserving that fine institution known as the modern family, this chapter includes a quick review of how to read a street map. (And I'll also tell you all about spreadsheets, which are a lot like maps.)

Spreadsheets Are for Dreamers

Spreadsheets are Man's answer to the little five-year-old within each of us that never stopped asking "yeah, but what if. . . ?"

Spreadsheets automate all of the calculations that used to take forever to do with calculators, adding machines, or fingers and toes. Because they let us change the values entered in formulas without erasing the whole page, they're perfect for creating business and financial plans, projecting sales figures, planning budgets, and keeping all kinds of financial records. I once used a spreadsheet to figure out how much tax I'll owe when I'm rich. The answer was so astronomical, I had to keep changing my definition of "rich" just to make it seem worthwhile.

Put It To Work

Here's what you can do with just one spreadsheet. Prepare a business plan spreadsheet to forecast your company's growth for next year or the next few years (these are your business goals). Estimate all of the revenues (sales) and all of the expenses (costs) for each year. Then subtract the expenses from the expected sales. What's left is the annual profit.

Use the same spreadsheet to keep track of actual sales and expense figures during the year. Compare your actual progress against the plan by having the spreadsheet automatically calculate the difference for you. If you're not reaching your annual profit goal, either increase sales, or lower costs, whichever you prefer!

Unfortunately, the "What If" game can only be played with numbers and calculations. We, in the real world, cannot yet get a verbal response to questions like "What if elephants could fly?" To solve mysteries like this, geeks have been furiously working on artificial intelligence and virtual reality: concepts that will one day let little Brad and Samantha sit down in front of (or perhaps inside) the home computer to get *all* of their questions answered intelligently, and in all-too-real living color.

Maps 101, or "How Does It Work?"

Spreadsheets are like city street maps that your computer uses to locate the numbers you want *crunched*.

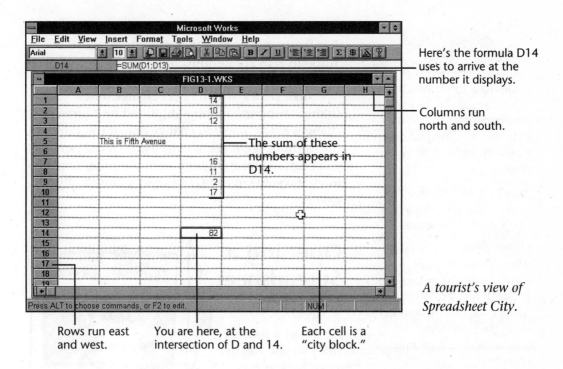

Here's the formula D14 uses to arrive at the number it displays.

Columns run north and south.

The sum of these numbers appears in D14.

A tourist's view of Spreadsheet City.

Rows run east and west.

You are here, at the intersection of D and 14.

Each cell is a "city block."

Spreadsheet City has two kinds of roads that criss-cross each other, forming a street grid. *Rows* run east and west (or left and right) and are numbered consecutively from 1st Avenue to 4,096th Avenue. *Columns* run north and south (or up and down) and are ordered alphabetically, starting with A Street. Since there are 256 columns, letters start repeating themselves after the first 26 columns, so that Z Street is followed by AA Street, and AZ Street is followed by BA Street, all the way down to IV Street.

You can enter numbers, formulas, or text in individual blocks called *cells*. Cells mark the intersection of columns and rows, and are labeled accordingly. The cell on the corner of D Street and 5th Avenue is known as D5.

If you want Works to add a column of numbers, you can tell it to add the contents of a group of cells and place the answer in another cell. Numbers entered into cells are called *values*. The instructions you give Works

SPEAK LIKE A GEEK

Crunch A semi-techie term that refers to the noise computers used to make when calculating large formulas with many variables. When numbers are **crunched**, they are calculated.

to perform calculations are called *formulas*. In that last figure, notice that the contents of cells D1 through D13 are summed in cell D14.

Unlike values, which never change unless you change them, the number displayed by a formula changes every time you change one of the values in the formula. So, if you changed any of the numbers you entered along D Street (or any intersecting row), the value in cell D14 would automatically change.

Opening a Spreadsheet Window

Let's start a spreadsheet so you can get a real look at one. First, get into Works if you're not already there: Open the Works for Windows program group and double-click on the **Works** icon. If you're still displaying the Welcome screen, select Start **W**orks Now to move on to the Startup screen.

If you were with me in the Word Processor, you'll remember I turned the Startup Screen into quite a major production. Basically, if you want to work on a Spreadsheet, you've got three choices:

☛ **Start a brand new spreadsheet** by clicking on the Spreadsheet button, or pressing **S**, in the "Create a new" box. (This is the route we want now, so click here if you're with me!)

☛ **Open a spreadsheet that you created recently.** To find out if your file is considered "recent" (within the last five or six spreadsheet files), check the Recently used files box at the bottom of the Startup screen. If your file is there, use the arrow keys or a click of the mouse to select it.

☛ **Open an existing document.** If your existing spreadsheet didn't appear on the Recently used files list, you'll need to go the long route. Click the **Open An Existing Document** button, and then select the file from the list.

By the Way . . .

Opening a spreadsheet file is the same as opening any other kind of file. You learned to do it earlier in the book. Just pick it from the list of files and click the **OK** button or press **Enter**. You might need to select the drive and directory from their respective lists, or set the file type to Works SS (*.wks).

Looking Out a Spreadsheet Window

A spreadsheet window holds the potential for the greatest Bingo game the world has ever known. Nevertheless, its only claim to fame so far has been its outstanding ability to display and crunch numbers. Here's how it works:

If double-clicking doesn't work for you, try one click and then press **Enter**.

At first glance, the most obvious difference between a spreadsheet and any other document window is the grid. So, although this may not be the logical place to start, we will.

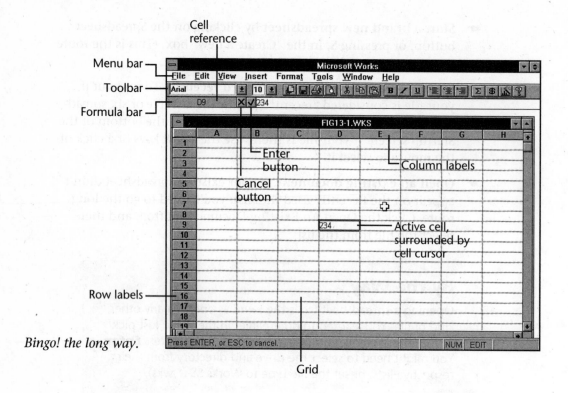

Bingo! the long way.

You've already learned that cells are the intersection of rows and columns. The *grid* is nothing more than lines on the screen to visually separate all of the cells in the spreadsheet. If you don't want to use the grid-lines, just switch them off by selecting Gridlines in the View menu.

The grid is enclosed in the spreadsheet's own document window. Notice that this window has its own title bar, Control-menu box, and minimize and maximize buttons. Outlining the grid, along the edges of the document window, are *row and column labels*. They identify your street map coordinates, so to speak, and help you find your place in the big city.

Speaking of finding your place, when you open a new spreadsheet, you always start in A1, the *active cell*. That doesn't mean you have to start working there, but if you do get lost it's always nice to have a place you can return to. You can tell it's active because of the dark outline around it, a.k.a. the *cell cursor*.

The *menu bar* and *Toolbar* in the Works program window (which you will remember from Chapter 5), are standard issue in all of Works' tools. They do, however, change slightly from tool to tool, so you may want to open each menu and look around, and also point at each Toolbar button to check things out. In the Spreadsheet, for example, you'll find only the File menu, Window menu, and Help menu are exactly as you left them in the Word Processor. All of the other menus have some new commands that you need only for Spreadsheet business.

The Toolbar contains three command buttons that you've probably never seen before, but which you'll use a lot in your spreadsheets:

 The Autosum button is used to total a column or row of numbers.

 The Currency button is used to turn your numbers into dollars and cents.

 The New Chart button is truly amazing. It turns the numbers entered in any rows and columns you select into a chart!

The *formula bar* is another addition to the spreadsheet document window that you won't find in a word processing window. The formula bar is used to enter and change cell formulas or values in an active cell or cell range. (You'll learn about ranges later.) It contains a *cell reference* (which always gives you the exact address of the active cell or range) and the formula or value itself. Between the two you'll find an *Enter* and a *Cancel* box that you can use to either accept or reject the information contained in the cell.

Remember that the Toolbar is customizable. That means there's a Toolbar button available for every spreadsheet command. When you're ready to customize yours, review Chapter 5 for the details.

The Three Faces of Mouse

To reveal your mouse's spreadsheet personality, drag it slowly straight down from the top of the Works title bar through the spreadsheet grid. Watch the face of the pointer as it changes.

This is the shaded cross pointer that appears in the spreadsheet grid. Use it to select the cells you want to work with.

This is the I-beam pointer, marking the point at which you can type to enter or change text in the formula bar.

This is the standard mouse pointer, used to select commands from the menu bar and Toolbar.

Selecting Cells and Ranges

By this time, you already know what a cell is (I hope!), but what is a range? That's an easy one: a range is an adjacent group of cells. For instance, cells C1, C2, D1, and D2 are a range, because you can draw a rectangle that encompasses all four of them and nothing else. Because the number of cells in a range can be huge (thousands!), ranges are usually abbreviated in a statement that looks like this:

top-left cell : bottom-right cell

A real range reference looks like this:

C1:D2

To select a single cell, you just move the cell cursor to it. You can do this by pressing the keyboard's arrow keys to move it around, or by clicking on the cell you want with the mouse. Easy enough. To select a range of cells, you can use either the keyboard or the mouse:

☛ To select a range with the mouse, click on the top left cell, press and hold the left mouse button, and drag the mouse pointer to the bottom right cell. Release the button.

☛ To select a range with the keyboard, move the cell cursor to the top left cell, hold down the **Shift** key, and use the arrow keys to move to the bottom right cell. Release the Shift key.

Take some time right now to practice selecting some cells and ranges! You'll need to be familiar with this process before you go on to the next chapter. As you select ranges, notice how they're identified in the formula bar.

You can even select more than one range at a time: Just select the first range, hold down the **Ctrl** key, and select the subsequent ones. Don't release the Ctrl key until you're finished selecting all the ranges you want.

The Least You Need to Know

Memories of our trip to the Spreadsheet City:

- ☛ Spreadsheets contain grids that are made by intersecting rows and columns.

- ☛ Columns run north and south (up and down). Rows run east and west (right and left).

- ☛ Cells are the boxes at the intersection of columns and rows. All of a spreadsheet's information (including text, numbers, and formulas) is entered in cells.

- ☛ You can enter labels (text) and values (numbers) into cells. You can also enter formulas, which perform calculations on values. Formulas are noted with an equal sign (=).

- ☛ The mouse pointer changes its shape in different parts of the spreadsheet window.

- ☛ To select a single cell, move the cell cursor to it. To select a range of cells, drag the mouse pointer across the cells you want, or hold down the **Shift** key while you use the arrow keys to move from one corner of the range to the other.

Geez, another @!*%& blank page!

Chapter 14
Constructing a Spreadsheet

In This Chapter

- ☛ Planning before you type
- ☛ Entering different types of data
- ☛ How a spreadsheet handles dates and times

So, you're eager to start number crunching? Well before you can crunch anything (data or otherwise), you need to do some basic planning. Figure out what you want to accomplish with this great spreadsheet of yours, and then plunk down the labels before you forget how to fill them in. Trust me, after you finish plugging all your data into the appropriate slots, you'll be prepared to do some real number crunching in the next chapter.

Plan Ahead

Whenever I have to do something over because I was too busy to do it right the first time, I remember this poster: scrawled in a kid's handwriting that doesn't quite fit in the allotted space, are the simple words "PLAN AHEAd."

If you decide to plan *your* spreadsheet ahead of time, here's what you need to think about:

The subject   Narrow the field. Don't try to cram everything you possibly can into one spreadsheet. (Especially your first one!) If you want to create a spreadsheet for your business travel expenses, don't try to turn it into an annual travel budget too. (There's time for that later.)

The calculations   What are you trying to count? Do you only need one final cost, or do you need separate subtotals for transportation and everything else? Do you need daily counts, or is one count for the whole trip enough? What equations would you be using in your head—or on paper—to calculate your subtotals and totals?

The pieces   What pieces do you need to count in order to make your calculations? In other words, you probably need to list airplane tickets, as well as hotel bills, meal expenses, rental car receipts, and so on.

The layout   How do you want this thing to look? Keep the structure as simple as possible and try to make it easy to trace the values (pieces) that were used in the calculations.

The Tools of the Spreadsheet Trade

Once you have an idea of what you want your spreadsheet to do, figure out what kind of information it needs. A spreadsheet can contain three kinds of information:

Text   Use text for headings, labels, notes and instructions.

Numbers   Numbers represent quantities, dates, or time. Unless you have entered a recalculating date or time, a number value will remain constant until you change it.

Formulas   Use formulas to calculate a new value from existing values. Formulas must always start with an equal sign (=), and can contain any of the following:

- ☛   **Operators**, which are symbols used to denote a mathematical operation such as +, −, /, and *.

- ☛   **Numbers**, such as 1, 12, 325, −45, and 36.4.

- ☛   **Cell and range references**, like B5, D14, and A2:C14.

- ☛   **Cell and range names**, such as Meals, Lodging, Total, and Subtotal.

☛ **Functions**, which are ready-made equations for common mathematical procedures, such as addition (SUM), average (AVG), and rounding off (ROUND).

These types of information are the tools at your command. Before you start entering data, you should plan what you want your final result to be, and then figure out how to use these tools to get it done.

For example, to create the spreadsheet that will let us calculate our business travel expenses, we probably want a column that lists the expense categories down the left side (i.e. transportation, hotel/lodging, meals, etc.) and a row that lists the travel days across the top. The cells that intersect the rows and columns are where we enter the costs of each daily travel expense. We'll need to total each day's expenses in a row at the bottom, and then perhaps add another cell to the right of the last column to add all of the daily totals.

A Few Quick Layout Tips

When you're planning your spreadsheet, think about layout as well as content, so you don't have to do major cutting and pasting later. Here are some hints to keep in mind before you start:

☛ Leave extra rows and a column around the edges of your spreadsheet for the title, row headings, and column headings.

☛ Start in the upper left corner of the spreadsheet window, and work your figures down the sheet rather than across, when possible.

An easy way to abbreviate the cell names for a big block of cells is to use the top left cell, a colon, and the bottom right cell, as in A2:C14. It's called a *range reference.* (We covered it in Chapter 13, remember?)

A **cell reference** is a specific location in a spreadsheet that marks the intersection of a column and row.

A **range reference** is a shorthand notation used to reference all of the individual cells in a group of adjacent cells. A range reference refers to the cells in the upper left corner and lower right corner of a range.

☞ Don't skip columns or rows between data entries just to separate them. You can accomplish the same thing by adjusting the format, column size, and alignment, as you'll see in Chapter 17.

Entry Level Skills

When you're ready to enter the information you need for the spreadsheet, use your mouse or the arrow keys to move the cell cursor to the cell in which you want to type. When the cell cursor is positioned on a cell, that cell is *active*. Anything you type will be entered in the active cell.

If the active cell already contains some data, the new data replaces it. (That's the way you change the contents of a cell!) You'll learn how to edit the contents of a cell without wiping it out later.

Your typing appears in the formula bar as well as in the cell.

When you press the Enter key or click the Enter button, the data is entered in the cell.

	A	B	C	D	E	F
1						
2						
3						
4						
5	Income	January	February			
6	Gross Sales	248765	286079			
7	Less Returns and Allowances	29851	30645			
8	Less Cost of Goods	94530	108700			
9						
10						
11						
12						
13						
14						
15						
16						
17						

Entering numbers: a no-frills basic skill.

Press ENTER, or ESC to cancel.

Whatever you type is placed in the active cell when you press enter.

As you can see, your entry is displayed in both the formula bar and the active cell as you type. When you finish typing, press **Enter** or click the **Enter** box in the formula bar to commit the information to the active cell.

Labels, Labels, Labels

Labels are anything that Works doesn't interpret as a formula, number, date, or time. Generally, this means text (A–Z); but a label can also be a combination of text, numbers, and/or symbols.

The major use for labels (not surprisingly) is to label the values in your worksheet. It is customary, for example, to include row and column labels, so the reader will understand what the numbers in those rows and columns represent. You may think that you'll remember what each value represents in your spreadsheet, but trust me—you won't. Therefore, it's best to label everything.

When you view a label in the formula bar, it always appears to have a double or single quotation mark before it. That's how Works separates labels from values and formulas. If you have a number that you would like Works to interpret as a label (for example, a ZIP code or a telephone number), just type a quotation mark before you type the number, and Works will consider it a label.

Don't worry about entering numbers in their proper format for now. You'll learn how to format each cell so it can display numbers as currency, percentages, fractions, or dates later.

The spreadsheet in the last picture has had its column widths adjusted so all the data fits nicely. We'll talk about doing this in Chapter 17, but if you can't wait, position your mouse pointer between two column headings and drag the dividing line between them to resize the column on the left. (The column on the right simply moves over; it doesn't change width.)

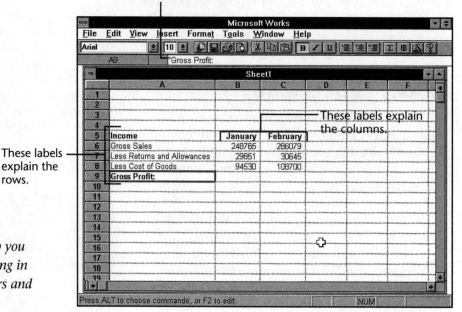

A quotation mark in the formula bar means that the cell contains a label.

These labels explain the columns.

These labels explain the rows.

Labels help you find meaning in the numbers and formulas.

When you need to enter the same information in adjacent cells, select the range of cells (as you learned in Chapter 13) and type the information. When you're finished typing, hold down the **Ctrl** key and press **Enter**.

Labels are automatically left aligned when you type them. If you don't like this arrangement, you can change *cell alignment,* as discussed in Chapter 17, when you learn how to format cells.

If you enter a label that is longer than the width of the column, Works overlaps the extra text into the cells to the right. If those cells happen to be full, Works only displays what it can fit in the active cell, but the entire entry remains stored in Works' memory. You'll learn to widen a column in Chapter 17, so that the entire contents are displayed. (Hint: use the mouse to drag the line between two lettered column headings to the right.)

What's the Value of All This?

To a Works spreadsheet, *values* are either quantities of something (such as money, shares, units, etc.) or dates/times. You enter values to describe a situation—for example, you made $150 profit, or the schedule is 3 weeks behind. (Of course, you'll want to enter labels for each value, so you won't get confused.) Then, once your values are in place, you can enter formulas that give you information about your situation. For example, a formula could tell you that if you had been only 1 week behind, you would have made $500. (Pretty depressing, isn't it?)

The position of text or numbers within a spreadsheet cell is the **cell alignment**. You can align characters within a cell both horizontally (left to right), and vertically (top to bottom).

Values can be entered as positive and negative whole numbers, decimals, fractions, exponents, dates, or times. Works is flexible—it can take almost any kind of number you can dish out.

When you type a value into a cell, it is automatically aligned to the right. If you enter a value that is too large for the cell, Works will either display ##### in the cell, or it will convert the number to scientific notation (for example, 4.23E+23). However, if you widen the column or change the format to one that will fit, the number will be displayed as you entered it.

To make sure Works doesn't read a fraction as a date, type a zero in front of it, like this: 0 2/3 or 0(Spacebar) 2/3.

Entering Many Values at Once

To save yourself time when you want numbers or dates to increase incrementally through a row or column of adjacent cells, Works can enter the series for you. For example, here's how you could create a timesheet and have Works automatically display each day of the week across the top row:

1. Move the cell cursor to the starting cell, and type the starting value (for example, 6/4/94 or June 4). Click the **Enter** button or press **Enter**.

2. Hold down the **Shift** key and press the right arrow key until the cells you want to fill are selected too.

3. Open the **Edit** menu and choose Fill Series.

4. In the Units box, select the units by which you want to advance the series, and then choose **OK** or press **Enter**.

Dealing with Dates and Times

All you have to do to change the amount of increase or decrease in a series is to highlight the series again. Then go back to **F**ill Series from the **E**dit menu and select a different unit or Step by amount.

The beauty of dates and times in Works' spreadsheets is that Works sees them as numbers. That means you can set up formulas (to be covered shortly) that perform calculations based on them. For instance, a formula could calculate when exactly 70 days from a given date would be, and can enter the answer into another cell.

When you enter a date like December 14, 1993, for instance, Works stores it in pure numerical form. It calculates the number of days that have elapsed from January 1, 1900 to the date being entered, and that number becomes the "date" that Works stores in its memory. The same thing with the time: Works calculates the number of minutes since 12:00 midnight. Unfortunately, these "pure" dates are nearly impossible to decipher at a glance.

If you're into science fiction, you've probably read or seen stories about alien beings who make themselves appear in earthling form so they won't scare people. Well, dates and times can do this same shape-changing trick, with a little help from you. All you need to do is change the date format that's displayed. Here's how.

If you're using Version 2.0, choose **T**ime/Date from the Forma**t** menu and select your format.

Choose Number from the Forma**t** menu. In the Format box, select either **D**ate or **T**ime, whichever you want to display. Use the Options box to the right to choose the exact format you want. When you're finished, press **OK** and check the contents of your cell. If the format you selected doesn't work for you, try another.

The Least You Need to Know

Spreadsheets take a little getting used to, but you'll be racing through them in no time. This chapter helped you get ready to enter your formulas by helping you set up the spreadsheet structure:

- ☛ It helps to plan what your spreadsheet needs to show, as well as what calculations you need to make, before you actually start creating a spreadsheet.

- ☛ You can put text, numbers, and formulas in spreadsheet cells. When you enter information, it is displayed in the cell and in the formula bar.

- ☛ To enter information in a spreadsheet, select the cell in which you want to enter the information, and type. When finished, press **Enter** or click the **Enter** box in the formula bar.

- ☛ Works 3.0 users can enter a series of consecutive numbers or dates with the Fill Series command on the **E**dit menu.

- ☛ When you enter a date or time, Works converts it to a number that it can use in calculations.

- ☛ To make the number display appear in a recognizable format, select **N**umber from the Forma**t** menu and select a different **D**ate or T**i**me format. (Works 2.0 users, select **T**ime/Date from the Forma**t** menu.)

**Another inadvertent blank page.
Creepy, isn't it?**

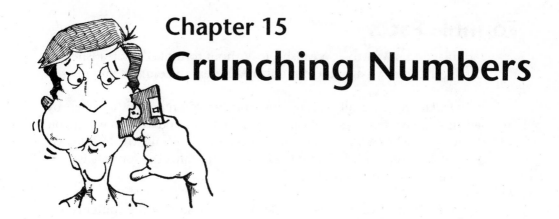

Chapter 15
Crunching Numbers

In This Chapter

- ☛ What is a formula?
- ☛ Much ado about operators
- ☛ Autosumming it up
- ☛ Cell and range references in formulas
- ☛ Functions: the formula shortcut

Don't you hate it when, at the end of your favorite television show, that guy with the big blustery voice tells you, "Don't go away, we'll be right back." And just because you really enjoyed this particular episode, you stick around—just in case. (Then they finally come back, and you've waited just to watch the credits roll.)

Well, we're not like that here in Idiot-land. We told you in Chapter 14 that we were gonna show you how to crunch numbers next, and "by golly" we are! Here goes.

Formula Facts

Formulas add power to a spreadsheet. Without formulas, a spreadsheet is just another pretty page full of numbers and text in columns and rows.

Formulas are powerful tools because they let you represent numbers by cell and range references that can be changed and updated. So when you change the value in a cell that is referenced by a formula, the formula is recalculated automatically, and the cell that contains the formula is updated with the new result.

If, for example, you wanted Works to add the sum of the contents of D5 and D6 and place the answer in D7, the value displayed in D7 would always depend upon the values entered in D5 and D6. If you changed the value of D5 or D6, D7 would automatically recalculate.

To see what I mean, try it yourself. Enter **4** in cell D5 and **6** in D6. Highlight cell D7 and type the following formula: **=D5+D6**. The answer is 10, and if you entered everything correctly it is displayed in D7. Now change one of the entries in D5 or D6, and notice what happens to D7.

By the Way . . .

In the default mode, Works displays the result in the cell, and displays the formula (of the active cell) in the formula bar. If you would like to view the formulas in their cells as you are setting up the spreadsheet, open the **V**iew menu and select **F**ormulas. The columns expand in this view to accommodate lengthy formulas.

Building a Formula

All formulas start with an equals sign (=) that tells Works that this is a formula and not just a string of text or numbers.

A simple formula, like =C8, may contain only one cell reference, telling Works to give the active cell the same value as the cell specified in the formula. If you want to perform calculations on values, you can use these common operators to build other kinds of simple formulas:

Use this operator	For this kind of formula
+ (addition)	=C4+C5+D7+E8
– (subtraction)	=D7–C2–4
* (multiplication)	=C4*D8
/ (division)	=D6/3

A formula can also include one of Works' built-in functions and cell references. Here's how you can have Works average a column of numbers: =AVG(C2,C3,C4,C5,C6). Or, to use a range reference in that formula (instead of individual cell references), the formula could be entered like this: =AVG(C2:C6). We'll look at functions more closely later in this chapter.

Just Following Orders

When Works runs across formulas that contain two or more operators, it follows these standard algebraic rules to decide which one to do first:

Don't leave any spaces in a formula. Use operators or commas to separate numbers and cell references.

☛ Contents of the innermost set of parentheses are evaluated first.

☛ Operators are evaluated second in the standard order of evaluation.

☛ And third, equations are evaluated from left to right.

Table 15.1 shows Works' operators and their order of evaluation:

Table 15.1   Order of Evaluation of Works' Operators

Operator	Order of evaluation
– (negative), + (positive)	First
^ (exponential)	Second
* (multiplication), / (division)	Third
+ (addition), – (subtraction)	Fourth

continues

Table 15.1   Continued

Operator	Order of evaluation
= (equal to), <> (not equal to)	Fifth
< (less than), > (greater than)	Fifth
<= (less than or equal to),	
>= (greater than or equal to)	Fifth
#NOT#	Sixth
#OR#, #AND#	Seventh

That's quite an impressive table, but what does it mean? Let's look at a few formulas until you get the idea how this works.

For instance, if you entered a formula that looked like this: =(C5*D5)–(A3+B3), you might wonder how Works decides what to do first. If cell C5 contained the number 8, D5 the number 2, A3 the number 6, and B3 the number 1, Works would see the following values: =(8*2)–(6+1). It would complete the equation in three steps. First it would do the multiplication, and arrive at 16. Then it would perform the addition for the second value, which equals 7. Finally, Works would perform the last calculation: =16–7, and come up with 9.

Great! But, how does it know what to do with something like this: =C5+A3/D5?

Good question, but actually that formula is even easier. Since there are no parentheses, Works knows to perform the division first (based on the standard order of evaluation), and then add the result to C5. Using the same numbers, here's how Works would solve the problem: =8+(6/2), or 8+3. The answer is 11.

One more. What happens if there are parentheses inside parentheses, like this: =(3*(C5*B3))–A3?

Like the rules say, the innermost set will be calculated first. So before doing anything else, Works will figure out that C5*B3 equals 8. Then, it will evaluate the outer parentheses (3*8), and come up with 24. Finally, Works will subtract A3 from 24, like this: =24–6. The answer, of course, is 18.

Doing a Quick Sum

One of the most common calculations most people do is to add a column or row of numbers. Here's a quick and easy way to get the job done:

1. Highlight an empty cell at the end of a column or row of numbers.

Click here to cancel.

Click here when the range
reference is correct.

Autosum button

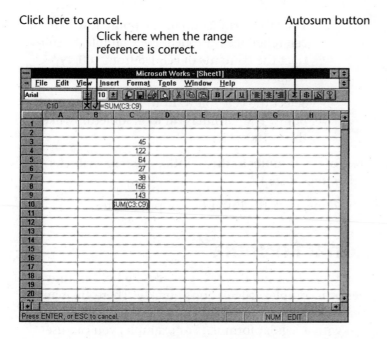

It's Autosum!

2. Click the **Autosum** button on the Toolbar, or press **Ctrl+M**. Works will look for cell references to include in the formula and then will propose the range to be summed in the formula bar.

3. If the range is correct, press **Enter** or click the **Enter** box. If the range is not correct, type the range references yourself. Use the mouse pointer to position the insertion point, and delete the existing reference. Then type the correct references and click **Enter**.

Referring to Cells and Ranges

As you're creating formulas, very seldom will you have a "pure math" formula, such as 2+3. More often, you'll be calculating the contents of other cells, as in D3+B5. There are lots of ways to insert a cell or range reference into a formula, but here's the easiest way:

1. Select the cell in which you want to type the formula.

2. Type the formula up to the point at which the cell reference is needed. For example, to subtract the contents of cell D5 from 100, type **=100–**.

3. Select the cell you want to include at that point. The formula will look something like this: **=100–D5**.

4. Type the rest of the formula to the point of the next cell reference, and then repeat step 3.

5. When you're done, click the **Enter** box or press **Enter**.

A Truly Functional Formula

Functions are a special type of formula. Works provides 76 built-in functions to help you perform complex calculations quickly. There are many functions that do quickly what it would take quite a bit of thinking and typing to accomplish with a regular formula. For example, you can use =AVG to average a group of numbers, like this:

    =AVG(C3:C7)

If you didn't have the AVG function, you would have to average the numbers like this:

    =(C3+C4+C5+C6+C7)/5

All functions contain a function name, a set of parentheses, and *arguments*. Arguments must be enclosed in a set of parentheses and separated by commas. Cell and range references are the arguments used most often.

You saw how easy it was to use functions with ranges, columns, or rows when you used the Autosum button on the Toolbar. The Autosum button is actually just a way of entering the =SUM function, which adds numbers. All you had to do was apply the function and highlight the range.

Arguments, the values used in a function to produce a new value, can include cell references, range references, other functions, numbers, or text. Arguments are always enclosed in parentheses.

Getting Functional

Functions are a particular kind of formula; all functions are formulas, but not all formulas are functions. Here's how to enter a function:

1. Highlight the cell in which you want to place the formula.

2. Type = (an equals sign) followed by the function, for example, =AVG.

3. Type an opening parenthesis.

4. If there is more than one argument, separate each one with a comma, but do not leave a space.

5. When you're finished, type a closing parenthesis. The formula now looks like this: =AVG(2,9,C6).

6. Press **Enter** or click the **Enter** button on the formula bar when the formula is complete.

A simpler way to enter a function is to select it from Works' list of functions. When you use these functions, Works enters the function name and the parentheses, and you need only supply the arguments to the formula. To use a function from the list:

1. Select the cell in which you want to place the formula.

2. Choose Function from the Insert menu.

3. Narrow your search by identifying the type of function you need in the Category box.

4. Choose a function from the Functions box and click **OK** to insert it into your spreadsheet.

5. Move the mouse pointer insertion point to the formula bar in order to replace each argument name with the values, cell references, or range references you want.

6. Click the **Enter** box or press **Enter** when you're done.

To simplify the function, use your mouse to capture the reference. (That's what you did when you used the Autosum button, and when you selected cells and ranges in formulas earlier in the chapter.) Just highlight the argument you're specifying in the formula bar, and then drag the mouse through the range. Check to make sure the range reference syntax is correct: a full set of parentheses, a colon separating cell references, no spaces. When everything is correct, click the **Enter** button.

First, type the function and the opening parenthesis here.

Third, finish the argument by entering the closing parenthesis here.

Second, highlight the range.

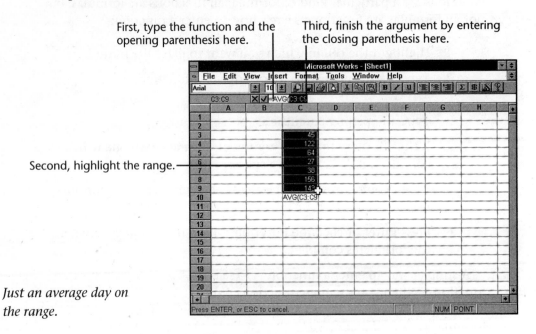

Just an average day on the range.

Making Changes: The "What If" Game

Now that you know how and what you can put in a spreadsheet cell, it's only fair to show you how to get it out or change it. That's what the "What If" game is all about, isn't it?

Sorry, Formula, You're Cancelled!

You can totally remove the contents of a highlighted cell or group of cells, without clearing the formatting and style, in any of these ways:

☛ Press the **Del** key to clear the contents.

☛ Type over the existing entry in a cell.

☛ Select Clear from the Edit menu.

TECHNO NERD TEACHES

Most dates don't spontaneously change themselves; you have to manually change them if you want them to be current. But wouldn't it be nice to be able to open a spreadsheet and have the current date and/or time always entered at the top?

The answer to this wish comes in the form of a function: =NOW(). The =NOW() function can report the current date and time, depending on which number format you assign the formula cell.

Change It—We Can Fix That!

To edit an entry in a highlighted cell instead of changing it completely:

1. Highlight the cell, and then move the insertion point to the formula bar by clicking on it or by pressing **F2**.

2. Use the arrow keys or the mouse to move around within the formula bar and make the editing changes you need.

3. When you are finished editing, click the **Enter** box in the formula bar or press **Enter**.

When you accidentally clear an entry, or if you don't like the changes you've made to a cell, use the **E**dit **U**ndo command to try to restore it, or click the **Cancel** button on the formula bar.

Besides changing the text or number in the cell, there are lots of formatting changes you can make to a cell to make it look more appealing. You'll learn about them in Chapter 17.

Saving What You've Got So Far

Until you save your spreadsheet for the first time, Works calls it Sheet1, or Sheet2, etc. depending on how many attempts you've made today. When you think you've got a "keeper," *save* it so you don't accidentally lose it. Saving is the same in all of Works' modules, so you're probably already a pro at it. Here's a quick refresher just in case you're rusty:

If you leave a space in the file name, or use an "unauthorized" special character (such as ? or .), Works will ask you to choose another name.

1. Choose **S**ave from the **File** menu.

2. Select the drive and directory in which you'd like to save the spreadsheet.

3. Type a name for your spreadsheet that is no more than eight characters long, and that is reminiscent of what the file contains. Works will automatically add the spreadsheet extension (.wks).

4. Tell Works if you want it to make a backup copy of this file, by selecting the **M**ake backup check box.

5. Click the **OK** button or press **Enter**. Hallelujah, another file is saved!

The Least You Need to Know

You've come a long way since Chapter 13, where you first met the Works spreadsheet! In this chapter, you learned to tie all the numbers together with formulas and functions. Here are the highlights for you to look at one more time:

☛ Formulas let you represent numbers by cell and range references that can be changed and updated. When the number values change, the results of the formula are automatically recalculated.

☛ Formulas must always start with an equal sign. Formulas can contain cell and range references.

☛ To quickly total a column or row, highlight the empty cell at the end of the range, and then click the **Autosum** button on the Toolbar or press **Ctrl+M**.

☛ Functions are a special type of formula that contain a function name, a set of parentheses, and arguments.

☛ Works has 76 predefined functions built in. To insert a Works function in a formula, choose **Func**tion from the **I**nsert menu.

☛ Don't forget to save your work once you've created a spreadsheet masterpiece!

**Computer nerds who made the list
of the world's sexiest people.**

Chapter 16
Simple Spreadsheet Tricks

In This Chapter

- ☛ Adding and deleting rows and columns
- ☛ The many ways to move and copy
- ☛ Sorting your data
- ☛ Finding and replacing specific chunks
- ☛ Printing the whole thing

It's always gratifying to be able to say you did something. If you've been keeping up with Chapters 14 and 15, you should already be able to say that you did a spreadsheet. But what if it's still not really what you want? What if you've got extra blank rows or columns, or some numbers that are noticeably out of place? In this chapter, you'll learn to make changes to your spreadsheet: adding, deleting, moving, copying—that sort of thing. Then, once it's perfect, you'll learn in Chapter 17 how to make it pretty.

What's a Few Rows Among Friends?

It's never too late to insert another row or column in a spreadsheet. Just drop it right into place. Here's how.

Select the entire column to the right of where you want a new one placed, or select the row below where you want to insert one. (Click on the column letter or row number to select it.) If you want to insert two columns, highlight two columns. If you want to insert four rows, highlight four rows. Then choose Row/Column from the Insert menu. Works inserts the additional rows or columns and readjusts the spreadsheet.

Deleting a row or column is just as simple. Just select the rows or columns you want to zap, and choose Delete Row/Column from the Insert menu. It's outta there, and Works re-numbers (or re-letters) the rows or columns that are left behind.

Moving (and Copying) Right Along

Now that you've got these extra columns and rows to fill up, it's easier to copy or move information from an existing column or row than it is to enter it all over again. (That is, of course, if it makes sense to repeat that info in the new space!)

There are several ways to move and copy in a spreadsheet; let's look at each of them individually.

Traditional Travel

You're probably already familiar with Windows-style moving and copying—we covered it pretty thoroughly in Chapter 6. If you've forgotten, review these pointers:

☞ Copying leaves the original in place and puts a copy on the Clipboard. Moving (cutting) moves the original from its home onto the Clipboard, leaving an emptiness where it once lived.

☞ Once something is on the Clipboard, it stays there until you cut or copy something else on top of it. You can paste the item from the Clipboard into any number of different locations.

☛ Since there's a single Clipboard that all Windows programs share, you can paste an item from the Clipboard almost anywhere—in the same spreadsheet or a different one, or even in a different kind of document (such as a letter or a database).

With all that knowledge under your belt, you should feel completely at ease with these tried-and-true moving and copying techniques.

1. Highlight the cell or group of cells with the information you want to copy or move.

2. Select Copy or Cut from the Edit menu, or click the **Copy** or **Cut** button on the Toolbar.

3. Move to your destination and select **Paste** from the Edit menu, or click the **Paste** button on the Toolbar.

4. Repeat step 3 if you want to paste more copies in other places.

Drag-and-Drop Travel

Feeling adventurous, ready to try something new? Good! The easiest way to copy and move is to use one of Works features that's new with version 3.0: drag-and-drop editing. This lets you highlight the information you need to copy or move and drag it to a new location. When you get to the destination, just release the mouse button to drop.

Users of Works version 2.0 can't drag and drop; sorry, but you'll have to use the "Traditional Travel" method.

To copy a selection within the same document, click the border of the selection and hold down the **Ctrl** key as you drag to the new location.

To move a selection within the same document, click the border of the selection and drag to the new location.

To copy a selection to another document, click the border and drag the selection to the new location.

To move a selection to another Works document, hold down the **Shift** key as you drag.

Quick! Fill 'Em Up!

If you want to copy the same piece of info into many adjacent cells, there's a quick way to do it.

First, select the cell, column, or row that contains the information you want copied, and drag the highlight to the right (for columns) or downward (for rows) to include the number of columns or rows you want filled. If you're copying into columns, choose Fill Right from the Edit menu; if you're copying into rows, choose Fill Down from the Edit menu.

When copying data into adjacent cells, Works will replace any existing data in destination columns or rows with the data being copied. If you don't want to lose the existing information, insert extra columns or rows before using Fill Right or Fill Down.

The Tricky Part: Relative and Absolute References

Moving and copying labels and values is easy—it works just like any other cut-and-paste operation. Moving and copying formulas is a little different, though. It may seem confusing at first, but this difference actually makes life a lot easier for you!

Let's say you have some numbers in C1 through C10 that you want added up, and you have a formula in cell C11 that does it. That formula might look like this: =SUM(C1:C10).

Let's move the entire production to column D. (You can use either method we just talked about; it doesn't matter which you choose.) Of course, the numbers don't change when you move them; they rest comfortably in their new home of D1:D10. But when you move the formula, you think it will continue to sum the values of C1:C10. But wait! Works is smart enough to realize that you no longer want it to give you the total of C1:C10—you now want it to total D1:D10. And sure enough, when you check out the formula in D11, it reads =SUM(D1:D10).

This miracle of modern spreadsheeting is called *relative referencing*. It means that whenever you move a formula or a reference to another cell, Works adjusts that formula in relation to the new location. If you move the formula two cells down and one cell to the left, all the cell references in that formula change accordingly.

If you ever need Works to keep the cell reference the same, no matter where you move a formula, you must give the cell an *absolute reference*. You indicate an absolute reference by preceding the part of the cell reference that you want to remain constant with a dollar sign.

For instance, if you always want =SUM(B1:B10) to refer to B1:B10, write it like this: **=SUM($B$1:$B$10)**. If you want parts of the reference to be able to change, just leave the dollar sign off that part. For instance, if the rows can change but the column letters must stay the same, it would look like this: =SUM($B1:$B10). If the opposite is true (columns can change, rows can't), use this: =SUM(B$1:B$10). See?

By the Way . . .

When you want to summarize or consolidate information from many spreadsheets into one, you'll often want to copy the result of a formula, and not the formula itself. Luckily, there's a special command that does exactly what you need: the Paste **S**pecial command in the **E**dit menu. After you've copied the formula cell, select **E**dit Paste **S**pecial, and then choose **V**alues only in the Paste Special dialog box.

All the Sorted Details

If you're storing long lists of data, such as inventoried parts or first and last names, it's worth the extra seconds it takes to sort them alphabetically or numerically. When Works sorts according to the contents of one specific column, it takes the entire row of information with it, so there's no messy cleanup! (Works will also adjust all of the relative references to compensate for the move, at no extra charge!)

To sort rows (you can't sort columns), select the rows you want to sort, and then choose Sort Rows from the Tools menu. You'll get a handsome dialog box.

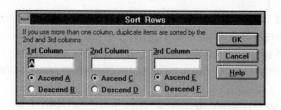

Your one-stop sorting shop.

Type the letter of the first column you want to sort in the 1st Column text box. Then indicate whether you want the sort to be in ascending (top to bottom) or descending (bottom to top) order. If you also want to sort the data in a second or third column (for example, when last names are listed in the first column, first names in the second column, and middle initials in the third), type the column letters in the 2nd Column and 3rd Column text boxes. When you're satisfied, click **OK** or press **Enter**.

Works will not automatically adjust absolute references after a spreadsheet sort. (That's what absolute values are for, remember? They don't get changed, no matter what.) You'll have to adjust them yourself.

Search and Ye Shall Replace

Works can help you find specific text, values, or formulas in your spreadsheet and, if you so desire, replace them with ones that are more to your liking (or perhaps more correct).

To have Works find and replace text or values, select the cells you want searched, or search the whole spreadsheet by not highlighting anything. Then choose Replace from the Edit menu. Another great-looking dialog box pops up.

Find (and Replace) lost values here.

In the Find What box, type the characters you want Works to find. In the Replace With box, type the characters you want to replace them with. Have Works search up and down by Columns or left to right by Rows by marking your selection in the Look By box.

To begin the search, choose the Find Next button. To replace found characters, choose the Replace button. If you want Works to search and replace all occurrences without asking for approval, choose Replace All. When you're done, choose the **Cancel** button, or press **Esc**.

If you just want to find some information, without replacing anything, use the Find command on the Edit menu instead. You'll get a dialog box that's basically the same as the Replace dialog box, but which has fewer choices to make.

Practical Printing Pointers

The most important difference between printing a spreadsheet and printing a word processing document is the way in which Works orders the pages. Word processing documents are consecutive. Spreadsheets, on the other hand, are laid out and printed in this order:

Spreadsheets that won't fit on a single page will print down first, and then across.

The reason for this, of course, is because very few people own printers large enough to print a 4,056 column Works spreadsheet on one humongous page. To compensate, Works prints the pages in this order so that you can tape your final pages together. Now why didn't I think of that?

This is why it's always best to take advantage of spreadsheet rows before branching horizontally into columns. If you don't, you'll have to live with a lot of blank page 2's when you print a wide spreadsheet.

By the Way . . .

You can print selected areas of your spreadsheet only by highlighting the cells you want printed, and then choosing **S**et Print Area from the Forma**t** menu. Once the area is set, see how it looks in Print Pre**v**iew, and then choose **P**rint.

Other than these few considerations, printing a spreadsheet is the same as printing any other type of Works document: just select **P**rint from the File menu, and you're off and running.

If your spreadsheet is wider than it is long, try turning the page sideways to get it all on one page. From the File menu, select Page Setup. On the Source, Size and Orientation tab, choose Landscape from the Orientation box.

The Least You Need to Know

Creating a spreadsheet is not much good unless you can make changes (and believe me, it won't be long before you need to make changes). Life is like that. Here's what you learned about handling it:

☞ To insert rows or columns, highlight a column to the right or a row below the place you want to add one. Then choose **R**ow/Column from the **I**nsert menu.

☞ If you want to delete a highlighted column or row, select it, and then choose **D**elete Row/Column from the **I**nsert menu.

☞ You can copy and move information between cells or between columns and rows by dragging and dropping, or using the **C**opy, Cu**t**, and **P**aste commands on the **E**dit menu (or the corresponding buttons on the Toolbar).

☞ Use the Fill Rig**h**t and Fill Do**w**n commands from the **E**dit menu to copy data into adjacent columns and rows. Just highlight the information and its destination first.

☞ Sort rows alphabetically or numerically by highlighting them first, and then choosing So**r**t Rows from the **T**ools menu.

☞ Spreadsheets print funny (see picture on page 181). Keep this in mind.

No, this is not a printing error.

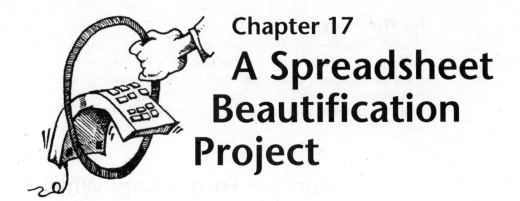

Chapter 17

A Spreadsheet Beautification Project

In This Chapter

- Formatting numbers (again)
- Resizing rows and columns
- Aligning data in a cell
- Fonts, shading, patterns, and borders
- AutoFormat—it's quick, it's cool

To be honest, there's nothing that puts me to sleep faster than uniform columns of spreadsheet numbers parading through a report—except maybe little white sheep jumping fences, and David Letterman.

So when I do a spreadsheet, I try to break up the monotony by adding a little style. There are just about as many ways to wake up a spreadsheet as there are to customize a word processing document. In fact, most of the tricks you learned in Chapters 9–11 work here as well. If you can't find a format option you need (like changing margin settings), refer to Chapters 9–11 for directions. If you wish Works could do all this formatting stuff for you, check out AutoFormat first!

By the Way . . .

It makes no difference whether you make formatting changes before you enter all your spreadsheet data or after. You can apply most formatting changes to one cell or to groups of cells, columns, or rows, regardless of whether they contain data. You can even format the entire spreadsheet at once!

To select a whole spreadsheet column, just click on the column label. To highlight an entire row, click on the row number. Keyboarders, press **F8** and use the arrow keys to highlight spreadsheet cells.

Instead of selecting the **N**umber command from the Forma**t** menu, simply select the formatting options you want from the list right at the top of the Forma**t** menu.

Number Formatting: What Kind of Number Is This?

When you created your first spreadsheet, you may have totally disregarded whether you were adding apples and oranges, dollars and cents, or percentages. (At least you did if you listened to me.) That's because the important thing was to get all of your data entered and your formulas working correctly. Now we have all the time in the world to go back and figure out what kind of numbers those happened to be.

For example, if you entered 1.75, which is a fixed, two decimal number, you could easily turn that figure into the price of an airport cup of coffee by simply changing the number's format to Currency.

First, select the cell or group of cells you want to format. Then choose Number from the Forma**t** menu. The Number dialog box will appear, presenting you with more number choices than you probably know what to do with. Select a format that remotely sounds like or resembles what you think you may need. To turn a fixed figure into dollars and cents, select Currency. To turn it into a Percentage, choose **P**ercent. Got the idea?

Choose a format.   Read about it here, and pick your options

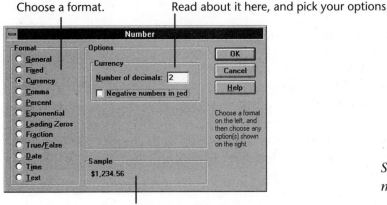

Test-drive your selection.

Suddenly everything makes cents!

Notice that **Currency** offers us the option of changing the number of places to the right of the decimal point, and of having all of our deficits appear in red. If you're not sure what an option selection will to do to your number, just change something and then look in the Sample box below.

When you've made up your mind, press **Enter** or click on **OK** to apply the number format to all of your highlighted cells. If what you see in the Sample box is not what you want, choose the **Cancel** button.

Number format—A format option that can be used to convey numbers or values as fixed values with a set number of decimal places or commas, currency, percents, exponents, fractions, date, time, text, true/false values, or leading.

By the Way . . .

Works automatically sets 2 as the number of decimal places used for all spreadsheet and database figures that display a decimal point. You can change the Default number of decimals by using the **T**ools menu's **O**ptions command.

Tailoring Rows and Columns

Since spreadsheet cells are created by the intersection of a column and a row, it's only fitting that they take on the height of the row and the width of the column they represent. Seems pretty logical, doesn't it? The off-the-rack default width of a Works spreadsheet cell is 10 characters wide. The row height is based on the size of the font selected, and the height of its tallest character. Text that doesn't fit in the cell width overlaps into the cell to the right if that cell is blank, or appears to be cut off if the neighboring cell is occupied; numbers that don't fit in the cell width are displayed as ###### (not a terribly readable format).

TECHNO NERD TEACHES

Instead of deleting columns or rows that contain sensitive information (such as salaries), you can hide them from view by changing their width or height to 0. Bringing them back into view is just a little tougher because you have to find them first! Try selecting the **G**o To command from the **E**dit menu and entering a cell reference that falls along the hidden row or column. When Works finds the cell, the cell will come ever so slightly into view. Select it and increase the row height or column width.

If you're tired of finding ###### in your columns because they're not wide enough for the numbers you've entered, choose one of the many ways available to resize columns and rows. Either adjust the column width and row height yourself, or let Works do it automatically with Best Fit, one of Works 3.0's newest features.

Best Fit: As Easy as Double-Click

To let Best Fit find the size that's right for your cells, double-click the row number if you want to change the row height, or double-click the column label if you want to change the column width. It's that simple!

If you don't have a mouse with which to double-click, you can still use Best Fit. Simply highlight each column or row you want changed and select either Column **W**idth or Row **H**eight from the Format menu. Check the **B**est Fit check box, and press **Enter** or click **OK** to finish.

Simple Do-It-Yourself Resizing

After Best Fit, if there's still an "easy" way to resize rows and columns yourself, it's to drag them to the size you want. Use the mouse pointer to drag the right side of a *column label* or the bottom of a *row number* to the size you want. For instance, to widen column A, grab the side between labels A and B; to lengthen row 4, grab the floor between numbers 4 and 5. You'll know you've got the mouse pointer positioned correctly when it turns into a directional arrow pointing out your dragging options.

Resizing, Keyboard Style

If you'd rather use the keyboard for this, choose either the Column **W**idth or Row **H**eight command in the Forma**t** menu, and enter your own specification. Columns can be set between 0 (zero) and 79, and row height can be set between 0 and 409.

Spreadsheet Chiropractic: Aligning Cells

Columns feel too tight? Rows pinched? Spreadsheet got that "spacey" look? Whenever I feel like that, I call Dr. Jack to get myself a quick adjustment. Works comes with its own built-in Dr. Jack to align the contents of spreadsheet cells in a hurry!

Since version 2.0 was born before Best Fit sizing was invented, you'll either have to drag your columns and rows to the size you want, or use the keyboard.

Just look at your alignment options:

This title was placed in cell A2 and
centered across columns A through E.

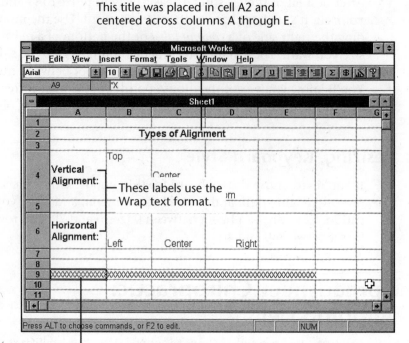

*Pick cell alignments
to suit your
spreadsheet's style.*

A single X in each cell becomes a
line of them when Fill is the
alignment choice.

To quickly change the horizontal alignment of a cell entry to one of the
three most popular (left, center, or right), select the cell(s) or column(s)
you want to adjust. Then click one of the alignment buttons on the
Toolbar or press a shortcut key:

To	Click	Or Press
Left align		**Ctrl+L**
Center		**Ctrl+E**
Right align		**Ctrl+R**

To change the vertical alignment of a cell entry, or to change the horizontal alignment to a special one, select the cell or group of cells you want to adjust. Then choose **Alignment** from the Forma**t** menu. In the Vertical box, choose **T**op, **C**enter, or **B**ottom. In the Horizontal box, select the alignment you want. You're already familiar with the three biggies; here's what the others do:

Your many alignment options.

☞ General sets the alignment back to the default for that cell: left for labels, right for values.

☞ Fill fills the entire cell. For example, if you type a single X and select Fill as the alignment option, Works fills the entire cell with Xs. If you widen the cell, Works creates more Xs to fill it.

☞ Center across selection centers an item across several cells. This is useful for spreadsheet titles.

☞ Wrap text indicates that you want labels that do not fit in the cell to wrap to the next line.

Fontasizing

Using different fonts can help highlight, emphasize, and organize a spreadsheet just as much as it can a word processing document. That's why we're not going to repeat all of the fascinating definitions of font, size, and attributes here. If you missed out on it, turn back to Chapter 9 and polish up your font skills. What I will do in this section instead is explain how to change fonts in a spreadsheet once you've decided which fonts you want.

Version 2.0 users can only adjust the Horizontal alignment. When you select the **S**tyle command from the Forma**t** menu, you have the choice of **G**eneral, **L**eft, **R**ight, and **C**enter. But think of it this way, you've got fewer decisions to make!

With a mouse, you can easily change the font, font size, and font style from the Toolbar. Highlight the cell or group of cells whose font you want to change. Then do what you need to do:

☛ To change the font, click on the font box arrow to display a selection list of fonts. Use the scroll arrows to move through the list, or click on the one you want.

☛ To change the font size, click the font size arrow, and choose the font size you want.

☛ If you'd like to liven up a spreadsheet entry, use the following Toolbar buttons:

B **Bolds** the contents of the selected cell(s).

I *Italicizes* the contents of the selected cell(s).

<u>U</u> <u>Underlines</u> the contents of the selected cell(s).

For more unusual changes (such as changing the font color), highlight the cells, and then select the Font and Style command from the Format menu. You'll see the Font and Style dialog box:

Change the font and other goodies from here.

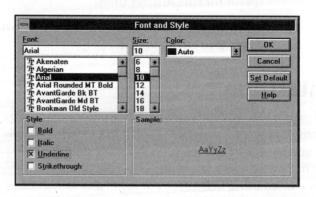

Go crazy with it; change all the characteristics you want. See how your entry will look in the Sample box. When you're satisfied, click **OK**.

Borders and Shading: Accentuate the Positive

Besides the formatting options you've already learned, you can use shading and borders to emphasize important data and help the reader understand important groupings. Use shading to emphasize totals and subtotals, or all of the figures for next year's projections.

Instead of printing the gridlines, try shading every other row to separate cells. Place a border around related groups to help the reader make associations and comparisons. Or, use a border to separate columns in a ledger.

To remove font styles, select the cells and press **Ctrl+Spacebar**.

If you're more than satisfied and want all your entries to look like this, click on the Set Default button. This will change the default font to the type, size, style, and color you've selected.

Made in the Shade(ing)

To add or change a shading pattern, first select the cell or group of cells you want shaded. Then choose **Patterns** from the Forma**t** menu. Select the pattern you want from the **Pattern** list box, and then adjust foreground and background colors or accept the automatic default. When you're finished, click **OK** or press **Enter**. To remove shading, repeat these steps, but set the Pattern selection back to **None**.

Run for the Border

Creating a border is just as easy as adding shading. Select the cell or group of cells you want to enclose. Then open the Forma**t** menu and select **Border**. Select the border enclosure: outline to place a border around all

Hate to disappoint you one more time (in a single chapter, no less), but while version 2.0 can place a border around in a spreadsheet, it can't **shade** them. To make matters worse, it doesn't have AutoFormat. Maybe you Auto Update!

If you use the Select **A**ll command in the **E**dit menu to highlight your whole spreadsheet for formatting, you'll get more than you bargained for. There are 256 columns and 4,096 rows that will be included when you do this. Your format will take a very long time to apply, and I'm almost certain it won't be what you expect! It's always best to just highlight the entire area of your spreadsheet.

sides, or any number of sides to limit the bordered sides to just a couple. Then choose your line style and line color and press **OK**.

To remove the border later, repeat the steps and select the border sides you want to remove. Selecting the border this time will remove the horizontal line from the selection box, turning your original selection off.

When All Else Fails, You AutoFormat

AutoFormat is another new Works 3.0 tool designed to make your life easier and boost your professional image. AutoFormat gives you a selection of "presentation-quality" formats that you can apply to the entire spreadsheet or sections at a time. Because it automatically sets all of the number formats, borders, cell alignment and size, fonts, and patterns to match whatever style you select, maybe you should check out your AutoFormat options first!

When you're ready to try AutoFormat, highlight the group of cells you want formatted. From the Forma**t** menu, choose AutoFor**m**at. Select each of the formats in the Table Format box one at a time, and look at the Sample box to see how it looks. Click **OK** when you've made your selection.

The Least You Need to Know

Now that you're a spreadsheet pro, isn't it time your spreadsheets started looking a little better? Take some fashion hints from someone who knows:

- ☛ You can format the numbers in a spreadsheet anytime you want by choosing **N**umber from the Forma**t** menu.

- ☛ Change a row height or column width by dragging the column or row to the size you want.

- ☛ Align cell contents left, right, or center by clicking the appropriate Toolbar button or by pressing **Ctrl+L** (to left align), **Ctrl+E** (to center), or **Ctrl+R** (to right align).

- ☛ Change the vertical alignment of the contents of a cell by choosing **A**lignment from the Forma**t** menu. In the Vertical box, choose **T**op, **C**enter, or **B**ottom.

- ☛ To center a spreadsheet title across several columns, highlight the entry and the columns you want to center it across. Then from the Forma**t** menu choose **A**lignment, and click the Center **a**cross selection box.

- ☛ You can change the font, font size, and bold, italic, or underline attributes from the Toolbar.

- ☛ To change the font, font size, style, or color at the same time, use the **F**ont and Style command in the Forma**t** menu.

- ☛ To change patterns and shading or add a border for emphasis, select the option you want from the Forma**t** menu.

"Here's that blank page thing again."

Part IV
Database: Keeping It on File

I once shared a secretary who everyone else thought was nuts. I was a young punk, and she had hopes and dreams for me. She taught me how to use file folders, seat them in proper outside folders, and use them to organize project records. She typed my letters, corrected my spelling, and significantly improved my grammar. She even wrote my weekly progress reports (as if I'd known we made any).

One day she asked to see my appointment book. Since I never had more appointments than I could keep in my head, the pages were pretty much blank. She made a phone list of all the people I worked with, and gave me a desk calendar and told me to use it. Then every morning (as if that wasn't enough), she'd come in and turn the page. She was my database. I was lucky!

If you're not lucky enough to have someone to take care of you like I did, you're just the person the Works database was designed for. And it just so happens we've penciled you in for the next four chapters.

Chapter 18
A Chart Is Worth a Thousand Cells

In This Chapter

- ☞ How charts are made—briefly
- ☞ Types of charts
- ☞ How to make a chart from different data arrangements
- ☞ Chart housekeeping tips
- ☞ Changing features of a chart
- ☞ About printing charts

Do you know that if your business reports only include words and numbers you're probably only reaching half of your target audience? Some of your readers may try to understand your information by drawing their own pictures . . .and conclusions. Others will simply give up.

With Works' Charting function you can turn pages and pages of professionally formatted but dull spreadsheets into powerful presentations. Do so and, most assuredly, your boss will be impressed—and your readers will be grateful!

The Miracle of Charting

Although it would be nice to think that Works can create a variety of charts with just the snap of a finger, the real truth is it needs your spreadsheet to work its miracles. When you ask Works to create a chart, it uses the text and values you've highlighted in the spreadsheet to create the chart.

A chart usually shows the values (on the Y axis, up and down) of several categories (on the X axis, left to right). For instance, you might chart the amount you spent on lunch in each of three months. The months, in this case, are the categories, and the amounts you spent are the values.

Some charts simply plot values in several categories.

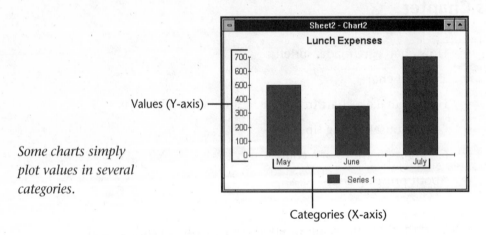

Values (Y-axis)

Categories (X-axis)

Some charts show several series at once. Series add another dimension to the charts. For instance, you could have a single chart that plotted the amount several salespeople spent on lunch over several months. The salespeople represent the series.

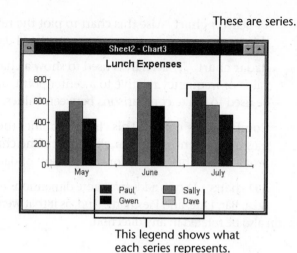

These are series.

This legend shows what each series represents.

Other charts plot values in several categories for several series, so you can compare the values of each series to one another.

The Eight Basic Chart Groups

If your data lends itself to something other than a bar chart, there are eight basic charts, each with its own variations, giving you a total of more than 60 chart flavors from which to choose. The best way to decide on a chart is to view the basic samples Works creates from your data in the New Chart window. Or, look in the Works for Windows 3.0 User's Guide to select a special flavor.

This list can help narrow your chart selection:

Area chart   Use this chart to show the amount of change in values over a period of time.

Bar chart   Use this chart to compare data between values represented by bars.

Pie chart   This chart is used to show proportion, or the ratio of one value to another.

Stacked line chart   This chart is used to compare the relationship of a value to the total of all values.

Sorry version 2.0 users: You don't have Area, Radar or 3-D charts. But you still have enough choices to wake up a dull report.

XY scatter chart   Use this chart to plot the relationship between two or more groups of related data.

Radar chart   This chart is used to show a change in value or frequency relative to a center point, and can be used to make comparisons between values.

Combination chart   This chart combines the message presented in a bar chart and a line chart, and provides another means for comparison of data.

3-D charts   Works adds two more dimensions to the Area, Bar, Line, and Pie charts. And, as if that weren't enough, 3-D charts can also be rotated in any direction.

Chart Making

Works creates charts from the values you select in your spreadsheet. If, in addition to numbers, you highlight column and row headings and other text tidbits, Works will figure out what they are and use them as labels in your chart.

To create a chart:

1. Select the group of spreadsheet cells, including text, that you want to include in the chart.

2. Select Create New Chart from the Tools menu, or click the **New Chart** button on the Toolbar.

3. To see how your data would be displayed in another type of chart, choose another type in the **W**hat type list box.

4. To finish it off, add a title, border, and/or gridlines in the Finishing touches box. Although you will be able to add all of these features later, this is a very opportune time to do it. If you don't like how any of the features look, you can always change them.

5. When the sample chart in the dialog box looks the way you want it to, click **OK** or press **Enter** to have Works create the chart for you.

The new chart will be displayed in a full Works window, with a Charting toolbar and menu bar. If you like the chart just the way it is, close its window. The chart will be saved automatically with the spreadsheet.

Organizational Change, Anyone?

Let's skip back to the moment between steps 4 and 5 in those last steps. At this point, if you're not sure you have charted the spreadsheet data in a way that can most effectively make your point, you can use the "How is your spreadsheet data organized?" box to look at your alternatives.

TECHNO NERD TEACHES

How does Works know what you want when it automatically creates a chart for you? The size and shape of the range you select determines how Works sets up the chart. Whichever your range contains more of (rows or columns) usually becomes the categories, and the other becomes the series.

☞ The information that's already selected within the box represents how the spreadsheet data was organized in the current chart. If you want to change the orientation of your row and column data along the X-axis of the chart, select the other series in item 1.

☞ Item 2 tells Works whether your first column contains labels (which will become the X-axis legend), or if it contains actual spreadsheet values (which should be another category on the X-axis).

The New Chart button on the Toolbar is the fastest way to create a chart.

☞ Item 3 tells Works whether your first row contains labels (which will become the X-axis category labels), or if it contains actual spreadsheet values (which should be Y-series values on the chart).

Experiment with each variable in the organization box until you are satisfied with the chart.

Adding and Removing Values on a Chart

If you want to add a series to your chart, add it to the spreadsheet on which the chart is based. Then switch to the chart you want to add the copied values to, by either clicking on the chart window, or selecting the chart from the **Window** menu. From the chart's Edit menu, select **Paste Series**. Works will show you a list of the value (Y) series and the category (X) series for the chart. (By the way, this list is a perfect opportunity for you to figure out this X-and Y-series stuff.) Choose the series in which you want to "dump" the copied data and click **OK**. Works automatically revises the chart to reflect its increased value.

Most charts show values that are right next to each other on the spreadsheet, but it doesn't have to be that way. All you have to do is chart the columns or rows that are adjacent, just like you would any other chart. Then add the non-adjacent series to the chart.

Oh, I almost forgot. You can delete series that no longer interest you using the Edit menu's Series command to view the same list. Only this time, choose the values you want to delete, and then press the **Del** key! Press **Enter** or click **OK** to have Works update the chart.

A Chart by Any Other Name

Every Works chart is endowed by its creator with two things: a typical Works name, and a window. You can change the name, but you're stuck with the window.

Working with the Inevitable Chart Window

The chart window sits on top of the spreadsheet from which it descended. You can either resize the chart window in order to see both at once (this really helps when you're trying to figure out the X and Y stuff), or switch back and forth between the two windows.

To switch back and forth, use the View menu in either window. Select Chart when you're in the spreadsheet, and select Spreadsheet when you're in the chart. If that's too confusing and all of the windows are open, use the Window menu no matter where you are.

To resize one of the windows, grab a side or corner of the window border and drag the mouse. Drag inward to make it smaller; drag outward to make it larger. To really organize your workspace, place the downsized window where you want it by clicking on the window title and dragging it to a new location.

Renaming the Chart Window

Charts start out with boring names like Chart1 and Chart2. To give your chart a more descriptive name, choose Name Chart from the Tools menu. Select the chart you want to rename. Then type it's new name, in fifteen characters or less, in the Name box. Choose the Rename button and click **OK**, and you're out of there! When it comes time to look for Chart 2 in the View menu, don't forget you renamed it!

Playing Musical Charts

Once you make a chart, you're not stuck with it. Aside from the fact that Works lets you create and save eight different charts with each spreadsheet, you can always change the chart you're currently working on. (Try turning a Line chart into a Pie when you crave an afternoon snack!)

Open the chart you want to change. Click the Toolbar button that represents the chart you want to change it into, or select the chart type from the list in the Gallery menu. Table 18.1 shows you the Toolbar buttons.

Table 18.1   Chart Toolbar Buttons

Button	Name
	Bar chart
	Line chart
	Pie chart
	Scatter chart
	Mixed chart
	3-D area chart
	3-D bar chart
	3-D line chart
	3-D pie chart

To view the list, which contains more selections than the Toolbar, open the Gallery menu and choose the type of chart you want. Works will show you several flavors. If you can't decide from what's available, click the Next or Previous buttons to see the other varieties and flavors. After you make your selection, choose **OK** to change charts.

If you just want to turn an Area, Bar, Line, or Pie chart into a 3-D chart, choose Make **3**-D from the Forma**t** menu.

If you decide you prefer one kind of chart over another, or if you find that most of the charts you use are of a particular flavor, you can set that chart type up as the *default* chart. Setting a chart type as the default tells Works that every time you create a new chart, you want that type. To change the default chart, open a chart window that contains the type of chart you want to set as the default. Then choose Se**t** Preferred Chart from the Gallery menu.

Let the Chart Doctor Help

Okay, so you've created a chart, but somehow the chart just doesn't do anything for you. There's something missing, but you're not sure what.

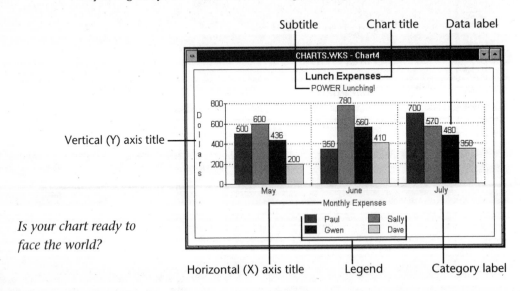

Is your chart ready to face the world?

Well, you know, nothing much is permanent in this changing world, and charts are no exception. If you want to add a little pizzazz to your chart and give it that look you've always wanted, try a little cosmetic chartistry.

Pump Up the Title

Titles help your audience understand what the chart's all about. If you've already assigned a title that's no longer relevant or that just doesn't grab you, you have to delete it before you can add a new one. To delete a title from an open chart, choose **Titles** from the Edit menu. Choose the title that you want to delete and press the **Del** key. Then press **Enter** or click on **OK**. (This is the same process you need to use to delete labels and legends too, except you delete them in their edit boxes.)

To add a new chart title, use the same Title dialog box. Either type the title you want, or enter the spreadsheet range reference that contains the title. Press **Enter** or click **OK** to add the title. You can change the look, and fit, of your titles by trying different fonts. Hang in there, we'll get to that soon.

If titles get chopped off, or are difficult to read, try changing the font and font size.

Improve Weak Category Labels

Chart labels tell the viewer just what your chart is measuring or comparing. Category labels, in particular, identify what it is you're plotting.

Once again, if you already have a label but want to change it, you must delete the existing label first. To delete a label, switch to the chart you want to change and choose Series from the Edit menu. Highlight the range in the **Category (X)** series box, and then press the **Del** key. Press **Enter** or click **OK**, and you can start to add the new label.

To add a category label:

1. First add the text or numbers you want to use for category labels to your spreadsheet.

2. Then highlight the labels in the spreadsheet and use the Copy command in the Edit menu or the **Copy** button on the Toolbar to copy them to the Clipboard.

3. Switch to the chart in which you want to place the labels.

4. Choose Paste Series from the Edit menu.

5. Select the **Category** button and click **OK**.

If you have too many category labels on your chart, you can reduce the number of labels displayed. From the Forma**t** menu, choose **H**orizontal (X) Axis. Highlight the contents of the **L**abel frequency box, and type a new value. Then click **OK**.

Beef Up Your Data Labels

Data labels provide the actual measurement, or values, of the data. You can only put data labels on Bar, Line, and Pie charts.

First, let's see how to add data labels for a Bar or Line chart. If you want to use the chart's plotted values for labels, switch to the chart you want to change and choose Data Labels from the Edit menu. In the Data Labels dialog box, click on the Use series data check box to select it. Once this box is turned on, Works will use the plotted values as labels. When you're finished, click OK.

If you don't want to use the plotted values, go back to the spreadsheet and enter the actual labels you want to use for the values. Then, like category labels, copy them into the chart. From the chart's Edit menu, choose the Data Labels command. Turn off the Use Series Data check box, and select the Value (Y) series you want to label. Click the **Paste** button and click OK to have your chart updated with new labels.

Adding data labels for a Pie chart is slightly different. Switch to the Pie chart you want to label and choose Data Labels from the Edit menu. Pie charts let you use two different types of labels on each chart. You can choose from a choice of four different types: value, percentages, cell contents, or sequential number labels (1,2,3...). Make your selection for either one or both of the data labels and then press **Enter** or click OK.

Be a Legend in Your Own Time

If your chart shows more than one value in each category along the X-axis, as my Lunch Expenses did, a legend helps to distinguish what each value is. Very similar to the legend that you'll find on a map, this legend tells you what the colors, patterns, and markers on your chart mean. If you didn't specify names for the different values in your spreadsheet, Works will assign them Series 1, Series 2, and so on.

To add or change a legend, first go back to your spreadsheet and add the identifying text or numbers you want to use for the legend. Switch to the chart in which you want to place the legend, and from the Edit menu choose Legend/Series Labels. If you just want to use the generic series labels, check Auto series labels at this point. Otherwise, choose the value (Y) series whose value(s) you want to add or change. Type the spreadsheet cell reference for each value series, such as A5, or go ahead and type the actual legend label. When you're finished adding or changing each legend value, choose OK to have Works update the chart.

To turn a legend off without deleting it, select the Add **L**egend command from the Forma**t** menu to get rid of the check mark. To turn it back on, select Forma**t** Add Legend again.

Add Inches to Your Axis Scale in Seconds!

When Works creates a chart, it assumes you want the scale of both the X-and Y-axis to begin at 0, and then proceed in either direction to your highest value. However, this may not be the case if you plan to use this chart to compare profits or sales this year and, for example, again next year. (If all goes as planned, next year's values should be way off this year's scale).

To change either the X or the Y scales, open the chart you want to change. From the Format menu, select either the Vertical (Y) Axis command or the Horizontal (X) Axis command.

To change the vertical axis, type the new minimum and maximum and the number of intervals you want displayed. If you want to add vertical gridlines too, while you're there, check the Show Gridlines box. Then click **OK** or press **Enter**.

You can only change the label frequency on the Horizontal axis. Enter a new number between one and fifteen in the Label frequency box. To add gridlines here, check the Show Gridlines box. Click **OK** when you're done.

Can You Do Anything for These Lines and Wrinkles?

Gridlines, which you had the opportunity to add while you were changing the axis scale, can make some charts (especially Bar charts) easier to read. Likewise, borders can make your chart more attractive, and droplines on an Area chart help the viewer match categories on the X-axis with their Y values.

To add a border around your chart, simply open the chart you want to control and choose Add **B**order from the Forma**t** menu. To turn off the border, choose Add **B**order again.

When you want to add droplines to an Area chart, switch to the chart and choose Horizontal (X) Axis from the chart's Forma**t** menu. Select Show Droplines, and then choose **OK**. To turn them off, select the Show Droplines option again.

Change the Color of Your Stripes

Works automatically creates color charts using assigned colors and patterns. If you know which colors look best on your color printer, or if you want to make particular categories stand out, change them. While you're at it, feel free to experiment with the patterns and markers that Works applies to each value series on the X-axis.

To change colors, patterns, and markers, open the chart you want to work on and choose **P**atterns and Colors from the Forma**t** menu. Choose the value (Y) series, or pie slice, that you want to change. Select your colors, oddly enough, from the Colors box first. Then move next door to **P**atterns. If your chart uses Markers, move over one more box to change them. If you prefer to use Works' judgment on any of these, select **Auto**.

If you'd like to use the same colors, patterns, and markers for all of your series, select Format All after you've made one set of selections. Your choices will be applied to each series. If you prefer to change each series separately, select Format after you finish one series' selection, and then go on to the next series. When you're done with all of your changes, choose Close.

Try On a Whole New Face?

It's important when working on a chart to resist "font" temptation, and let the picture tell the story! That's why Works limits your font selection to two: one set for the chart title, and another for everything else.

To change a chart title's font, size, style, and color, select the chart title by clicking it, or choose Select Title Text from the Edit menu. Once you've got a hold of the title, choose Font and Style from the Format menu. You can select any combination you want. When you're done, choose **OK**.

When you're ready to change the remaining text, click outside the chart title to release it, or choose Select Title Text again from the Edit menu. From the Format menu choose Font and style, and then select the combination you want for all of the other text. Click **OK** when you're ready.

Putting a Chart Out to Pasture

Works lets you keep eight charts with each spreadsheet, which should be more than enough to cover all of your spreadsheet bases. But if it's not, you have two options: (1) copy the spreadsheet file, save the copy under another file name (like an alias), and then create new charts in the original file, or (2) put some of the charts you don't use anymore out to pasture.

It's a tough call to make, but considering that charts aren't totally free (they take up quite a lot of computer memory), you may want to think about door number 2 once in a while.

To delete charts from your spreadsheet file, choose Delete Chart from the Tools menu. From the list of charts, select the one you want to dump, and then choose Delete. Keep doing this until you feel like you're done, and then choose **OK** or press **Enter**.

Printing Particulars

Printing a chart is like printing anything else, except for these two things:

☛ If you don't have a color printer, you may want to preview your chart the way it will look on a black and white printer. To do this, select Display as Printed from the View menu. Colors and patterns may change a little. To return your screen to the way it was before, select View Display as Printed again.

☛ To resize the chart to fit the paper you're using, choose Page Setup from the File menu,. Choose the Other Options tab, and look at the Size options listed. Select the one you want and choose **OK**. This is a good time to select Print Preview from the File menu to see your chart before you actually print!

The Least You Need to Know

This is what you need to know about charting, without all the "graph"ic details:

☛ Works can't create a spreadsheet without a chart. It uses the values you select in your spreadsheet to plot the coordinates on the chart.

☛ Once you highlight spreadsheet values, create a chart by clicking the **New Chart** button on the Toolbar, or by selecting **C**reate New Chart from the **To**ols menu.

☛ Add more values to a chart by copying them from the spreadsheet and pasting them into the chart as a series. Delete values, too, using the **S**eries command in the **E**dit menu.

☛ View both the spreadsheet and the chart at the same time by resizing one of the windows, or using the **W**indow **T**ile command.

☞ Change the type of chart you've created by selecting a new one from the **G**allery menu. Change the default chart that way, too.

☞ Use cosmetic chartistry to improve chart titles and text; create legends; change the X-and Y-axis; add borders, gridlines, droplines, and markers; change fonts and colors; and chart patterns and colors.

☞ Since you can only save eight charts with one spreadsheet, delete charts you don't need. To do so, open the **T**ools menu and choose De**l**ete chart, of all things, and then press **Enter**.

☞ Use Pa**g**e Setup in the **F**ile menu to make your chart fit on the page the way you want it to. Choose the **O**ther Options tab, and select one of the Size options listed.

A page is a terrible thing to waste.

Chapter 19
Database-ics

In This Chapter

- ☞ What is a database?
- ☞ Starting a new database
- ☞ The parts of a database window
- ☞ Creating fields
- ☞ Saving your work

Some people (and you know who you are!) will skip over this chapter and keep playing James Bond: stuffing business cards and scraps of paper in or under every book, blotter, and secret compartment they can find. The rest of you will get a grip on the database part of Works, and finally get your desk cleaned up.

Database Defined

A *database* is, as the name implies, a base full of data. Fine. So, what's a "base"? Right, that's what I said. Who's on first. What's on second. The *base* is what they're standing on. Can't you keep this game straight, mister? Hey, maybe you need a database?

SPEAK LIKE A GEEK

A **database** is a computer program that's used as an automated filing system to organize address and phone numbers, personnel records, client lists, inventories, recipes, appointments, and anything else we can think of.

SPEAK LIKE A GEEK

Form A boilerplate, fill-in-the-blank outline that you create in a database to gather the same information about many subjects. A filled-in form is one database record. Works' database provides Form view so that you can see and work with all of the fields in one database record at a time.

Field (1) Where Kevin Costner is said to have some of his better dreams. (2) Categories of information on a database form. Each **field** is made up of a field name and a field entry that can contain text, numbers, or formulas.

A database, gang, is what helps you keep all that stuff running around your brain, tucked in your briefcase, stuck on the walls, slid under desk blotters, stashed in drawers and crumpled in jacket pockets, organized. A database is Man's answer (how come we women never answer any of this?) to all the information we're bombarded with all day long.

A database is a place to store information: put it away in neat little categories, take it out as fancy reports, rifle through it to find what we need, or feed it once in a while and just watch it grow!

A database is the most important ingredient for mailing out form letters. While the form letter is typed and stored in the word processor with special instructions, the addresses remain part of a database that's stored in a database document. When you're ready to do a mailing, the two files are merged. Works automatically personalizes each letter based on it's mailing address data, and prints an address label or envelope.

How Does It Work?

When you create a database, you start by designing a *form* in which to dump all of your data. If you wanted to create a client list database, for example, you would leave spaces on your form, called *fields,* in which to enter specific information about each client. You'd probably want to include enough

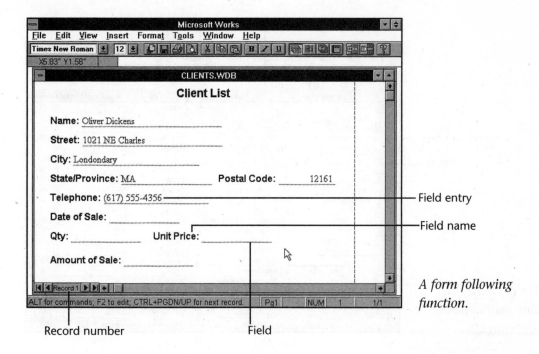

Field entry

Field name

A form following function.

Record number   Field

fields to have at your fingertips everything you'd ever want to know about a client.

The form would be your "boilerplate," or fill-in-the-blank outline, for every client. When you fill in a form, you have a client *record*. When you have enough records to put them together, you can create a client *list*.

Field name   Field entry

	Name	Street	City	State/Prov	Postal Code
1	Mary Deeton	18732 Forrest Rd.	Aberdeen	WA	98259
2	Mike Jones	101 Highview Court	Boston	MA	13134
3	Joy Yarrow	26 East Carroll St.	Friday Harbor	WA	98259
4	Roger Armstrong	1824 Fernwood Ct.	Port Townsend	WA	98368
5	Jane O'Reilly	2421 4th Avenue	Portland	OR	97111
6	Leah Shirigean	126 Elm St.	Carnation	WA	98644
7	Lin Guthree	Rt. 2, Box 28	Sunnyside	OR	97219
8	Keith True	P.O. Box 101	Eastsound	WA	98245
9	Ellen May	10 South Lucille	Seattle	WA	98116
10	Jane Browning	4832 South Mead	Seattle	WA	98114
11	Betsy Davis	67 Brilliant Drive	Tulalip	WA	98118
12	Cary Grable	199 Laguna Avenue North	Hollywood	CA	90048
13	Carla Jung	122 Inner Circle	Psyche	MA	12199
14	Dorothy Peyton	2601 Elliott	Santa Paula	CA	93004
15	Oliver Dickens	1021 NE Charles	Londondary	MA	12161
16	Will Gates	2449 152nd Ave.	Redmond	WA	198052
17	Jehovah Weatherby	44 Rain Drive	Astoria	OR	97267
18	Tim Christmas	77 Precious Parkway	Portland	OR	97219
19	Pat O'Brien	4104 Madison	Champion	VA	99221
20	Edward Milne	79 Christopher Lane	Lincoln	NE	88709

Record number

Record

Microsoft Works - [CLIENTS.WDB]

File   Edit   View   Insert   Format   Tools   Window   Help

Arial   10

"Will Gates

Press ALT to choose commands, or F2 to edit.   NUM   16   20/20

The database list: junk mail's humble beginnings.

The client list lets you view all of the records in your entire client database at once. You can sort the list alphabetically, numerically, or chronologically to help you find what you need fast.

If you only wanted to view specific information (such as all clients in Washington state, or all clients who hadn't placed an order in 3 months, or all clients in Washington state who hadn't placed an order in 3 months), you could quickly sort through all of the records by conducting a database *query*. When you query the database, Works finds only those records that match your query, and creates another client list to display the results. This is where you really get to fine tune those mailing lists!

SPEAK LIKE A GEEK

The **query** process lets you sort through all of the records in a database to find the ones that match the criteria you specify.

If you wanted to change the layout of the regular client list by displaying only certain fields, to group and summarize information, or to calculate field data for every record in the database, you could create a database report.

Where Do I Start?

You can view your database in either Form or List view. The best place to start a database is in Form view, where you can decide what information you want to include in the database and then design a form to collect it. When the form is ready, you can stay in Form view to fill in each database record. (To change views, select your choice from the View menu.)

You can also create a database in List view, but it's not quite as easy. We're going to start with Form view and then show you how to modify the database list in List view, later. If you'd like to create your database working entirely in List view, check the Works for Windows 3.0 User's Guide.

There are many AutoStart **T**emplates available for common database applications. Also check the Wor**k**sWizards if you need a "push."

Opening a Database Window

To open a new database document from the Startup screen, click the **Database** button. The Database program opens. If you get an instruction box, click **OK** to get rid of it for now, or click **Cancel** to get rid of it permanently. (Instructions? We don't need no stinkin' instructions!)

If you want to open a database file you've worked in before, check to see if it's listed on the Startup screen in the **Recently used files** box. If it is, select it there. If it isn't, choose the **Open An Existing Document** box, and then select it from the File **N**ame box. Make sure

If you're already in the Database program and want to start a new database, click the **Startup** button on the Toolbar to get back to the Startup screen, and then choose **D**atabase. Or, from the Database program's **F**ile menu, select Create **N**ew File.

you've got the right file extension listed in the List of Files of **T**ype box. Works database files use (.wdb) for their extension.

Running the 'Bases

When you finally get into the Database tool, the first window you'll see is the Form view screen.

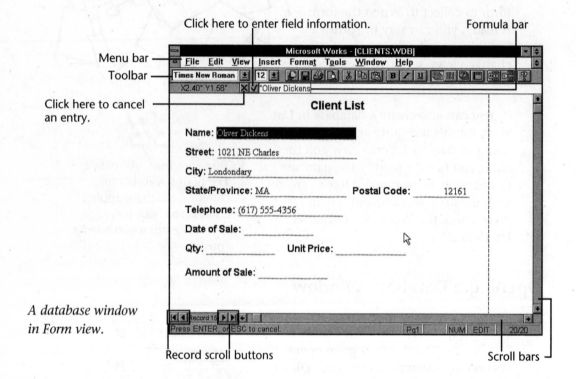

Click here to enter field information.

Formula bar

Menu bar

Toolbar

Click here to cancel an entry.

A database window in Form view.

Record scroll buttons

Scroll bars

As you can see, this window is a basic Works document window. Much like the word processing window, it contains a menu bar, Toolbar, status line, scroll bar, and insertion point.

Hey, what's that formula bar doing here? You may remember the formula bar from your work with spreadsheets. Well, if you think back just a few pages ago, I said database fields could also contain formulas, in addition to text and numbers. (If I didn't I should have, because they can and that's why you need a formula bar.) We'll get into it more later. I'm in no hurry, myself. Let's just enjoy the serenity of an empty window a little while longer.

Here's what you'll find in the Database window:

Menu bar   A typical Works menu bar, this gives you access to all of the database commands. Since some of the commands within each menu, (except File, Window, and Help) are different, you might want to peek inside each one.

Toolbar   The Toolbar gives you the quickest access to the most commonly used database commands. To interpret each icon, point the mouse pointer at each button—but don't click. If you don't have a mouse, it doesn't matter. You can't use 'em without a mouse. Sorry.

Formula bar   This formula bar displays the insertion point (or cursor position) in X, Y coordinates within the document area. It also contains Enter and Cancel buttons, and displays information about the field you're working in.

Scroll bars   By clicking in either scroll bar with the mouse, you can move to different places within the database window. Click on or near the arrow facing the direction in which you want to move.

Version 2.0 users: Stop pointing your mouse at the Toolbar buttons to read the Toolbar tips! You don't have tips. But that's okay, because you don't have the full complement of Toolbar buttons either.

Record scroll buttons   By clicking on scroll buttons you can move forward or backward through different records in the database. The scroll buttons work as described here:

 Use this button to go back to the first record.

 Use this button to go back to the previous record.

 Use this button to go to the next record in the database.

 Use this button to go to the last record in the database.

Farmer John Does Forms

It wouldn't hurt to think of your database form as a farm, and you're the farmer "planting the field." Each field has its own crop, and with proper planning and care, you can reap a small harvest in each one.

What that means, basically, is that it's important to think about what kind of information you want to get out of your database—before you start planting fields. Much of what you can do with a database depends on how you've set it up. For example, if you wanted to be able to sort through the data in each record (or form) to identify residents on a particular street, or with a particular ZIP code, you'd have to create a separate field for street addresses and ZIP codes. If you wanted to find all the Harry Smith's in southern California, you'd have to set your form up with a field for first names, a field for last names, and separate fields for city, state, and ZIP codes. It's a good idea to keep each field as specific as possible. No sense planting both apples and oranges in one field.

By the Way . . .

A database form can be more than just a tool for gathering information. You can eliminate handwriting on preprinted forms by creating a database form to match the preprinted ones you're already using. Once you fill in the database form, you can print the contents on the preprinted one to deliver professional receipts, inventory lists, and purchase orders. You can even include formulas in forms to create invoices that you can mail to clients using your client list. Then tie the amount owed from the invoice into a balance on the client list database form to keep it updated as the invoice is paid.

Planting a Field

A database form can have as many as 256 fields. After you've planted a field, you can format it, edit it, move it, even add drawings and clip art to it. You'll learn how to do all that later.

To create a field:

1. Plant the cursor where you want the field to be. You can move the cursor by clicking the mouse where you want the cursor, or by pressing the **Shift** key while you use one of the arrow keys.

2. Type a field name, followed by a colon (:). The field name can't have more than 15 characters, and it can't begin with an apostrophe ('). For example, type:

   Last Name:

3. Press **Enter** or click the **Enter** button in the formula bar. Works will display a field size dialog box so you can specify the size field you want for entries. If you don't want the field to be 20 characters wide and one line long, change the figures entered in the **Width** and **Height** boxes. A field can hold a maximum of 254 characters. If you would rather have a narrower field with multiple lines, like this:

Comments: _____

_____

enter the number of lines you want in the Height box.

4. When you're finished, press **Enter** or choose **OK**.

Saving a Database Form

When you create a new database, Works temporarily calls the form DATA1 or DATA2. When you save it for the first time, you get the chance to be more creative and descriptive.

You can enter the field name and size at the same time by using the **Insert Field** Toolbar button.

To save a database for the first time, choose **Save** from the File menu. In the File **Name** box, type a name that you prefer, with up to eight characters. If you want Works to create a backup copy every time you save this document, click the Make backup copy of old file box. When you choose **OK** or press **Enter** to complete the save, Works will automatically add the Database extension (.wdb) to the file name.

Whenever you want to save the database from then on, you can just click the Toolbar **Save** button, or select **Save** from the File menu.

The Least You Need to Know

For those who want more out of life than just another list:

☞ You can use a database to organize just about anything.

☞ A database is made up of individual records, each of which is made up of the same fields.

☞ A database can be viewed as individual records in Form view, or as a complete list of all the records in List view.

☞ The easiest way to create a database is to start by creating a form. Use the form to create individual records, and then view all of the records in a list.

☞ You can organize the list in alphabetical, numerical, or chronological sequence. Or, query the database to sort out only those records that meet your predefined criteria.

☞ You can sort, query, modify, and format database lists any way you'd like and present the results in a fancy report.

☞ When you want to save a database for the first time, use the **S**ave command in the **F**ile menu. It doesn't matter which database view you are working in (Form, List, Query, or Report) when you save your data. All views are saved as the same database.

Chapter 20
Diving into a Database

In This Chapter

☞ Getting the data into the fields

☞ Setting up formulas

☞ Switching views

☞ Entering lots of numbers or dates at once

☞ Changing the data in a field

☞ Adding and deleting records

☞ Copying and moving fields

When last we saw our valiant hero, Database, he created fields in a form and saved them to a file. (If you missed that thrilling episode, turn back to Chapter 19.) Now, let's rejoin him as he continues his quest for a complete and useful database file.

Meanwhile, Back on the Farm: Sprouting Field Entries

As you know, a *field entry* is the information you store in a field, for instance, "Smith" in the Last Name field or "14590-3" in a Product Number field. And, as we said before, field entries can be made of text, numbers, or formulas, just like a spreadsheet.

The one-size-fits-all approach to entering text or numbers in a field works like this: highlight the field in which you want to enter information (the field is always to the right of the field name). Then type the entry, which will be displayed in both the field and the formula bar. Press **Enter** to secure it in place in the field.

When you finish working in one field, press **Tab** to move to the next field, or press **Shift+Tab** to move to the previous field. To move on to the next record, click the scroll button in the lower left-hand corner, or press **Ctrl+Page Down**. Press **Ctrl+Page Up** to move back to the previous record.

By the Way . . .

To show or hide field lines in Form view, use the Field Lines command in the **V**iew menu to turn them on and off.

Yes, Virginia, Fields Can Have Number Formats

If you want to format a field to display number values as currency, percentages, fractions, etc., highlight the field (or fields) you want to format and choose **Number** from the Forma**t** menu. Then choose the type of format you want. Read a description in the Options box, and see how it looks in the Sample box.

By the Way . . .

If you want to format more than one field at a time with a number format, select the whole group before you choose the Forma**t** **N**umber command. To select a block of fields, drag the mouse across them, or hold down **Shift** while you use the arrow keys to highlight. To select a group of fields that aren't necessarily adjoining, click on each one while holding down **Ctrl**.

"Formula"ting a Database

Formula entries aren't any more complicated than number or text entries, but I think you should understand *how* and *why* to use them in a database before we get carried away with planting them. The formulas you use in databases are the same as the ones used in spreadsheets, except you refer to field names instead of cell addresses. (Turn back to Part III if you need to brush up on your formulas.)

To format a number in version 2.0, select one of the formats listed in the Forma**t** menu. Don't bother looking for the **N**umber command. It's not there.

Why Use a Formula?

Formulas can be used in a database to calculate the contents of one field, based on the contents of other fields within the same record or form. For example, if you set up the following fields in a customer invoice, you could use a formula in the Balance Due field to automatically subtract the deposit amount from the total price.

Total Price: 123.00

Deposit Amt.: 70.00

Balance Due: $53.00

(The formula you would enter in the Balance Due field would be: **=Total Price–Deposit Amt.**

You can also use a formula to automatically enter any piece of information that is unlikely to change from one record to the next, like a State field in a local mailing list. Suppose you were creating a database to gather a list of all the members in your club, all of whom live in the same state. Rather than typing that state's name each time, you could enter a formula containing the state name or abbreviation. Using a formula, the State would be entered automatically each time, unless you entered regular text for the occasional exception.

If the state in which they all lived happened to be Confusion (which, I understand, is one of the names being tossed around for the remnants when they spin off part of California), your formula would look like this: **="Confusion"**.

Making a Formula into a Field Entry

To enter a formula as a field entry, highlight the field entry area in which you want to type the formula. Type an equal sign (=) and then the formula. Don't leave a space between the two. If other fields on which the formula is based are empty, a 0 will be displayed in the field. To keep track of your database updates, you may want to include a date or time field. If you do, a quick way to enter the current date is to hold down the Ctrl key and press the semicolon, like this: **Ctrl+;**. To enter the current time, hold down the Ctrl and Shift keys together and then press the semicolon: **Ctrl+Shift+;**.

The Big Picture (List View)

Once you've created the form and entered a few records, you'll probably want to see how "fruitful" your efforts have been. To get the big picture, switch over to List view by selecting List in the View menu.

By the Way . . .

If you think List view looks like a spreadsheet, you're right! Your database is displayed in a grid that contains rows made up of records, and columns made up of fields. As a matter of fact, many of the features (such as highlighting and hiding columns and rows) work the same in both.

Field name

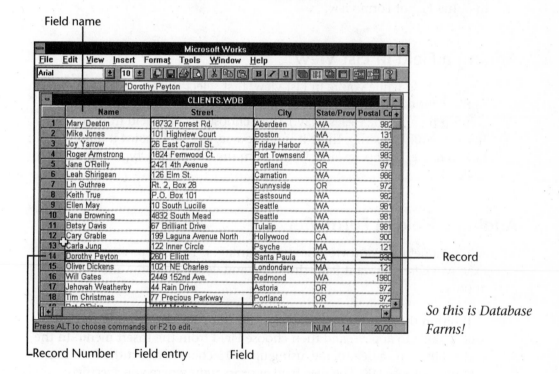

Record

So this is Database Farms!

Record Number   Field entry   Field

List view can be easier to work in when you want to:

- ☞ Work with and change all or many of your records at once.

- ☞ Copy field entries from one record to another.

- ☞ Delete and clear records and fields.

- ☞ Look at the results of a query, sort, or search.

- ☞ Add a series of numbers or dates to your records.

We'll make most of our database changes in List view, but you'll be able to see the result of the change in either view. If it's easier to switch back to Form view, I'll let you know.

Adding a Field or Two

Once you start using your database, you may find that you need another field in each record. Luckily, it's fairly easy to add fields, and you can do it in either List or Form view.

Adding a Field in List View

To add a field while you're in List view, first select the entire field that lies to the right of where you want to add the new field. (Clicking on the column name is the easiest way.) Then choose Record/Field from the Insert menu. Whoomp, there it is. Of course, as of this point it doesn't have a name, so choose Field Name from the Edit menu, type a name, and click OK.

Adding a Field in Form View

Adding a field in Form view has its advantages. You can position the field exactly where you want it on the form, and define its name and length all at once.

Position the insertion point where you want the first letter of the new field's name to appear, and then choose Field from the Insert menu. In the dialog box, type a field name, using up to 15 characters. Set the field size, and then choose OK. The new field appears right where you specified.

> ### By the Way . . .
> You might have noticed that the Insert menu's commands are different from List view to Form view. In List view, you add fields and records with one command: Record/Field. In Form view, there are two separate commands.

Get That Field Out of Here!

You can delete an entire field in List view by highlighting it and choosing **Delete Record/Field** from the Insert menu. In Form view, it's a little harder to delete a field. Highlight the name of the field, and then choose Delete Selection from the Insert menu. When you're asked to confirm, choose **OK**. Remember, when you delete a field, whether in List view or Form view, it's totally deleted in every record!

Getting Series-ous About a List

One thing that you can do in List view that you can't do in Form view is enter a series of numbers (from 1 to 200) or dates that progress evenly from one record to the next. When you want to insert consecutive invoice numbers, or assign a number to parts or customers in each of your records, this simple procedure makes it easy.

First, you'll need an empty field in your list; add one using the instructions from the last section. Then enter the starting number or date in the first record of the series. If you want the series to start with 20, type **20**. Then highlight that field in the record and the same field in the records below it.

From the Edit menu, choose Fill Series and then choose the unit of measure you want: number, day, weekday, etc. If you want the series to increase or decrease by more than one unit, type the new increment in the **Step by** box. For example, to decrease 2 units, type **–2**. To increase by 3 days or units, type **3**. When you choose **OK** or press **Enter**, Works inserts the values.

Re-Planting: Editing

You can change a field entry or field name by editing it in either Form view or List view. The changes will appear in both places.

Editing Field Entries

To edit a field entry, highlight the entry you want to edit and click the formula bar, or press **F2**. Use the arrow keys or the mouse to move the

If you're trying to clear a field that contains the result of a formula, you must first clear the formula.

insertion point in the formula bar to the characters you want to change; delete and retype them. Click the **Enter** box or press **Enter** to confirm your changes.

To clear a field entry without losing the formatting, highlight the entry or entries you want to clear, and then choose Clear Field Entry or Clear Formula from the Edit menu.

Renaming a Field

Renaming a field is really easy in List view. Just select the entire column, choose Field Name from the Edit menu, and type a new name in the text box.

From Form view it's just as easy, but in a different way. Click on the field name to highlight it, and then change the text in the formula bar in the same way that you would change a field entry.

Resizing Your Fields for Maximum Economy

Field sizes will vary in each view, so unless you like what Works comes up with, you have to size the fields in each view separately.

Resizing: Form View

You learned how to size a field in Form view, when you entered the field. Here's a quick refresher, though:

1. Highlight the field (not the name).

2. Position the mouse pointer at the right edge of the highlighted rectangle, so the cursor turns into a square with the word "Resize" under it.

3. Drag the edge to resize the box.

Another way to resize a field in Form view is to select Field Size from the Format menu and type a new size in the **W**idth box.

Resizing: List View

In List view, you can size both the field width and the record height. The field width can be between 0 and 79 characters, and the row height between 0 and 409 points. You can even specify "best fit," which means Works will automatically adjust the field size to accommodate the longest entry.

There are two ways to give the field width and record height the "best fit":

- Double-click the field name or record number

- Select Field **W**idth or Record **H**eight from the Forma**t** menu. Select the **Best Fit** check box, and press **Enter** or click **OK**.

2.0

Poor 2.0 users, you can't benefit from Works 3.0's Best Fit. But you still can adjust field size by using the Format menu.

By the Way . . .

If you set width or height to 0 (zero) the field will be hidden. To get it back, use the **G**o To command in the **E**dit menu to track it down, and then use the **F**ormat menu to resize it.

Records: More or Less

You can always add records to the end of the list without much effort; just move to the next record when you get to the end. But what if you want to add one in the middle, *before* an existing record?

In List view, highlight the entire record below the line you want to insert, and choose Record/Field from the Insert menu. When the record is inserted, Works automatically renumbers all the records that follow. Delete a record by highlighting it and choosing Delete Record/Field from the Insert menu.

In Form view, it's basically the same story, except you select Record instead of Record/Field, and Delete Record instead of Delete Record/Field.

Copying and Moving Fields (Form View)

Once you have fields set up in one database, you may find you'd like to use them in another database or another Works document. If you want to duplicate a field someplace else, but leave it in it's original location, that's a *copy*. If you want to remove the information from one place and paste it in another, that's a *move*. (Is this copying and moving business beginning to sink in? Good.)

The quickest way to copy or move information from within the database to another location is to highlight it in Form view, and then drag and drop it where you want it. Keep both document windows open (or split your window if you're working in the same document), with the destination document scrolled to the point at which you'd like to drop the information.

Table 20.1 shows you four methods that you can use to complete the copy or move:

Table 20.1   Four Methods for Copying and Moving

To	To This Destination	Do This
Copy information	Within the same Works document	Click within the highlighted selection and hold the **Ctrl** key as you drag to the destination.
Move information	Within the same Works document	Click within the selection and drag to the destination.
Copy information	A different Works or Windows document	Click within the highlighted selection and drag to the destination.

To	To This Destination	Do This
Move information	A different Works or Windows document	Click within the highlighted selection and hold the **Shift** key as you drag to the destination.

You can also copy and move highlighted fields by using the Copy and Cut commands in the Edit menu (to copy and move, respectively). When you have the cursor at the destination, choose Paste from the Edit menu. You can Paste the information as many times as you like, as long as you don't copy or cut something else to the Clipboard in between pastes.

To copy field information to the fields below, highlight the fields you want copied and the fields you want to copy them in. From the **E**dit menu choose Fill Do**w**n.

Copying and Moving Records (List View)

You can easily copy or move an entire record within your database or another Works document using List view. To do so, highlight the record you want to copy or move, and choose Copy or Cut from the Edit menu or click on the appropriate Toolbar button. Move the cursor to highlight the row, or record, in which you want to paste the information, and choose Paste from the Edit menu.

A Field Re-Org (Repositioning Fields)

You may find after creating your database that you'd like to reorganize or change the location of a field to make the form easier to use in Form view. While a move could accomplish the same thing, a reposition is more precise. With it you can

If you copy or move information into a record that already contains information, the old information will be replaced. If you don't want that to happen, add an extra record row.

use the snap to grid feature, which will move the insertion point and field placement in even increments.

To turn on the snap to grid feature in Form view, choose the **Snap To** command from the Format menu. Then either drag the field to a new position or highlight the field you want to change. Choose Position Selection from the Edit menu, and use the arrow keys to move the high-light in even increments to the new location.

While you have the Snap To grid turned on, if you have two fields of data on your form that you want to position side by side, just drag the field on the right closer to the one on the left. With the Snap To grid on, they will remain on the same line.

Moving or repositioning a field in Form view has no effect on its place-ment in List view. You may want to do your own List view re-org so that you can view related fields side by side.

To rearrange a field in List view, highlight the entire field you want to move, and then choose Cut from the Edit menu or use the Toolbar button. Highlight the field to the right of where you want the moved field to go, and choose **Paste** from the Edit menu or click the **Paste** button on the Toolbar.

Want a Hard Copy?

You can print a database in either List view or Form view. If you print in Form view, you'll get one record printed per page. So if there are 10 records, you'll print 10 pages. (Unless, of course, each record takes up more than one page.)

In List view, each record in the database is printed on one line, just like it appears on your screen. In either view, if a record is wider than a piece of paper, it will be continued on another page. And, like the spreadsheet, Works will print all of the left-hand pages before going back to print all of the right hand pages. (The intent is that you can go back and tape the two pages together later.)

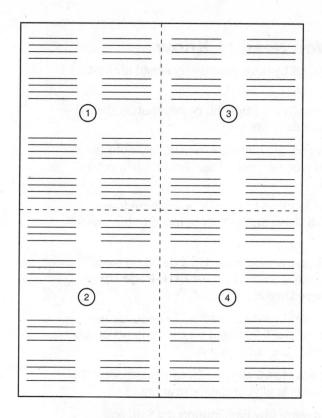

Printing by number.

By the Way . . .

If you want to hide records in the printed copy of a database list, use List view to select the records you want hidden. Then choose Hi**d**e Record from the **V**iew menu. If you want to hide more than one record and they are not right next to each other, repeat the procedure. When you're done, print.

The Least You Need to Know

If you know this much by now, you're way ahead of most people:

☞ A field entry is the single bit of information that is stored in a database field.

☞ To enter text or numbers in a field, highlight the field and type the entry. Press **Enter** when you're finished.

☞ To move from field to field in a database form, press **Tab**. Press **Shift+Tab** to move to the previous field.

☞ To move to the next record in a database form, click the scroll button or press **Ctrl+Page Up** or **Ctrl+Page Down**.

☞ Use formulas in a database field to calculate the contents of one field based on the contents of other fields within the same record.

☞ Use List view to list all records, so you can view the entire contents of your database at once.

☞ Edit field entries by highlighting the field and making corrections in the formula bar. When you're finished, click the **Enter** box or press **Enter**.

☞ The easiest way to give field height and width the "best fit" is to double-click the field name or the row number.

☞ To copy information from the database to another location, highlight it in Form view and drag and drop it where you want it to go.

☞ Use the Snap To grid feature to reposition fields in Form view. Simply choose **S**nap To from the Forma**t** menu and drag the field to its new position.

Chapter 21
More Database Goodies

In This Chapter

- Putting a smile on your database face
- Adding labels and text to your forms
- Aligning cells
- Sorting, sorting, sorting
- Overcoming query anxiety

If databasing didn't do much for you, wait till you see what happens when you put one in overdrive! Stay tuned. But first, a word for our format fans. I'll go over how to liven up your format, and then I'll show you how to sort through all that data. You'll even learn how to speak "Query" (yes, you're heading right into the BIG TIME!). From simple sorts, you'll move to creating tailored subsets of your database that you can use for special purposes.

Tired Old Forms Got You Down? Lifeless Lists?

Welcome to the club. Your lists never seem to line up right. Fonts look like yesterday's leftovers. One darn thing after another. Nothing seems to move you. What's a d'baser to do?

Change your point of view, that's what! Go back to Form view. Run through the fields. Wake everything up! (Go get a cup of coffee, this may take a while.)

Start with a Label

If you're the only one who knows what this form is for, we've got a problem. What you need is a label and text to show the world what you just spent the past two days working on.

This label describes the database.

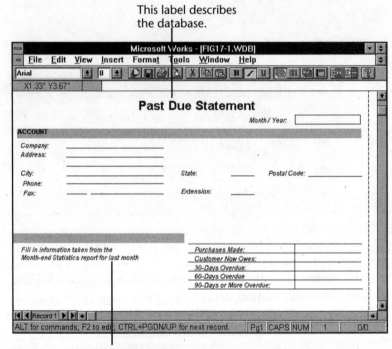

Labeling: sometimes it just can't be helped.

This label helps "idiot-proof" your form.

Add helpful notes and titles in Form view by following these simple steps:

1. Move the cursor to where you want to place a label.

2. Type the text for the label.

3. That's all folks! Press **Enter**.

If you don't like where you just stuck your label, you can always move it! You do remember how to move things, don't you? Just put a click and a drag together and run like the wind.

Don't add a colon to a label or note! If you do, Works will think it's a new field!

Paint Rainbows All over Your Blues?

Well, not exactly. But you can change the font, style, size, and color of your text. And you know from the word processor and the spreadsheet how much that can get people's attention.

To liven up the font, highlight the field, field name, or label whose font you want to change. Click on the font box arrow to display a selection list of fonts, and use the scroll arrows to move throughout the list. When you find one that intrigues you, click on it and give it go.

To change the font size too, click the font size arrow and choose the font size you want. To add some text attributes, use the bold, italic, and underline buttons on the Toolbar.

You can't paint rainbows, or rather change font colors, using the Toolbar, so we'll have to saddle up to the menu bar. To change either the font, font size, font style, or color with the menu:

1. Highlight the fields and labels you want to change.

2. Select Font and Style from the Format menu.

3. Change all the characteristics you want in the option boxes, and check out your selections in the Sample box.

4. If you want all of your entries to look like this from now on, click on the Set Default button. This will change the default font to the type, size, style, and color you've selected.

5. When you're finished for sure, click **OK** or press **Enter**.

If you have trouble highlighting more than one field at a time with the mouse, I'll bet you're not holding the **Ctrl** key while you click on each field. I'd also bet that you dragged a couple of fields around while trying. Well I hope you got to the **E**dit **U**ndo command in time. And I'll bet you won't do that again. Right?

Separate the Wheat from the Chaff

You can outline fields with fancy borders, or draw a rectangle around related crops to draw attention to specific groups and categories. Use shading or color to add accent or to mark off special areas "For Management Use Only!"

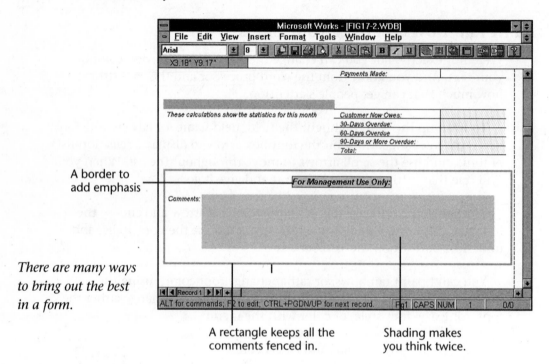

A border to add emphasis

There are many ways to bring out the best in a form.

A rectangle keeps all the comments fenced in.

Shading makes you think twice.

To add a rectangle around a group, position the cursor where you want to insert the rectangle. From the Insert menu, choose Rectangle. Then drag it to the size you want by grabbing the sizing handles. Or, move it into position by clicking and dragging.

To add a border around individual field elements, select all of the field elements (name, entry, and labels) that you want enclosed. Then open the Format menu and select Border. Choose the line style and line color you want around each border, and select OK. Each field element will have its own border.

If you want to remove the border, go back to the Format menu and select **B**order again. This time choose the first box, "Empty," as your Line Style, and then click **OK**.

To add color and shading, highlight just the fields you want shaded, or don't highlight anything if you want the whole form shaded or colorized. Then choose **P**atterns from the Format menu. Select the pattern you want from the Pattern list box. Select the foreground and background colors in the **F**oreground and **B**ackground boxes. If you choose a solid pattern, you will get to select only a foreground color. When you're finished, click **OK** or press **Enter**.

To remove color and shading, repeat these steps, but set the Pattern selection back to **None** and color back to **Auto**.

By the Way . . .

You can always add special interest to a not-so-interesting form by adding **W**ordArt, Clip**A**rt, pop-up Not**e**-Its, Draw**i**ngs, or **Sp**readsheets. Select the added attraction you want from the **I**nsert menu, and then resize it to fit. (Check back in Chapter 12 to learn about creating drawings, WordArt, and ClipArt. Note-Its are very similar.)

Align 'Em Up!

One of the biggest challenges in List view is getting all those columns (fields) lined up in some kind of orderly fashion. The problem stems from the fact that all text is left aligned, and numbers, dates, and formulas are right aligned. So, if you have a text column surrounded by two number columns, the text will look squished on one side, and vice versa.

Another challenge arises when a field entry doesn't fit the field, even though you've widened the column as much as you can without pushing a column onto the next page. A possible solution here is to wrap the text in the column, if you don't mind extending the row height another full record.

Here's what all of your alignment choices will look like:

This field is formatted 16-point bold.

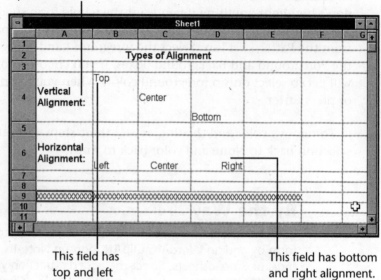

Places, everyone!

This field has top and left alignment.

This field has bottom and right alignment.

To change the horizontal alignment of a field, highlight the field you want to change, select Alignment from the Format menu, and select the Alignment option you want. Or, from the keyboard press:

Ctrl+L	to left align
Ctrl+E	to center
Ctrl+R	to right align

To change the vertical alignment of a cell entry, highlight the field you want to change, and then open the Format menu and choose Alignment. In the Vertical box, choose Top, Center, or Bottom. Click **OK** or press **Enter**.

To wrap text in a field so that it flows to a second line if the field width is too narrow, highlight any cell in the field in which you want the text to wrap.

OOPS!

In a spreadsheet, you can specify different formatting for each cell. In a database, however, formatting you set for a cell will apply to the entire column (field). You can't have different field entries for the same field formatted differently.

Then from the Format menu, choose Alignment. In the Alignment dialog box, select **Wrap text**.

> ### By the Way . . .
> When you change a field's alignment in List view, it does not change in Form view. But you can use the same procedures to change field alignment on forms.

Where in the Heck IS Carmen Sandiego?

What good is a list if you have to search through 26 pages of random names to find the one you need? Same goes for part numbers, car numbers, membership numbers, house numbers, dates, times. Who needs all this information if it takes forever to find what you want?

Works has the solution. But before I explain, I just want to make one thing perfectly clear: Works can put your records in such good order, it won't take an FBI investigation or an act of congress to find what you're looking for!

You can sort all of your records logically: in alphabetical and numerical order, from first to last, lowest to highest, or reverse. Here's a sample of what you can do with a sort:

- ☛ Print names in alphabetical order, sorted by last and first names (and middle initial, if needed).

- ☛ Inventory parts by part number, or catalog them for customers by price.

- ☛ Print mailing labels in order of ZIP code or street address.

- ☛ Chronologically list dates and times to find a missing hour or two.

Works lets you sort each database on three fields. So if you have an extremely large address database, for example, you can specify Last name as the most important field. Then have Works sort First names as the second priority, in case there are duplicate last names. And, as a third priority, have Works look for and sort the middle initial or city, in case there are duplicate first and last names.

If you ever need to sort more than three fields, you can run a sort on three fields, and then run another sort. If you do, though, run the least important sort first, and the most important sort last.

To sort a database:

1. Open the Tools menu and choose Sort Records.

2. Under the 1st Field, choose the name of the first field you want to sort the list on. Works will automatically select the first field as the first field to sort in your database. Change it if it's not what you want to do.

   ☛ Choose the direction of the sort: Ascend A to Z or Descend Z to A.

   ☛ Select the name of the 2nd and 3rd Fields (if you want to sort on more than one field) and the direction of sort.

3. Choose OK or press Enter to begin the sort.

The Hunt for Red October

A sort won't help you find something as easily as a search will. When you need to get to a particular piece of information fast, do a Find.

To Find Specific Information

Choose Find from the Edit menu. Type the text or values you're looking for in the Find What box. Choose Next record if you want Works to find each occurrence one at a time. Or, choose All records if you want Works to search through all records in the database and then show you the ones in which your characters were found. To start the search, choose OK or press Enter.

When the search is over, the only evidence will be a list of the records found. To display all of the records again, choose Show All Records from the View menu.

The Quick Switcharoo

If you're hunting for a piece of information so you can change it quickly, do a Find and Replace. But, sshhh! (We don't want anyone to know.)

> If you need to search only a specific field instead of the whole database, use List view and highlight the field before you start the search.

To replace specific information, choose Replace from the Edit menu. Type the text or values you want to find and replace in the Find What box. In the Replace With box, type the characters you want to replace the found ones with. In the Look By box, tell Works whether you want to search by Records (rows) or Fields (columns). To begin the search, choose Find Next.

If you want Works to replace the found characters, choose Replace. Then choose Find Next again to continue like this through the whole database. If you want Works to get the whole thing over with at once, choose Replace All and be done! When the mission is over, choose **Cancel**.

By the Way . . .

You can protect your own files from illegal search and replace, or just plain curiosity. Works automatically locks all fields in a database. But this lock isn't active until you turn it on. If you want to protect some fields but not others, unlock the fields you don't want to protect, and then turn on the protection.

To lock or unlock a field, highlight the ones you want to change. From the Format menu, choose Protection and turn the **L**ocked check box on or off, depending on what you want to do. Then turn on the **P**rotect Data box if you want any fields locked. (Turn it off if you don't.) Choose **OK** when you're done.

Queries: Narrowing the Field

Sorts make it easier to locate information in records. And searches let you riffle through records to track down characters one at a time. But queries sort through all your records and find those that match whatever criteria you've set, all at once!

For instance, a query can help a discount warehouse locate all of the office supply items they have in stock that cost more than $10 and that come from XYZ Suppliers. Or, a supermarket can locate all of the dairy products they've received from Dairies Are Us since last Wednesday. You could even identify all the men in your address book who are over 5'1", speak English, and are still alive, if that's the kind of information you like to keep.

Queries let you search and select records based on the following criteria:

Criterion	Searches for records that contain:
Is equal to	a specific value or text string, such as "Jones" or "$100.00"
Contains	part of an entry. Lets you use a wild card (*) to indicate where an unknown can be located. For example, *123 finds *123*, 3*123*567, and 234*123*
Is greater than	values larger than the given value
Is less than	values less than the given value
Is greater than or equal to	values larger than or equal to the given value
Is less than or equal to	values less than or equal to the given value
Is not equal to	values or text that DO NOT match those specified

The Simple Three-Criteria Query

When your query contains only three criteria or less, you can use Works' Query dialog box. Define the simple query by specifying the field you want to compare, how you want to compare it, and what you want to compare it against. To create and apply a simple query:

1. From the Tools menu, choose Create New Query. The New Query dialog box is displayed.

2. If you want to rename the query, enter a new name for it; otherwise accept Works' name: Query1. The name cannot exceed 15 characters.

3. In the Choose a field to compare box, choose the field you want to use for the first criterion.

4. Choose the mode of comparison in the How to compare field box.

5. Type the information you want to compare the field to in the Value to compare the field to box.

6. If you want to add another set of criteria to the query, choose "And" or "Or" before entering the next query statement. Use "and" to find all records that match both the first and next (second) statement's criterion. Use "or" to find all records that match either the first or the next (second) statement's criterion.

> Version 2.0 users don't have the choice of using the Query dialog box. You'll have to use the Do-It-Yourself method described in the next section.

7. Repeat steps 3 through 6 to add additional query statements.

8. When you're done entering criterion, choose Apply Now. Works displays a list of the records that match your query.

To show all of the records that don't match the query, choose Switch Hidden Records from the View menu. To display all records again after a query, choose Show All Records from the View menu.

By the Way . . .

Like spreadsheet charts, Works will automatically save each query when it saves the database. To view an existing query when you're working in a database, select the query you want with the **V**iew **Q**uery command.

Also like charts, you can only accumulate eight queries for each database. So if you find you need to use more than eight, either delete existing queries or duplicate the database and create new ones. To delete a query, use the **T**ools Dele**t**e Query command.

Do-It-Yourself Queries: Are You Ready for the Big Time?

When you want to define more than three criteria or use a mathematical formula or Works function in a query, you'll need to use this "by hand" method.

Query view basically takes your blank database form, and lets you specify your criterion in each field, as needed. You'll need to use query instructions, which are nothing more than equation operators, such as >, <, =, etc. The most common operators are included on the chart provided in the earlier section, "Narrowing the Field."

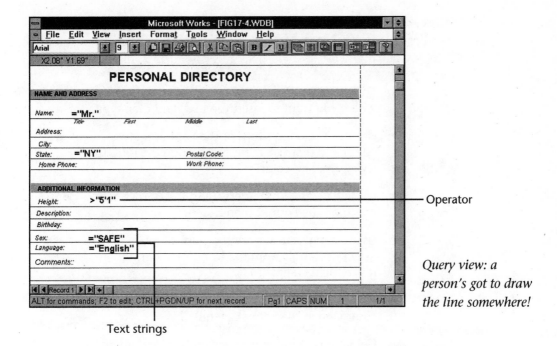

Operator

Query view: a person's got to draw the line somewhere!

Text strings

Here's how to set up a database query based on more than three criteria.

1. From the Tools menu, choose **Create New Query**. The New Query dialog box is displayed.

2. If you want to rename the query, enter a new name for it; otherwise accept Works' name: Query1. The name cannot exceed 15 characters.

3. Choose the Clear button.

4. Choose the Query **V**iew button. When Works switches to Query View, you can specify your query criteria. Use the **Tab** key to move from one field to the next.

5. Type a query instruction in one or more fields. Make sure you enclose any text in double quotations marks, like this: =**"text"**.

6. Switch to another view (i.e. List view, Form view, or Print view) to see the results.

7. Repeat steps 2 through 6 for each query.

The Least You Need to Know

Here's all the stuff we covered, in case you were sleeping:

☛ To add labels (Form view only), move the cursor to where you want to insert the text, and then type.

☛ Use the Toolbar buttons or the **F**ont and Style command (Forma**t** menu) to change the font, font style, size, and color.

☛ Outline fields with borders using the **B**order command on the Format menu.

☛ Use rectangles to surround groups of related fields. Select Recta**n**gle from the **I**nsert menu and then resize the rectangle to fit.

☛ Add color and shading by using the **P**atterns command in the Forma**t** menu.

☛ Get your cells in List view into proper alignment by choosing the **A**lignment command from the Forma**t** menu.

☛ Use the So**r**t Records command in the T**o**ols menu to sort the contents of your database along three fields.

☛ Choose **F**ind from the **E**dit menu to find specific information. Choose Rep**l**ace from the **E**dit menu to find and replace specific information with new, improved information.

☛ Choose **C**reate New Query from the T**o**ols menu to conduct a simple three-criteria query.

☛ To conduct a more complex query, choose **C**reate New Query from the T**o**ols menu, but this time press the **C**lear button. Then choose the Query **V**iew button. When a blank database form is displayed, enter your query criteria in the fields you want to cover.

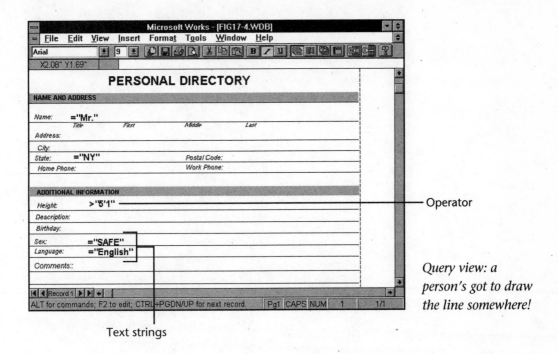

Query view: a person's got to draw the line somewhere!

Here's how to set up a database query based on more than three criteria.

1. From the Tools menu, choose Create New Query. The New Query dialog box is displayed.

2. If you want to rename the query, enter a new name for it; otherwise accept Works' name: Query1. The name cannot exceed 15 characters.

3. Choose the Clear button.

4. Choose the Query View button. When Works switches to Query View, you can specify your query criteria. Use the **Tab** key to move from one field to the next.

5. Type a query instruction in one or more fields. Make sure you enclose any text in double quotations marks, like this: =**"text"**.

6. Switch to another view (i.e. List view, Form view, or Print view) to see the results.

7. Repeat steps 2 through 6 for each query.

Chapter 22
Give Me a Full Report!

In This Chapter

- Reports vs. printouts
- Creating a simple report
- Adding stats
- What's a Report view?
- Customizing a report
- Adding more data

Why do you need to make a well-planned, presentation-quality, summarized/customized report, when any old printout will do? Because all your great information won't mean diddly if you can't make it palatable. Remember, if you don't catch their eyes in the first blink, you've lost 'em.

Besides, I'm going to make this little seminar as short and sweet as I possibly can. If you've made it this far in Works, you know enough about it to fill in your own blanks.

Re-Engineering a Printout

Database reports give you the freedom and flexibility to turn acres of fields into a few pages of carefully analyzed, well-planned solutions sprinkled with your usual amount of wit, wisdom, and charm. They let you organize and summarize key information, draw statistical inferences from groups of data, or just present database records in the simplest, yet most advantageous light.

By creating a report instead of using a database printout, you can:

☛ Limit your report to include only the fields or records you need.

☛ Place fields anywhere you want on the page.

☛ Sort and group field entries.

☛ Make database calculations (for example, count, add, and average field data).

☛ Format and embellish with all the fonts, art, graphics, colors, and borders you want.

There are two kinds of database reports: simple and complex. As usual, we'll create a simple one first. You can make it as complex as you want with the information that follows. Before we start, you should know that there's nothing you can do to harm or damage your original, underlying database data while generating a report. But this would be a good time to Save just in case!

> ## By the Way . . .
> Whenever you change or add information to the underlying database, Works will automatically update your database report.

Starting Simple

Works walks you through the simple database reporting process very carefully. It only takes two standard dialog boxes to create a simple report.

Here's what to tell the first:

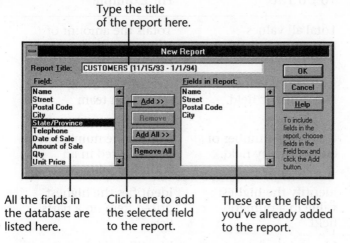

Type the title of the report here.

All the fields in the database are listed here.

Click here to add the selected field to the report.

These are the fields you've already added to the report.

Talking about the new report.

To create a simple, standard report, first open the database you want to work on. Then select Create New Report from the Tools menu. Type a title for the report in the Report Title box. This title will appear on the report, so be serious.

In the Field list box, select the field that you want to have appear in the first column of your report, and then select the Add button. Repeat this for each field you want to add to the report. If you want all fields listed to appear in the report, select the Add All button. When you're finished, choose the OK button. The Statistics dialog box is displayed.

Statistical Significance

Don't let the term "statistics" turn you off. What this dialog box really lets you do is draw some valid conclusions (i.e. summaries) from all of the information you've collected in the database fields.

If you make a mistake and don't really want to add one of the fields, remove it by selecting it in the **F**ields in Report box and choosing the **R**emove button.

It's the type of work that used to take some real long hours and a lot of figuring. But now all you have to do is tell Works what operation (or statistic) you want performed, and Works does it all.

Use This Function	To Do This	For Example
SUM	Total all values in a numeric field.	Totals the amount of all outstanding invoices.
AVG	Average all values in a numeric field.	Averages bowling scores in a team database.
COUNT	Count the number of entries in any field.	Counts the number of people listed in an address book.
MAX	Identify the highest value in a numeric field.	Identifies the highest priced item on a parts list.
MIN	Identify the lowest value in a numeric field.	Identifies the lowest test score.
STD	Calculate the standard deviation for a numeric field.	Calculates the standard deviation for a series of test scores.
VAR	Calculate the variance, or standard deviation squared, for a numeric field.	Finds the amount of variance in a series of test scores.

To add statistics to the report, select the field in which you'd like to perform calculations from the Fields in Report box. Then click the type of calculation you'd like to have performed on that field, in the Statistics box.

The Name field
is the one you've
selected.

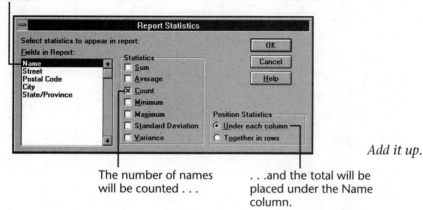

Add it up.

The number of names
will be counted . . .

. . .and the total will be
placed under the Name
column.

Repeat this procedure for each field in which you want a calculation performed. Then in the Position Statistics box, choose where you'd like all of the calculations to be displayed in the report.

When you choose **OK**, the dialog box will close and the Report Definition will be displayed. More on that in a minute. If you'd like to see how the report will look when printed, check it out with the Print Preview command in the File menu.

This Report Just In:

The Report Definition is Works' first shot at creating and defining your report. The Report Definition window is organized in rows and columns, much like the database in List view. But instead of the numbered records for row headings, Report Definition tells you how each piece of information will be used in the report. For example, the first Title line listed in the row headings column is the same title you entered in the Create New Report dialog box.

These are the field headings.

	A	B	C	D
Title		CUSTOMERS (11/15/93 - 1/1/94)		
Title				
Headings		Name	Street	Postal Code	City
Headings				
Record	=Name	=Street	=Postal Code	=City
Summary				
Summary	Count Of Name:	=COUNT(Name)		

Row headings define the parts of the report.

This is Report view, and you're looking at a Report Definition window.

OOPS!

If your mouse acts strangely when you've been creating a report, it may be that your database is getting too big for your computer's memory.

A Report Definition can contain six different types of rows, although not every type will be used in every report. To save you time and frustration later when you want to modify the report, let's go over the purpose of each row heading used in the Report Definition window:

Title rows   Most reports need two title rows: one to display the report title and the other left blank to leave a space between the title and the report contents. The title only prints on the first page of the report.

Heading rows   Most reports also need two heading rows: one that displays each column's field name, and another left blank to leave space between the headings and the data. Headings print at the top of every page.

Record rows   These rows display all of the data from your database that you want used in the report. The symbols that you see in Record row cells (for example, =Name in the figure above) are report instructions that tell Works what to display in that position. These instructions are based on your earlier selection in the Create New Report dialog box. Most reports have one Record row containing several different fields, but you can have as many record rows as you need. In the final report, you will have one line for each record in the database.

Intr (*fieldname*) rows   In this type of row, Works replaces the field name with one that you specify. It's useful when you want to add blank lines or headers above data that's been sorted and grouped into logical sort breaks, like all of the S's in an address book. In that case, the Intr LastName row would identify the sort field and tell Works what to use to separate each group into subgroups. You can include one or more Intr rows for every sort break. Works prints the text specified in an Intr row as headings for each subgroup.

Summa (*fieldname*) rows   Summa rows are also used to organize sorted groups of data by placing field *subtotals* after each group. The Summa (field) rows provide a place for you to insert group statistics, such as number of items in the group (=count), total cost (SUM), etc. Include one or more Summa rows for every sort break. Works will print any text entered, as well as the results of calculations requested.

Summary rows   These rows display the results of calculations you've performed on the entire report. You can use them to total all of the report subtotals, or as final totals on their own. Works prints Summary rows on the last page of the report. You can use as many Summary rows and explanatory text as you need at the end of the report.

If you're wondering what your report will look like, choose Print Preview from the File menu. Here's mine:

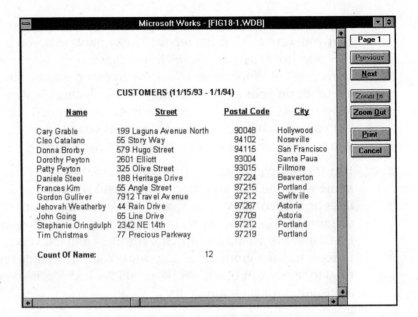

This is what Report Definition was trying to tell us.

By the Way . . .

You can create your own custom report without the aid of the Create New dialog box. Immediately after you select Create **N**ew Report from the **T**ools menu, choose **OK**. Works will close the dialog box and display a blank Report Definition for you to fill in yourself.

Fine Tuning

You can customize any report to display data the way you want by modifying rows in the Report Definition. Add subtitles and explanatory text by typing text or formulas into a field; sort and group report information; or just add and delete rows and columns to make room for more text or more blank space!

And, of course, you can always change the look and style of your report by changing the standard formatting options, such as number format; font selection, style, size, and color; field alignment; margins; page breaks; and headers and footers.

> When you're ready to get back to the whole database again, select List or Form view from the **V**iew menu or Toolbar.

In the remaining sections of this chapter, we'll cover some of the changes you may want to make to your database report. For more information about customizing database reports and using standard formatting options, check the Microsoft Works for Windows 3.0 User's Manual.

Tweaking Field Entries

It's easy to change, rearrange, or correct mistakes in rows or fields. To change an entry by inserting new information over existing information, follow these steps.

1. Highlight the text or report instruction that you want to change.

2. Type the new entry in the field or formula bar, or insert a new report instruction by choosing the appropriate command from the Insert menu.

3. Click the **Enter** box in the formula bar or press **Enter.**

If you want to edit an existing entry without changing it completely, just highlight the entry you want to change, and then make your changes in the formula bar.

You can clear an entire field, without losing the formatting instructions that go along with it, by highlighting the field or group of fields, and then pressing **Del**.

One More Row to Hoe

When you add a row to a Report Definition, Works asks you to specify what type of row you'd like: Title, Heading, Record, etc. Since rows are grouped according to their type in Report Definition, Works will automatically place the extra row with the group to which it belongs.

To add a blank row, highlight the entire row below where you want the new one. (Highlight as many rows as you want to insert.) Choose **Row/Column** from the Insert menu, and then select the type you want from the list shown. When you choose **OK**, the row(s) is inserted above the highlighted row(s).

If you decide you're better off without a row, delete it! To delete a row (and all of the report information contained in it), highlight the row you want to delete and then choose **Delete Row/Column** from the Insert menu.

Set That Column Down There

Inserting a new column is just as easy as it was in List view, unless you just happened to pick this one up at the Parthenon.

To add a blank column, highlight the entire column to the right of where you want to place the new one. (If you want to insert more than one, highlight more than one.) Choose **Row/Column** from the Insert menu, and the new one(s) will be placed to the left of your highlight.

You can delete a column in the same way that you deleted a row. And the warning still stands: you will delete any information contained in it as well.

Details, Details

You can add explanatory labels to columns or rows, or add notes at the end, to define the calculations used in the report. You can easily add anything you want to use as text by highlighting the field or row in which you want to place the text and typing the entry. When you're done, press **Enter** or click the **Enter** box on the formula bar.

Telling a Report What to Do

Report instructions tell Works what data to use in the report, based on the choices you made in the Create New Report dialog box. If you've added a column and don't intend to leave it blank, you'll need to use a field-entry report instruction to have Works fill it with data, and a field name report instruction to have Works label it.

To add a field name label, first move the highlight to where you want the field name (usually in a Heading or Intr Row). Then choose Field Name from the Insert Menu. Works lists the field names that are already in the database. Take your pick. Choose **OK**, and Works will place the field name where you wanted it.

To add a field entry instruction, move the highlight to where you want the instruction (usually in Record rows). Choose Field Entry from the Insert menu. Works lists all of the fields that are listed in the database. Choose one, and then click **OK** or press **Enter**. Works will insert an equal sign (=) followed by the appropriate field name, for example, **=ZipCode**.

Yes, It's Possible: Report Instructions for *More* Calculations

You can enumerate your findings by adding extra calculations to your final report. Adding calculations can be as easy as using the built-in functions provided by the Statistics dialog box, or defining your own.

Calculations must be inserted into Summa (field) or Summary rows in order to work correctly. To insert a calculation instruction into a Report Definition:

1. Add a Summa (field) or Summary row for the information, if there isn't one available.

2. Move the highlight to where you want to place the instruction.

3. Select Field Summary from the Insert menu. In the Fields box, choose the field in which you want to perform a calculation.

4. In the Statistic box, choose the calculation you want performed. Choose **OK**, and Works inserts the calculation formula.

You can also create your own formulas using field names and standard mathematical operators. You could keep an accounts receivable database with fields named "Previous Balance," "Payment," and "New Balance," current by using the following instruction to calculate the New Balance=Previous Balance–Payment formula.

Just enter the calculation instructions in a Record, Summa (field) or Summary row. Don't forget to start each formula with an equal sign (=), and don't use spaces between letters or words.

The Least You Need to Know

I'm sure you know everything about databasing now! But in case you forget, I've filed a report:

- ☞ Start with a simple report by choosing Create **N**ew Report from the **T**ools menu.

- ☞ Add statistics to draw conclusions and summarize your findings. The Statistics dialog box is displayed when you're done with the Create New dialog box.

- ☞ Works generates a Report Definition based on what you asked it to create. The Report Definition means you're looking at the report in Report view.

- ☞ Modify the Report Definition to add more data or take some away. Add columns, rows, subtitles, and explanations. Change fonts and colors, field alignment, margins, page layout, and text.

Chapter 23

Sharing: The Good OLE Days!

In This Chapter

- ☞ All the different ways to share
- ☞ Sharing files with other programs
- ☞ Copying, linking, or embedding?
- ☞ Foolproof linking and embedding methods

Works eagerly supports two behaviors that most of us learned as kids: sharing and copying. While copying was rarely encouraged back then, as adults, we recognize its value with the simple phrase "Why reinvent the wheel?"

As you've already seen, Windows programs use a common Clipboard, enabling you to share words and pictures among almost any Windows programs, as well as some non-Windows ones. (There are other ways to share too, as you'll see shortly.) Also like most Windows-based programs, Works supports a little wonder called OLE (object linking and embedding, pronounced "oh-lay"), which makes it possible to . . .well, link and embed. Stay tuned and you'll find out exactly what that means.

Doing Your Share

Works encourages us to work with what we've got in order to create something new and better. We can easily mix and match pieces of one Works file with other Works files, or files that were originated in separate Windows or DOS programs. That's what sharing is all about, and here are all the ways we can do it:

☞ Share Works files between different Windows, DOS, or Macintosh programs.

☞ Share pieces of Works files between different Windows applications or other Works files via *copying*.

☞ Link objects created in other Windows applications or Works tools to Works files through *object linking and embedding* (OLE!). (Much more to come on this.)

Swapping Files (Like Trading Cards)

Back in the old days (say, the early 1980s), file formats couldn't be changed. If you had a file in WordPerfect, and you wanted to give it to your buddy who used Wordstar, you were basically out of luck. There were a few fancy conversion programs, but they didn't work very well.

Nowadays, almost all programs (including Works!) have simple file converters built in. You can save a file in any of a whole list of formats, and the file is converted to that format as it is saved. And if someone gives you a file that is in a foreign format, Works' file converter can usually convert the file to Works format as it opens it.

Preparing a File for Another Program

Let's say you want to give a file to a friend who uses a different program, such as WordPerfect. All you need to do is use the Save As command in the File menu to save it as that type of program file. Then just copy the file onto a floppy disk for your friend.

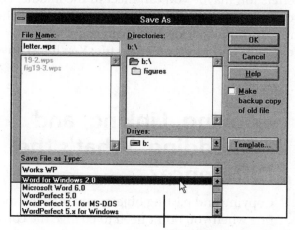

Choose the format you want this file converted to.

It's nice to have something to share.

Getting Files from Other Folks

One way to get a file from a friend, of course, is to ask him or her to convert the file to Works format for you using his or her program's conversion feature. (That's what you just did in the previous section. It's not exactly brain surgery.)

OOPS!

If the exact file type is not listed in the Save File as **T**ype box, try saving the file with the Text format. You'll lose all the formatting, but the text itself will come through intact.

If your friend can't do it and ends up giving you the file in his program's native format (like WordPerfect, for instance), go ahead and try to open it in Works. Works will probably convert it and open it automatically for you—with no fuss at all.

If this is not the case, try opening the file using the Open Existing File command on the File menu. Change the file type in the List Files of Type box to match the incoming format. When you're all set, select the file and click **OK**. Works will convert the file for use in Works.

If that program's format was not on the list and Works won't open the file, talk with your friend and see if there is a file format that both your programs have converters for; maybe you can meet in the middle. For instance, if Works won't convert to Quickie-Write, and Quickie-Write won't convert to Works, perhaps Quickie-Write can convert to WordPerfect, and Works will open a WordPerfect file. You'll just have to experiment.

Linking is the process by which an object created in a "source" document is shared with another document, while still maintaining its link with the source. When the source is changed, the linked document is updated automatically.

Embedding is the process that allows you to create an object using a different program while remaining in the originally active program. Since an embedded object carries it's own source with it, when you select an embedded object, the tool that created it is opened. In Works, drawings, ClipArt, WordArt, and Note-Its are embedded objects.

Copying, Linking, and Embedding: What's the Difference?

Copying and pasting objects and information work fine when you don't need to change the copied material after it has been copied. For instance, let's say you've created a spreadsheet with last year's sales figures, and you want to include it in a word processing document. This would be a great occasion for copying, since last year's numbers are not going to change.

But when you want copies to be updated every time the original changes, you need to link the object. For instance, if the spreadsheet contains this year's figures, since the year is not over yet, the numbers will continue to change each time you update the spreadsheet at the end of the month. When you link the spreadsheet to the word processing document in which you want it to appear, every time you make changes to the spreadsheet, the version in the word processing document will change also.

If you've got memory to spare and want the convenience of creating and modifying an object right inside your document, you can embed it. Embedding is just like linking except that you can actually make changes to the linked object right there in the program. For instance, if a spreadsheet was embedded in the word processing document and you wanted to make a quick change to the spreadsheet, you could simply double-click on the spreadsheet, and the Spreadsheet program would open up before your eyes, without your ever having to leave the Word Processor.

The basic difference between *copying*, *linking*, and *embedding* objects is where the tool used to create the object resides.

☞ Once an object is *copied* to a new location, it loses all connection to its source.

☞ With a *linked* object, the object is still linked to its creating tool, but the tool remains outside the new document.

☞ With an *embedded* object, the creating tool is part of the package and can be called up from inside the new document to make changes.

Since you already know how to copy and paste objects within Works tools and other Windows applications, we'll get right into linking and embedding.

By the Way . . .

There are two more things you should know about copying. When you copy database or spreadsheet data into a word processor document, you will lose the original document's format. To compensate, Works inserts tabs between cells and fields to keep columns aligned.

When you copy a word processor table or a spreadsheet into a database, each cell will have its own field. If you copy word processor text into a database or spreadsheet, it will be contained in one field, or cell.

Embedding Basics

Let's start with embedding, since it's the most full-service way to go. When you embed an object in your document, the application needed to modify it will pop up with a click of the mouse whenever you need it.

There's a slight difference in the procedure for embedding objects that are created with Works tools (such as Draw) and programs outside of Works (such as Paintbrush, which comes with Windows). So let's look at them separately.

Putting Together the Works Pieces

When you learned how to use Microsoft Draw to create a drawing in Chapter 10, you were embedding an object in a word processor document. Remember, the only way you could even get near the drawing was to open the word processing document first. They were really tied to each other— just "bound" to be together.

Don't bother trying—you can't link or embed an object in a Works spreadsheet or chart. But you can link and embed spreadsheets and charts into other Works documents.

Within Works, you can embed ClipArt, WordArt, Note-Its, charts, spreadsheet tables, and drawings into word processing and database documents in the same way.

Just position the cursor where you want to embed the object and then use the Insert menu to select the type of object you want to embed: Chart, Spreadsheet/Table, ClipArt, WordArt, Note-It, or Drawing. The application opens, and you create your object. When you're finished, close the application and the object appears in your Works document. It's as simple as that. If you want to modify the object later, just double-click on it, and the application will reopen.

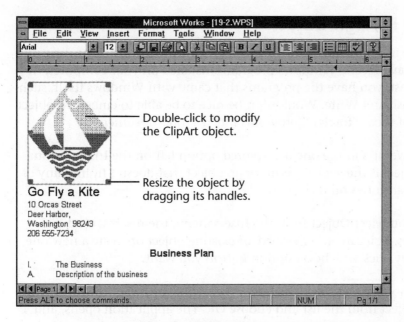

Double-click to modify the ClipArt object.

Resize the object by dragging its handles.

A deeply embedded object.

By the Way . . .

You can change the size of a linked or embedded object in any document. Just click the object to select it, and then drag a resize handle or two until the object grows to the size you want. You can also resize a selected object by selecting Picture/Object in the Format menu, but it's not as much fun that way.

If you want to move an object without resizing it, click on the object to select it. Then position the mouse in the center (anywhere but on a resize handle) and drag to the new location.

Embedding Foreign Objects

Besides the few programs that come as part of the Works package, you probably have several Windows programs installed on your computer. At the very least, you have the programs that came with Windows itself, such as Paintbrush and Write. Wouldn't it be nice to be able to embed an object from one of those "foreign" programs into a Works document?

The answer lies in the one unexplored option left on the Insert menu: Object. Object is the generic term for an object that doesn't fit into any of the other categories on the menu.

When you select Object from the Insert menu, the Insert Object dialog box appears. You can either embed an existing object or create a new one immediately. Pick whichever option button you want.

If you choose Create New, pick the application you want to use to create the new object from the list and choose **OK**. The application opens, and you're home free—from here on, it's just like embedding with one of Works' own apps.

If you choose Create from File, the list of programs disappears, and instead you must type the file name in the File text box. (Use the **Browse** button to find the exact name if you're not sure of it.) Then choose **OK**, and it's back to the regular procedure from here on.

Creating a "Link"age

Linking is a good option if you want to embed an object but your computer is low on memory. When you link, any changes you make to the object in its native program will automatically be reflected in your Works document in which the object is linked. Here's what you do to create a link:

1. Create the file you want to link. For example, if you want to link a Paintbrush picture, create it using Windows Paintbrush.

2. Highlight the object (still in the original program).

3. Choose Copy from the Edit menu.

4. Close the original program (or just minimize it to get it out of your way).

5. Open Works, and position the cursor where you want to insert the linked object or information.

6. Choose Paste **S**pecial from the Edit menu, and then choose the **Paste Link** option. (If the Paste Link option is dimmed and unavailable, the source application may not be able to create a link or support OLE.)

7. Choose **OK** or press **Enter**, and Works will paste the link in the word processing document.

File Linking

You can use an entire file as another object and create a link to a Works document. Here's how to edit and link an entire file to a Works document:

1. Choose **O**bject from the Insert menu, and then click the Create from File button.

2. Either type the file name, or **B**rowse and select the name of the file you want to link with the main document.

3. Click the Link check box and choose **OK**. The source application and file will open. Make any changes you want to make to the source document.

4. When you're finished changing the source document, click anywhere outside the source document window, or press **Esc**. Works will insert the linked file into the Works document.

To edit a linked object, double-click the object and make the changes you want. Save the main document that contains the link, and the changes will be saved in the source document too.

Linking Spreadsheet Data

Linking a spreadsheet to a word processor document is a good way to make sure a report you're developing stays current. Whenever you change the spreadsheet, the word processor report will be updated too.

To link spreadsheet data into a Works document, first name the range of spreadsheet cells that you want to link in the other document. Once you have named the cell range and saved the spreadsheet, you can open the spreadsheet again.

Then switch to the document (either a word processing document or a database form) that you want to place the spreadsheet cells in, and position the cursor where you want to place them. From the Insert menu, choose Spreadsheet/Table and select Use existing spreadsheet range option in the dialog box.

In the Spreadsheets box, choose the name of the spreadsheet you want to link. In the Ranges box, choose the particular cell range. Choose **OK**, and the spreadsheet will be linked to your document.

Linking Spreadsheet Charts

Charts are a good way to summarize spreadsheet data and to present findings, conclusions, and solutions in a word processed report.

To link a chart to a Works document, open the spreadsheet that contains the chart you want to link. Then switch to the word processor or database document in which you want to link the chart. Move the cursor where you want the chart to go and choose Chart from the Insert menu. Then select Use existing chart. In the Spreadsheets box, choose the name of the spreadsheet on which the chart is based. In the Charts box, choose the name of the chart you want to link. When you choose **OK** or press **Enter**, the chart will be linked in the document.

The Least You Need to Know

Just wanted to share this brief summary with you:

- ☛ When information is copied from one document to another, it is no longer connected to its source program.

- ☛ When information is linked or embedded in a document, it is referred to as an object.

- ☛ When an object is linked to a document, it remains connected to its source, and automatically receives updates whenever the source document is changed.

- ☛ When an object is embedded in a document, the object's source comes along for the ride. Embedding takes up more computer memory than linking because the source document remains with the object.

- ☛ To link an object, copy it from the source like a regular copy, and then paste it into the main document using the Paste **S**pecial command in the **E**dit menu.

- ☛ To link an entire file to a document, choose **O**bject from the **I**nsert menu and click the **Create from File** button. Type the file name in the File box, click the **L**ink check box, and then choose **OK**.

- ☛ Before linking a spreadsheet into another document, you must first name the cell range you want to use for the link. Then make your link through the main document's **I**nsert menu. Choose S**p**read-sheet/Table and select **U**se existing spreadsheet range.

- ☛ To link a spreadsheet chart, choose **C**hart from the main document's **I**nsert menu.

Meditation page (insert mantra here).

Chapter 24
Big-Time Mergers

In This Chapter

- ☛ Creating a form letter
- ☛ Mail-merging to your heart's content
- ☛ Creating mailing labels

Have you ever picked up a book because you wanted the answer to a specific question, read the entire book, and still not had the answer? I hate that. That's why I want to make sure that I've covered everything you need to know to get 99% of your common, everyday home and office business done with Works.

In the last chapter, we talked about copying and linking objects, which is what you need to do if you want to, for instance, put some data from a spreadsheet into a word processor document, or include a picture in a database.

But there's one other way that Works' programs can work together, and that's by merging two files. This is usually called "mail merge," because you usually mail the items that you create. In this chapter, we'll delve into the mysteries of merging, and surface a few pages later, able to crank out junk mail with the best of them.

Dear FirstName LastName . . .

As the name implies, a *form letter* is part database and part word processor. A form letter merges the benefits of both so that you can print multiple copies of the same letter and have Works automatically insert appropriate information, such as name and address, in each copy. Works prints a customized copy of the letter for each record in your database.

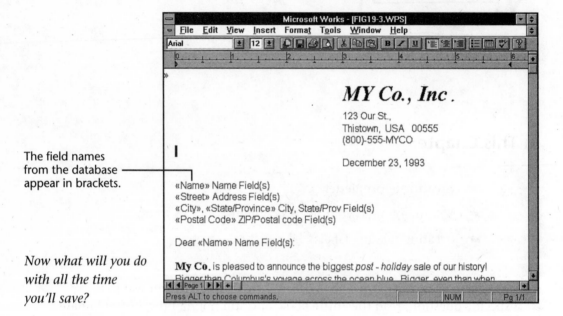

The field names from the database appear in brackets.

Now what will you do with all the time you'll save?

Typing the Letter

To print form letters like this, it's a good idea to start with the letter.

> ### By the Way . . .
> It doesn't always have to be a form letter. You can do the same thing with invoices, invitations, personalized sales messages, and so on.

Type out the whole letter, including placeholders for addresses and names, so that you have a better idea of what you want your database fields to contain. For example, do you want to use first names in the greeting, or is Mr. and Ms. more appropriate? Do you want to include a date, and if so, should it be the current date or a future date that reflects the time of the actual mailing?

Making the Database

Once you've ironed out the letter, you need to create a database that contains the information that you want Works to add. Open a new Database file, and set up the fields the way you want them; then enter the records. (If you need a refresher on this, turn back to Chapters 19 and 20.)

Fields are the categories in a database that hold a specific piece of information for each record. For example, in a database of names and addresses, City is a field. For each record (each person), there is a field entry in the City field (column) that lists that person's city.

Telling the Word Processor Which Database to Use

The next step is to specify the database file in the word processor. To do this, open the word processing document containing the letter, and move the cursor to where you want to insert the placeholder.

Choose Database Field from the Insert menu, and then click the Database button to see your database list. Choose the Works database that you already set up for this. (You can only use one database with each form letter).

When you choose **OK**, the Insert Field dialog box is displayed. Don't close it! You'll need it in the very next section.

Inserting Placeholders in the Letter

From the Insert Field dialog box, choose the database field that you want Works to print at the location of your first placeholder. Then click the Insert button, and Works inserts the placeholder.

You can copy, move, or edit placeholders once they're inserted. So although your cursor may not be positioned exactly where you want to place them, you can enter all of your placeholders now. Or, you can close the Insert Fields box, go back to the letter, reposition the cursor for the next placeholder, and then insert the next one. It's up to you. When you are finished inserting placeholders, choose the Close button.

If you need to add text, spaces, or punctuation before or after any of the placeholders in the letter, do so now.

Print 'Em, Danno!

The merge takes place when you print. (You can't make the merge output appear on-screen.) When you're ready to print, print from the word processor document, not the database. Use the Print command in the File menu, and make sure the Print merge box is turned on.

You can create a form letter with the help of the Works Wizards. Then, whenever you need to, you can open it as a regular word processing document and modify it.

Make Labels, Not War

Mailing labels are great for large envelopes or mass mailings, when your printer won't accept envelopes. The biggest difference between creating mailing labels and form letters is that labels don't have all that other text around them. You also need to use the Tools menu instead of the Insert menu to create them. (I guess the Insert menu got too crowded). Here's how to create and print mailing labels.

Specifying the Database

As with mail merge, you must specify the database that the label text is coming from. First open a word processing document for the mailing label placeholders. Then choose Envelopes and Labels from the Tools menu and click the Mailing Labels tab. Click the Fields button, and then accept the current database listed or select the database you want to use by clicking the Database button.

Inserting the Placeholders

Next we'll insert placeholders in the form letter. In the Fields list box, choose a field name that you want to use as a placeholder. Choose the Insert button, and Works will insert the placeholder into the Label box. Repeat this until you have all placeholders inserted in labels.

> **By the Way . . .**
>
> If you want any text to repeat on each label, such as "ADDRESS," type it in the **L**abel box.

Setting Up the Label Size

Open both the database and the word processor document containing the mailing label placeholders. Then select Envelopes and Labels from the Tools menu and choose the Mailing Labels tab.

On the Mailing Label tab, select the kind of label you're using in the Label style box. If yours isn't listed, choose the Custom Label button and enter the number of labels on the page and the label spacing dimensions. Select OK, and then set the margins, paper size, and orientation. Click OK to return to the Mailing Label tab. When you're ready, choose the Create Label button, and Works sets up the labels in the word processing document.

The Label Printing Extravaganza

When you're ready to print, load the labels into your printer and open the word processor document containing the labels. Choose Print from the File menu, and make sure the Print merge box is turned on. Choose OK, and then select the database. When you select OK this time, the labels will print. No problem!

By the Way . . .

If your printer can handle envelopes, you can use the same process you used to create mailing labels to print on envelopes instead. Just select **E**nvelopes and Labels from the **T**ools menu and use the **E**nvelopes tab.

The Least You Need to Know

Ready to tackle any merge project now? Actually, if you know how to do the mail merge and the labels, everything else you might need is just a variation of one or the other. Keep these pointers in mind as you bravely venture out on your own:

- ☞ Form letters let you combine a database mailing list with a word processor letter.

- ☞ With a form letter, you can automatically create personalized letters for each name in the mailing list.

- ☞ To create a form letter, you need to start with a database and a letter. Then tell Works which database to use and where to place database information in the letter.

- ☞ The actual merge takes place at the printer; you won't see it on-screen.

- ☞ You can create mailing labels and envelopes as easily as form letters. The biggest difference is the page and printer setup, since mailing labels and envelopes come in many sizes.

Can We Talk?

In This Chapter

- ☛ "Talking" through the computer
- ☛ What it takes to make a connection
- ☛ How to start an on-line conversation
- ☛ How to save connection info to reuse later
- ☛ What if someone wants to call you?
- ☛ Sending and receiving files

Communications. Reaching out. Sending messages and files across thousands of miles in less time than it takes to read them. Placing orders. Checking stock prices. Buying airline tickets and holiday gifts. People who have never met sharing computer links and common interests. Finding information in the Information Age. Letting information find you.

Everybody's Talking

If you have a modem and I have a modem, our computers can talk to one another through the telephone lines. Everybody's doing it these days. All you need is a modem and a communications package like the one included with Works to transfer information or files from one computer to another.

Once you place a call, you can converse with the party on the other end by typing text back and forth. You can send and receive text, copy it for use in other Works files, or save it to file for future reference. You can even send and receive complete Works files.

> ### By the Way . . .
> If all you need is to share files between two computers in the same office, forget the modem. What you need instead is the Works Communications tool and a special cable, which I'll tell you more about later in the chapter. Rather than traveling through the phone line, information will flow through the cable between the linked computers.

A **modem** is a communication device that lets you send and receive information from one computer to another through a telephone line. Modems can be hooked up inside the computer (internal) or as an accessory outside the computer.

The On-Line Services Option: Why Leave Home . . . at All?

For a small fee and the price of a telephone call, you can also tap into any of the on-line information services and bulletin boards available today.

Most bulletin boards and on-line services have special sign-on procedures that you'll learn about once you sign up with them. They include special instructions and communication settings that let Works' Communications tool interface with their modem and communications package.

Getting Ready to Call

Bulletin boards and on-line services will be waiting patiently for your call, but another personal computer won't be. When you want to communicate with another PC, it's a good idea to call its owner (using your voice, not your computer!) so he or she can set it up to receive your call.

The most basic thing you need to know about the party on the other end, of course, is the phone number of the line that is connected to the modem. You may also need to know some technical settings for the modem that will be answering the phone, but we'll cross that bridge when we come to it.

By the Way . . .

Don't forget, if a number is long distance, you'll need an area code, and you may need to dial 1 to get long-distance. In some offices, you have to dial 9 for an outside line, too. Make sure all these special prefixes are included in the number you dial.

Making That First Modem Connection

Once your modem is properly hooked up, tuned in, and turned on, select New and Recent Documents at the Startup screen. Then click the Communications button. The first time you use the Communications tool, it will display the Modem Setup dialog box. Click the Test button to have Works determine which port your modem uses, and then click **ok** to continue. The Easy Connect dialog box appears. If you've used the Communications tool before, the Easy Connect dialog box appears immediately, without modem Setup.

Type the number you want to reach in the **Phone number** box. Remember to include all of those extra numbers (9, 1, 0 etc.) if they're needed from your phone line. Type the name of the person you're calling or the service you're reaching in **Name of service** box. This will be the name you select in the Phone list the next time you want to call that person. When you're done, choose **OK**.

Commas give the system time to access outside lines.

Hyphens are optional.

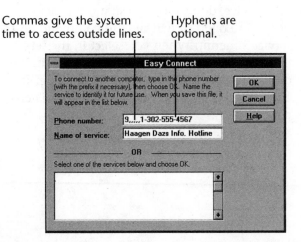

Reach out and touch somebody new.

TECHNO NERD TEACHES

When dialing to reach an outside line or phone service, your computer may dial too fast to allow time to make the proper connection. If you need to dial access numbers before the actual phone number, try adding commas between the access number and the phone number to allow the computer to pause longer. You can add as many commas as you would like, but do not leave a blank space between numbers.

OOPS!

If you get cold feet or just want to cancel while the call's being dialed, press **Esc** or choose the **Cancel** button in the Dial Status dialog box.

OOPS!

If the computer you're connected to ignores your commands or won't quit an operation, try sending a break signal by choosing **B**reak from the **P**hone menu.

When you click **OK**, Works dials the number using the standard communications settings. If a connection can't be made using these settings, you'll have to change them. (I'll show you how in the next section.)

When the other computer finally answers the phone, its response will be displayed on your screen. It may look something like "CONNECT 2400" (if you're connected at 2400 baud). If you're calling a bulletin board, on-line service, or mainframe, you'll most assuredly have to identify yourself and use their sign-on procedures. Most services will be friendly enough to display instructions for first time callers. Look for them on your screen.

If you're calling a friend's modem, with no special bulletin board installed, you may not see anything at all on the screen. If that's the case, try typing something (like "Hello!") and see if the person on the other end types a reply back to you. If you want to send or receive text or files once you've gotten through, hold on. I'll tell you how later in the chapter.

When you're finished and want to hang up, if you have been connected to a bulletin board or on-line service, don't forget to sign-off. (There is usually a Logoff or Exit or Quit command on the service's menu.) When you select it, the service or bulletin board will usually disconnect you. If you didn't sign on, you need to hang up yourself: choose Hang up from the **P**hone menu. Then choose **OK**.

Making a Few Adjustments

When you connect to a computer, computer service, bulletin board, or network for the first time, if your modem's settings do not match those of the modem you are calling, interesting things will happen. Garbage characters will appear on-screen. You might hear some beeps. You might be rudely disconnected. Any way you look at it, it won't be pretty.

If you get a busy signal or the other computer doesn't answer, just choose Dial **A**gain from the **P**hone menu.

If this happens to you, you need to change Works' standard settings. These adjustments can be made from the **S**ettings menu. When you select any of the first four options on this menu, a dialog box with four tabs opens. You can switch among the tabs by clicking on a tab.

Phone   This tab lets you change the type of phone you're using (tone or pulse) and the phone number you're dialing.

Communication   These settings signal your computer to get ready to send (or receive) at a certain speed (baud rate). It should be set to match the highest rate that both modems can achieve, even if one of the modems can go higher. The other settings—parity, data bits, and stop bits—are methods of controlling and understanding the data flowing through. It doesn't matter what they're set at, as long they're set the same at both ends.

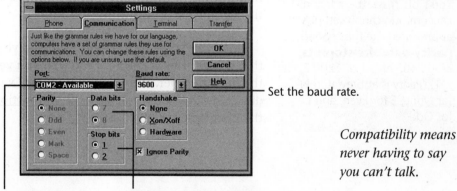

Set the baud rate.

Tell Works which port your modem is connected to.

Make sure parity, data bits, and stop bits are set the same for both computers.

Compatibility means never having to say you can't talk.

Terminal   This dialog box tab tells the other computer what languages and formats you can send and receive. If text is coming into your screen with double characters, turn Local Echo off. If you get no characters when you should be receiving, try turning it back on. Use the End of Line box to control text that comes in as one big line.

When all the settings have been adjusted to your heart's content, click **OK** to close up shop.

By the Way . . .

Adjusting modem settings can get fairly complicated, so don't feel bad if you don't understand all the settings. You really don't need to. Just call the person (by voice) who's in charge of the computer you're trying to call, and find out what settings the receiving computer uses. Then hunt around in the Settings dialog boxes until you find those settings, and make yours match theirs (except for modem port, of course: this setting should always reflect the port your modem is connected to).

You'll often see these technical communication settings abbreviated like this: **speed parity-databits-stopbits**, as in 2400 N-8-1 or 1200 E-7-1. (Parity is abbreviated N for None, E for Even, and O for Odd.)

Saving Your Connections

Whew! It's quite an ordeal to get connected for the first time, isn't it? Luckily, you don't have to go through all this every time.

Once you've made a connection, you've proven that the settings are correct and that you've dialed the right number. Why mess with fate? Even if you didn't get to say a word, save the connection for the next time you need it.

All of your settings and special instructions are saved in a communications file. When you need to call again, select the file from the **Phone** menu, and let Works set everything up and dial for you.

To save your connection as a communications document, choose **Save** from the **File** menu. In the File **Name** box, type something you'll remember the connection information by. Remember, no more than eight characters and no spaces in a file name! Choose **OK** when you're done.

To call a number that's been saved before, choose the file from the **File** menu or existing communications files.

Receiving Calls: The Other Side of That Coin

The more calls you put out there, the more likely it is you'll get one back—sooner or later. To have Works answer an incoming call, create a new communications document, or open an existing one, just to get into Works' Communications tool. From the **Settings** menu, choose **Phone**. Check your communications settings in the Communications tab to make sure they match the sending computer's settings. Then click on the **Phone** tab, and choose **Auto** answer in the Connect option box.

TECHNO NERD TEACHES

You can record a tedious sign-on procedure, or access sequence, in the Communications document file and have Works play it back automatically whenever you make a future connection. To record a sign-on script, choose **Record** Script from the **Tools** menu of the Communications document. Choose **Sign-on** as the Type of Script you want to record, and then press **OK**. Works will begin to record all of your entries as you sign on, as well as the other computer's responses. When you're done signing on, choose **End** Recording from the **Tools** menu. Now that the sign-on is part of the communications file, Works will automatically sign on for you whenever you call this number.

"Whom shall I say is calling, sir?"

Click here for the "answering service."

What then? Wait until the phone rings. But don't answer it; let the computer answer. From there on, it's just like any other call.

Extra, Extra! Cable Connections

If your computer is connected to another one via cable, use this procedure on both computers to get both of you "communicating."

Check each computer to make sure the cable is installed properly, and note which ports it is connected to (COM1, COM2, etc.). Also make sure the other computer is running the Works Communications tool or a compatible program.

Get into the Works Communications tool by either creating a new communications document, or opening an existing one. From the **Settings** menu, choose Communication and set the Baud rate and COM Port you're using. (Cable communications usually use the highest baud rate, 19200). Then choose **OK** or press **Enter**. From the Phone menu, choose Easy Connect, leaving the Phone Number and Name of Service boxes empty. Press **Enter** or choose **OK** to connect.

Once you're connected with the other computer, you can type text or copy files between the two. The message in the communications window status line will change, displaying the time elapsed while connected.

Say It with Files

When you're doing the talking (sending), you
can either say it with text or say it with files.
When you send text, it appears on the
receiver's screen without character or paragraph formatting. When you send a whole
file, such as a word processing document, the
other computer saves it on disk, so it doesn't
appear on that person's screen during the
transmission.

Baud rate refers to the
speed with which a commu-
nications device, such as a
modem, can send and
receive data back and forth.
One baud is equal to one
bit per second.

Sending Text

Text is sent to the receiving computer's screen whenever you type something during a communications session. You can send text the same way
by copying it from an existing Works file (word processing, spreadsheet, or
database) and pasting it in a communications document window.

   To send text that's been copied from a Works tool into the communications document window:

1. Make your connection to the other computer.

2. Open or switch to the Works document that you want to copy
   from.

3. Highlight the information you want to copy, and select Copy
   from the Edit menu or use the Toolbar button.

4. Switch back to the communications document window and
   choose Paste Text from the Edit menu. Works will automatically
   send the unformatted text to the other computer.

   You can also send text to the receiver's screen without even viewing it
on your screen. Just make your connections, as usual, and then choose
Send Text from the communications document window's Tools menu.
Choose the file you want to send from the File Name box. (If you can't
find the file in the list, change the directory or drive selection.) Once
you've found it, press **Enter** or choose **OK**. The contents of the file will be
sent and displayed on the other computer.

If you want to cancel a text or file transfer, just press the **Esc** key.

Sending a File

When you send a file to another computer, Works uses a transfer *protocol* to check for errors that may occur during the transmission. Works has several protocols from which to choose. So, before you begin sending, check with the other computer or service in order to match your Works protocol with theirs. You can set the Works protocol from a communications document window by choosing Transfer from the Settings menu. Then choose one of the following protocols:

Xmodem   The most common protocol; transfers only one file at a time, so it is slow, but reliable.

Ymodem   Faster than Xmodem because it sends big blocks of information and can download several files at once; however, it doesn't do well with poor phone connections.

Zmodem   Faster than Ymodem and as reliable as Xmodem.

Kermit   Designed for transferring information between different types of computers, such as mainframes and PCs. Although it's very slow, it's very reliable and compatible with almost everything.

Once you have set your transfer protocol, choose Send File from the Tools menu. Choose the file you want to send from the File Name box, and then press **Enter** or click **OK**.

By the Way . . .

For best results, when you send the contents of a Works file, save it in the format the receiving computer can recognize. If the receiving computer uses WordPerfect, for example, rename the Works file and save it as a WordPerfect file, using the Save **A**s command in the **F**ile menu. If Works doesn't have the exact format, save it as a text file.

Sometimes It's Better to Receive

What happens to all the text you receive from someone else's computer? Works stores it in a *buffer* while it's being transmitted to you. You can either copy it to another Works tool and save it as a file, or get rid of it when you're done reading it.

As for *files* that are sent to you, they are automatically saved as a file in your hard drive as they're received. Keep reading for more details.

Buffering Text

It would seem that a 256,000-line buffer has plenty of room to store anyone's text. But, in the unfortunate event that it doesn't, Works starts deleting old text to make room for the new. If you need all of the text, the best thing to do is to pause the transmission, and then save the text you've received so far to another file.

Buffer A temporary storage area in your computer for text that is sent from another computer. The buffer can hold a maximum of 256,000 lines of text, after which it starts deleting text.

To pause communications when receiving too much information, first make sure you've chosen a Handshake in the Communication settings. (You can't "pause" without a handshake agreement between both parties.) From the **Settings** menu, choose Communication. In the Handshake box, check Xon/Xoff if you're using a modem. If you're using a cable, select Hardware. Then choose Pause from the **Phone** menu, or use the Toolbar. (To restart the transmission after you've copied the text into a file, just select **Pause** again.)

Highlight the transmitted text that you want to copy to another file, or choose Select All from the **Edit** menu. From the **Edit** menu select Copy Text, and then switch to or open the document you want to copy the text to. Place the cursor where you want to insert the text, and choose Paste from the **Edit** menu or click on the **Paste** button on the Toolbar. Save the new file and then switch back to the communications document window to continue the transmission.

When you drag the mouse to highlight the text received in a transmission, Works automatically pauses the transmission.

Capturing Text

When you know ahead of time that you are about to receive a very large text transmission or something that you'll want to save, you can have Works save the text to a file.

Before you actually start receiving the text, but after you're already connected to the other computer, choose Capture Text from the Tools menu. Type the name of the file you want to save the text to in the File **Name** box. You must include your own file extension, such as .TXT. Choose **OK** when you're ready to begin.

When you want to stop capturing text, choose End Capture Text from the Tools menu.

What Every Inmate Wants for Christmas: Receiving a File

Instead of receiving pages of text, you can receive complete files and have them saved on your hard drive as they are sent. But before you receive a file, make sure the other computer is using the same transfer protocol as you are. Then tell the other computer to begin sending. From your communications document window, choose Receive File from the Tools menu.

If you're using the Xmodem protocol, you have to enter a file name of 8 characters or less in the Receive File box. If you're using one of the other protocols, the file is automatically saved under the file name used by the other computer. When you're ready to start receiving, choose **OK**.

The Least You Need to Know

Time for a chat:

- ☛ You can only communicate with another computer if both computers have modems, or if they're in the same room and are connected with a cable.

- ☛ You need to know the other party's phone number and any special sign-on procedures. Just ask—they'll be happy to tell you.

☞ When you call someone for the first time, use Works Communications tool to **C**reate a New File.

☞ When you're done with the call, choose **H**ang up from the **P**hone menu.

☞ Commas represent pauses. They give the phone service extra time to make the outside connection for you.

☞ If you get a busy signal or no answer while dialing, choose Dial **A**gain from the **P**hone menu.

☞ To save the connection as a communications file, choose **S**ave from the **F**ile menu.

☞ To have the Works communications tool answer an incoming call for you, choose **P**hone from the **S**ettings menu in any communications document. Then choose **A**uto answer.

☞ You can send text in a document file without sending the whole file by choosing the Send **T**ext command from the communications file's **T**ools menu.

☞ To send a whole file through a modem or cable, set the transfer protocol to match the receiving computer, and then select **S**end File from the **T**ools menu.

☞ When you know that a lot of text is coming your way, plan to have it sent directly to a file. After connecting to the other computer (the sender), choose **C**apture Text from the **T**ools menu.

A page is a terrible thing to waste.

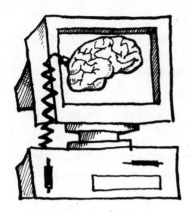

Great Ideas

Now that you've bought the program and read the book, it's time to put it to work. Here are some cool things you can do with Works!

Word Processing Ideas

Use Microsoft Draw, ClipArt, and WordArt to design your own letterhead or personal stationery with the Works word processing tool. To get started, open a new word processing document. If you already have a name picked out, save the document file and name it before you start drawing. Then press **Enter** to page down to the point on the blank page where you'd like to start being creative. Choose the Drawing, **WordArt**, or ClipArt tool you want to use from the Insert menu and have fun! (Unless, of course, this is business.)

Here are some more bright ideas:

- ☛ If you have your own business, use WordArt, ClipArt, and Draw to design simple mailing brochures or in-store handouts to advertise special sales and promotions.

- ☛ Teachers, use the word processor to create customized *Mad Libs* for all of your classroom subjects. Students will have fun working together and learning, too, as they fill-in the blanks with all of their latest Science, English, History, Geography, or even current events material. (They can create their own *Mad Lib* stories, too.)

☞ Create personalized greeting cards (and envelopes) for every occasion. Start by folding a piece of paper in quarters, so you can see where you'll have to enter your text and art on the flat page. Set your margin settings to keep your greetings in the right place, and go for it!

☞ Create a newsletter for your own neighborhood, or bring it into the classroom and let students do it.

☞ Start a simple, one-page newsletter for your office and ask different people to contribute each time. It won't be just a page for long.

☞ Teachers, create Official Certificates, and award a different one every day!

Spreadsheet Suggestions

Prepare your own income tax spreadsheet. Use the IRS' basic 1040 Form to identify the calculations you need to make, as well as the schedules and support data you'll need to come up with, for the formula values. Then start laying out the spreadsheet with each spreadsheet row corresponding to a line on the form.

When you get really good at this, add the totals from your business expense and tax deductible household expense spreadsheets to the original IRS spreadsheet, and have your taxes automatically updated every time you enter a receipt.

Want more? Try these:

☞ Keep a running tab of your net worth, and update it annually. Find the value of your assets by listing all of the money you have coming in plus your major assets. Then do an AutoSum total. Do the same for all of your liabilities (that's money owed). When you're done, subtract the total liabilities from the total assets. What's left is what you're worth—monetarily speaking, of course.

☞ Use a spreadsheet to keep track of all of your business expenses as you incur them, so that closing the books on a year doesn't take a week anymore!

- Design a spreadsheet to track actual household expenses (that's money spent, not just budgeted). Do this for a couple of months, and then prepare a real budget based on those expenses. Be sure to include money stashed away.

- Take the bowling score sheets home at the end of bowling night and enter all of your team members' scores. Keep track of everything, including the highest scores and individual averages, over a number of games and by frame.

- Teachers, develop a spreadsheet to keep track of individual scores on assignments and tests, and then automatically calculate each student's grade point average at the end of the semester.

- Create pie charts or line charts to show each student how his/her scores measure up to the class average.

- Business owners, automate your company's bookkeeping by preparing spreadsheets for all of your income/sales and accounts receivable/payable.

Database Ideas

Not everyone has the equipment to videotape every item of their home for insurance purposes. But now that you have a computer and Works, you can keep an inventory list that's easily updated. Before you begin, decide what kind of information you need to collect for insurance purposes (for example, date of purchase, price, quantity, size, condition), and which items you want to include in the inventory.

Open a new database document and make sure you're in Form view, in the View menu. Start creating the fields you need for the data you want to collect. Move the cursor where you want to place the first field, and then type a field name followed by a colon (:). For example, type **Date Purchased:**.

Press **Enter** when you've finished typing, and the field size dialog box will be displayed. Enter the amount of space you'd like to have for the field entry, and then click **OK**. Move the cursor to enter the next field, and repeat this procedure for all of the fields you need. If you'd like to be able to sort the inventory by categories later, include a special field in which to identify each item as electronic equipment, art, jewelry, etc.

After you've finished creating your form, fill one in for each item of your database. Remember to use the Tab key to move from field to field. Every now and then switch to List view in the View menu to see how big your list is getting. When you're done, print a copy of the list and keep it in a very safe, fireproof place.

Don't panic! I wouldn't leave you with just one idea. Here are some more:

☛ Although you can use a WorksWizard to do this, it's good database practice to create a special address book for members of your club, a class, or friends and relatives—or one big one for everyone you know!

☛ Add a field for birth dates and special occasions in your client list or your personal address book. Sort the list at the beginning of each month to see who's due for a card!

☛ Start a database of your favorite local restaurants. Include the phone number and address, as well as your own comments about the food, price, and service. Next time you feel like going out, check your restaurant file. When you try someplace new, add it to the list.

☛ Create your own on-line daily planner and set it up the way you always wanted to set one up!

☛ Prepare a cookbook of your favorite recipes. If you want to get fancy, include a field that tells you how many servings you can expect from the recipe. Then use a formula (like X * 1(tsp.))in the ingredient quantity field, that will let you automatically recalculate the amount of ingredients based on the number of servings you need.

☛ Dig up your own family tree by creating a form to record the family history. Enter what you already know, and keep adding to it as you ask around.

Communications

Test drive your modem on one of the following on-line services. In each case, all you have to do is literally pick up the phone (don't use the modem for this) and call one of these toll-free numbers to obtain a free 30-day trial subscription and/or a sign-on package.

To test drive . . .	Call this number . . .
America OnLine	1-800-827-6364
CompuServe	1-800-524-3388, operator 370 (Ask for the Intro Pak Offer. Check out WinCIM, to view CompuServe through Windows.)
Prodigy	1-800-PRODIGY. (Which is really: 1-800-776-3449. Don't you love getting a phone "word" that's easy to remember . . .but hard to use?)
Delphi	1-800-695-4005
GEnie	1-800-638-9636 (first monthly fee waived, plus 14 free hours through August 31, 1995)

Once you've set up your free trial subscription, create a new communications document. Enter the access phone number and service information in the Easy Connect dialog box. Press **OK** and have Works dial the number for you.

Follow the sign-on procedures given to you by the service you're connecting to. When you're finished with the session, don't forget to sign off, and then select **Hang Up** from the **Phone** menu. If you were instructed to adjust your communications or phone settings before dialing, use the dialog boxes in the **Settings** menu.

What else can you do with your communications program? Here are some suggestions:

- ☞ Another way to test drive your modem is to call a friend or co-worker who also has a modem. Make sure both modems are set up at the same baud rate and have one of you set to answer the phone. (If you're the designated answerer, use the **Phone** tab in the **Settings** menu and select **Auto answer**.) Once you've made contact, start typing your conversation back and forth.

- ☞ Modem a file that you've been working on all day at the office to your computer at home so you can put the finishing touches on it tonight.

- ☞ Connect to one of the local bulletin boards in your area to see what's going on. You can usually find many listed in the free computer magazines you pick up at computer stores and trade shows.

Speak Like a Geek: The Complete Archive!

active cell   The only cell, or cell range, in the whole spreadsheet that could possibly be doing anything at this moment, because it is the only one highlighted.

application   A bigger word for software program or tool.

arguments   The values used in a function to produce a new value. Arguments can include cell references, range references, other functions, or numbers.

baud rate   Refers to the speed with which a communications device, such as a modem, can send and receive data back and forth. One baud is equal to one bit per second.

bookmark   A Works function that lets you mark your place in a document so that you can easily go back to that spot. It works along the same lines as bending the corner of a page.

buffer   A temporary storage area in your computer for text that is sent from another computer. The buffer can hold a maximum of 256,000 lines of text; when those lines get full, it starts deleting text.

cell   The smallest unit in a spreadsheet that can be viewed with the naked eye. A cell reference is a specific location in a spreadsheet that marks the intersection of a column and row. A cell can contain text, numeric values, or formulas.

cell alignment   The position of text or numbers within a spreadsheet cell. You can align characters within a cell both horizontally (left to right) and vertically (top to bottom).

cell range   A group of active cells right next to each other that are grouped so that they do everything together. The cell reference used to describe a cell range refers to the upper-left and lower-right cells in the range.

cell reference   A specific location in a spreadsheet that marks the intersection of a column and row.

chart   A graphic representation of numeric data plotted against X and Y coordinates of a graph. Works can automatically create charts from the values in a Works spreadsheet.

Clipboard   A temporary storage place somewhere inside Windows where recently copied and cut items hang out. Since there's only room for one item at a time, as soon as you cut or copy new information, the old information has to move out.

column   Aside from those that are crumbling at the Parthenon, columns refer to lists of data that are lined up vertically, up and down a page.

commands   Orders that tell the computer what to do. Before there was Windows, computer users had to memorize commands and type them blindly into the computer. Now that Windows has given us menu boxes and bars, we can select our commands from a list instead.

configured   A big word to describe how the geek who sold it to you installed the computer's brain, memory, and software.

copying   The act of duplicating text, data, and objects that lets you retain the original in one place while inserting copies (that have no link to the creating tool) in other places. You can copy information within the same file, between files, or between different Windows applications and tools.

crunch   A semi-techie term that refers to the noise computers used to make when calculating large formulas with many variables. When numbers are "crunched," they are calculated.

database   (1) A collection of similar records, such as names and addresses or accounts, that you can organize in a way that will actually let you sort out valuable information. (2) A computer program that's used as an automated filing system to organize address and phone numbers, personnel records, client lists, inventories, recipes, appointments, and anything else we can think of. The most commonly known database application is junk mail.

database form One of two ways in which you can enter and view data compiled in a database. In Form view, you can only see and work with one record at a time. For example, if you had a recipe database (like a cookbook) and each recipe was a record, the database form would be the index card on which the recipe was written.

desktop publishing (DTP) A program that lets you combine text and graphics on a page more fancifully than a word processor is inclined to. DTP programs are more complicated, but they allow you to do more with sizing and placement of text and objects.

dialog box When there are too many ways to carry out a command that you've chosen, or too many important decisions to make, Works will display a dialog box to let you decide. That way, you have no one to blame but yourself.

directory A separate storage area on your hard disk that is used to store and organize files. If you think of the hard disk as a file cabinet, a directory is a file drawer containing many separate files.

document An important word that refers to the file of information created in a word processor, database, or spreadsheet to make it sound like the legal evidence it could someday be.

drive Short for disk drive, which is a device that is used to read and write magnetic data. A computer can have a hard disk drive, which is a permanent storage device, or a separate disk drive, which is used for temporary storage and transfer of data to and from the computer hard drive to diskettes.

edit The process of changing existing information. In a word processing document, editing includes format changes, content changes, and spell checking until the document is considered complete or until a deadline is reached, whichever comes first.

embedding   The process that allows you to create an object using a different program, while remaining in the originally active program. Since an embedded object carries its own source program with it, when you select an embedded object within a document, the tool that created it is automatically started. In Works, drawings, ClipArt, WordArt, and Note-Its are embedded objects.

ergonomic   A sophisticated way of saying it fits you like a glove—and won't cause carpel tunnel syndrome.

extension   Each file name consists of two parts: the file name (that you give it) and an extension. The extension can be up to three characters long, and usually denotes the file type. For example, Works uses different extensions to distinguish between each of the Works tools: word processing (.wps), spreadsheets (.wks), databases (.wdb), and charts (.wcm).

field   (1) Where Kevin Costner is said to have some of his better dreams. (2) Categories of information on a database form. Each field is made up of a field name and a field entry that can contain text, numbers, or formulas. Each field entry contains a single piece of information, such as last name, ZIP code, or telephone number.

field entry   The information that is contained in a field of a database, for example "Smith" in the Last Name field of a client list database.

file   A place where DOS saves all of its information. Each of the documents you save is placed in its own file. Fortunately, you get to name the files that you save, so you can find them when you need them again.

font   Any set of characters that share the same typeface, like Courier, Times New Roman, or Arial. Fonts help set the mood and style of a document.

font color   Allows you to type text in 16 different colors. Even if you can't print them all, colors can help you quickly identify special sections in a document, or identify negative numbers in a spreadsheet.

font style   Any special emphasis, like bold, italic, or underline, that is applied to a font.

form   A boilerplate, fill-in-the-blank outline that you create in a database to gather the same information about many subjects. A filled-in form is one database record. Works' database provides Form view so that you can see and work with all of the fields in one database record at a time.

format   The size, shape, and general layout of something printed.

formula   (1) A type of race car. (2) A mathematical equation containing a sequence of cell references, functions, or operators that is used to calculate a new value from existing values in a spreadsheet. In Works, formulas are noted by an equals sign (=).

formula bar   (1) A high protein, quick energy source for over-stressed infants. (2) A section of the Works spreadsheet and database program window that displays the contents of the active cell. You can use the formula bar to enter or change values and formulas in the active cell.

hanging indent   A paragraph in which the first line hangs closer to the left margin than the rest of the lines in the paragraph do. A hanging indent is often used to create bulleted or numbered lists.

hot key   The underlined letter in the name of a command or menu is called the hot key, or selection letter. It's your key to keyboard use; press the key that corresponds to that letter to activate the menu or command.

indent   An indent is the amount of space between the page margin and the edge of your paragraph. Normally a paragraph flows between the margins, but an indent allows you to move an edge of the paragraph closer or farther from the margin, to mark the beginning of the paragraph.

Insert mode   The default typing mode that allows you to insert characters and text to the right of the cursor, without wiping out entire armies of existing text.

insertion point   Another word for cursor, which is the blinking vertical bar that you see inside a text box and a word processor. It tells you where the next character you type will appear.

jump   A highlighted term or topic in the Works for Windows Help system that, when selected, jumps you right to that section of the Help system.

linking   The process by which an object created in a "source" document is shared with another document, while still maintaining its link and its ability to be updated with the source. When the source is changed, the linked document will be updated automatically.

list   A collection of all the records in a database that Works displays in List view.

margins   Margins determine the distance between text and the top, bottom, left, and right edges of the paper. The margin number refers to the amount of distance left between the edge of the text and the end of the paper.

modem   A communication device that lets you send and receive information from one computer to another through a telephone line. Modems can be hooked up inside the computer (internal) or as an accessory outside the computer.

number format   A format option that can be used to convey numbers or values as fixed values with a set number of decimal places or commas, currency, percents, exponents, fractions, date, time, text, true/false values, or leading zeroes.

object   Any information (including text, spreadsheets, charts, database forms, drawings, WordArt, and ClipArt) that is linked or embedded in a document.

object linking and embedding   Affectionately referred to in the techie world as OLE. A techno term that refers to a program's ability to use and update objects that were created in a different application program.

on-line   An old techno term that's been mainstreamed, that means on the computer.

Overtype mode   The ruthless typing mode that wipes out anything in it's way. When you're in this mode, anything you type at the cursor marches right over existing text in it's path.

placeholders   A marker in a word processed document that indicates the placement of a database field. A placeholder contains a field name from a database and double chevrons that set the placeholder off from the other text, for example, <<Last Name>>.

point size   The type size of a particular character. Point size affects the readability of your text, and how many words will fit on a page. There are 72 points in an inch. Using an Arial 72-point font, it takes almost four pages to type this definition, and probably ten minutes to print it.

program   A software application or tool that accomplishes a particular task, such as a calculator, Word Processor, Database, and Spreadsheet—even the Solitaire game is a program.

program icon   A graphic symbol of an application or program, like Works for Windows, that appears in the Windows Program Manager. The program can be started by double-clicking on the icon.

protocol   (1) A Goldie Hawn movie about life in the Diplomatic Corps. (2) Defines the language two computers will use to speak to each other during the transfer of files.

query   A process that lets you sort through all of the records in a database to find the ones that match the criteria you specify.

quotation indents   Indents used to offset a paragraph from the rest of the text by indenting both sides of the paragraph. Use quotation indents when you are quoting someone else's work.

range   A group, or block, of neighboring cells in a Works spreadsheet.

range reference   A shorthand notation used to reference all of the individual cells in a group of adjacent cells. A range reference refers to the cells in the upper-left corner and lower-right corner of a range.

record   All the information contained in a database about one particular subject (for example, a person, a client, a recipe in a cookbook, a part in an inventory).

row   Lists of data that are lined up horizontally, side by side, like houses.

scroll   To move horizontally and vertically through a document or list box, using the arrow keys or a mouse and scroll bars.

sort break   A self-imposed moment of pause that separates the results of a sort into related groups. If a list is sorted alphabetically, a sort break can be placed to leave space between the last entry of one letter and the first entry of the next.

source   The document in which information that you want to copy and link to another document was originally created. The source document must be named and saved before it can be used as a link to another document file.

spreadsheet   Comes from the term worksheet, which is what men in little green visors used to use to crunch numbers before there were spreadsheets. A spreadsheet organizes numeric information in columns and rows, and calculates new values from existing ones.

status bar   (1) A place for old yuppies and dinks to sample high-priced water while they wait for their beepers to beep. (2) A road sign at the bottom of the Works screen that tells you where you are in a document, and what you can do there. It describes what each command, or tool, you select will do.

subscript   Subscript characters are positioned below the rest of the text and are often used in scientific formulas and equations.

superscript   Superscript characters are positioned above the rest of the text and are used to denote exponential powers, scientific notation, and temperature.

system   A short way of referring to all of the components and equipment that make up your computer system.

template   A preformatted document window that can have pre-set margins, page layout, tabs, and font styles. Templates can save you a lot of time when you create many documents of the same type.

values   Numbers, dates, and times entered in the cells of a spreadsheet.

word processor   A program that lets you enter, edit, format, and print text. Word processors are used in lieu of typewriters because they make it easier to correct mistakes and make changes to letters, reports, envelopes, and other documents.

word wrap   A text formatting feature that automatically starts a new line as your typing reaches the end of the current line. Works uses word wrap in word processing documents, and within spreadsheet and database cells.

WYSIWYG   A friendly acronym for "What you see is what you get," which refers to how your document looks on the screen versus what it will look like when you print. Before Windows, what you saw on your screen barely resembled what appeared on the printed page.

Index

E

L

Who cares what you think? WE DO!

We take our customers' opinions very personally. After all, you're the reason we publish these books. If you're not happy, we're doing something wrong.

We'd appreciate it if you would take the time to drop us a note or fax us a fax. A real person—not a computer—reads every letter we get, and makes sure that your comments get relayed to the appropriate people.

Not sure what to say? Here are some details we'd like to know:

- ☞ Who you are (age, occupation, hobbies, etc.)
- ☞ Where you bought the book
- ☞ Why you picked this book instead of a different one
- ☞ What you liked best about the book
- ☞ What could have been done better
- ☞ Your overall opinion of the book
- ☞ What other topics you would purchase a book on

Mail, e-mail, or fax it to:

Barry Pruett
Que
201 West 103rd Street
Indianapolis, IN 46290

FAX: (317) 581-4669
CIS: 75430,174

Special Offer!

Que needs people like you to give opinions about new and existing books. Product testers receive free books in exchange for providing their opinions about those books. If you would like to be a product tester, please mention it in your letter, and make sure you include your full name, address, and day-time phone.